IMAGES
of America

AROUND CRANBERRY LAKE

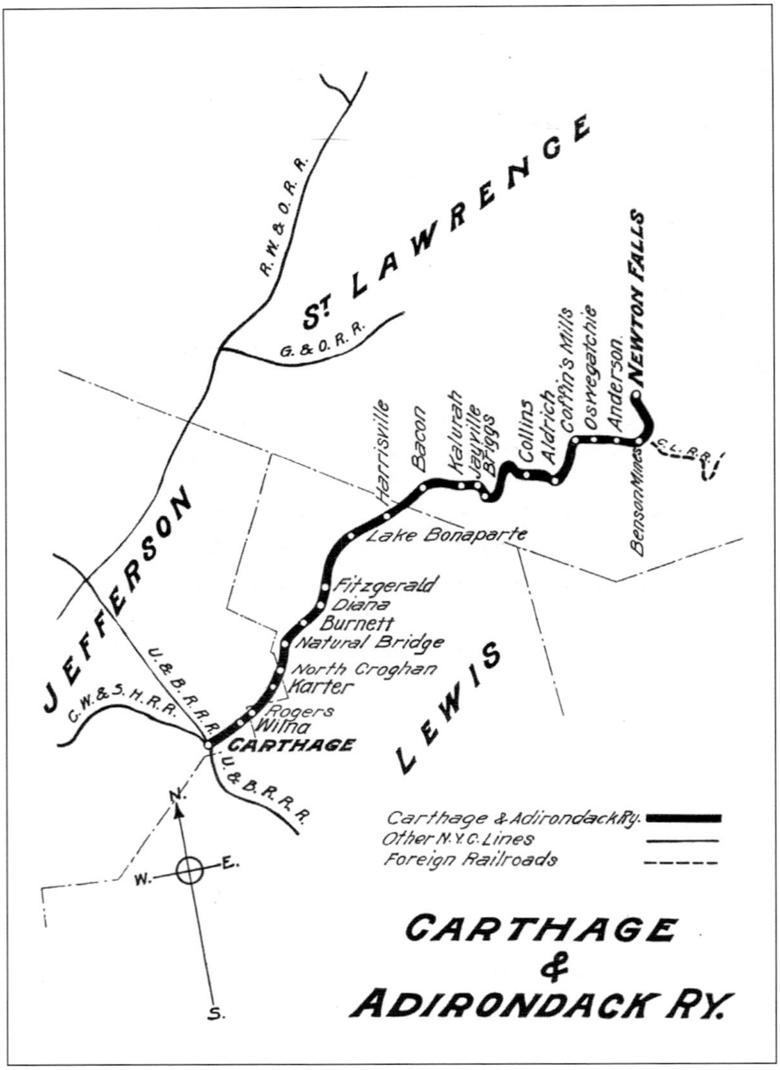

This map of the Carthage & Adirondack (C&A) Railway was included in a 1912 financial report by the New York Central & Hudson River Railroad Company. For the purposes of this book, the Cranberry Lake region begins at the Kalurah station, about 27 miles from Carthage. (Author's collection.)

ON THE COVER: The Ellsworth Hotel at Benson Mines is pictured next to the C&A Railway depot and tracks, with iron ore concentrating buildings in the background. Club automobile touring was a sensible precaution in an era of frequent breakdowns and flat tires. This c. 1915 postcard was produced by Santway Studio of Star Lake. (Author's collection.)

IMAGES
of America

AROUND CRANBERRY LAKE

Susan Thomas-Smeby

ARCADIA
PUBLISHING

ISBN 978-1-4671-0311-4

Published by Arcadia Publishing
Charleston, South Carolina

Printed in the United States of America

Library of Congress Control Number: 2018959080

For all general information, please contact Arcadia Publishing:
Telephone 843-853-2070
Fax 843-853-0044
E-mail sales@arcadiapublishing.com
For customer service and orders:
Toll-Free 1-888-313-2665

Visit us on the Internet at www.arcadiapublishing.com

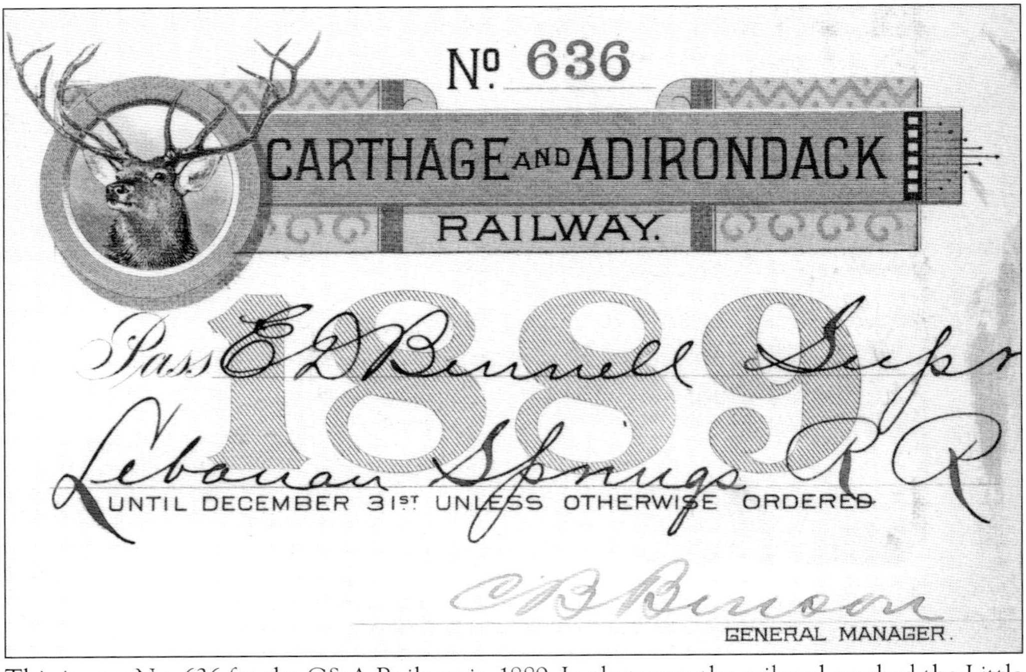

This is pass No. 636 for the C&A Railway in 1889. In that year, the railroad reached the Little River iron ore beds, later called Benson Mines. This pass was issued to E.D. Bennett, general superintendent of the Lebanon Springs Railroad. It was signed by Cadwell B. Benson, treasurer of the C&A. Courtesy passes like these were often exchanged between railroad company officials, whether of main or short lines. (Author's collection.)

Contents

Acknowledgments

All images used in this book appear courtesy of the author, with the following exceptions: the photograph of the Jayville Depot is courtesy of the Town of Diana Historical Museum, the two photographs of the Grasse River Club are courtesy of John Hancock and the Grasse River Club, and the photograph of the Emporium dock on Cranberry Lake is courtesy of Mark Friden.

I am grateful for the assistance of several individuals. Timothy Gates of Oswegatchie reviewed and clarified local images. Gaylord Kerr answered questions regarding Aldrich and Oswegatchie. Jeffrey James, an operator at the Browns Falls Hydro Plant, allowed me to tour the installation and explained the process of generating power from falling water. Maxwell Watson and Anne Hynes of Star Lake reviewed the Newton Falls chapter. The late Howard Rowand, engineer and geologist with Jones & Laughlin Steel, imparted his knowledge of the Benson Mines, along with boxes of labeled mineral specimens. My husband Bruce's working knowledge of crane and heavy equipment operation helped make sense of technical references. Bruce, a native of Star Lake, also accompanied me on field trips; his memories of locations featured in the book, revived while exploring the woods and waters of the region, were a valued contribution.

I relied on a number of books for reference material beyond those mentioned in the text. Michael Kudish's *Where Did the Tracks Go in the Western Adirondacks?* and *Where Did the Tracks Go in the Central Adirondacks?* were great sources of rail-related data. William Gove's *Logging Railroad of the Adirondacks* offered perspective along with facts. *A History of the Grasse River Club*, by William Myers and John Hancock, provided a history of both the club and the Grasse River Railroad. A small booklet, *Browns Falls: Where the Oswegatchie Once Rumbled and Roared*, by Joseph Brownell and Jean Grimm, allowed me to include Browns Falls images in the book. There was little published previously to help explain its history.

Finally, I must thank the state of New York for supporting the Historic Newspapers website. It provides free online access to over eight million pages scanned from New York newspapers, dating from 1795 to 2014. Search results from this site led to most of the articles quoted in the book. They have greatly enriched it.

INTRODUCTION

By the early 1800s, the northwest Adirondacks were acknowledged to be rich in natural resources: timber and iron ore, plus the waterpower needed for industry. Yet taking advantage of these assets depended on cost-effective methods of extracting them. Dubious schemes were organized and capital was raised in early, failed attempts to profit from the region's raw wealth. A typical example was the Harewood Iron & Mining Company of St. Lawrence County. In 1864, this company issued capital stock of $100,000 in 20,000 shares of $5 each to strip mine magnetic iron ore on its property east of Cranberry Lake. It proposed to set up forges and smelting works at the foot of the lake, near the present location of Cranberry Lake village; a dam to provide waterpower would also be constructed. Ore would be drawn by ox cart to the lake, then barged or sledded to the foot, where it would be manufactured into charcoal blooms or pig iron. From there, it would be brought by wagon road some 30 miles to the nearest rail connection, on the Rome, Watertown & Ogdensburg Railroad. The prospectus also noted that the surrounding lands were ideal for agriculture, and could produce the staples needed to support the manufacturing population. From the company's headquarters in Boston, this all sounded promising, but the 1864 Report of Directors was the first—and last—summary of the Harewood Iron & Mining Company's plans. This, and many other Adirondack projects, were thwarted by a lack of economical transportation.

In 1869, construction started on a new railroad that would begin to reach into the Cranberry Lake region: the Black River & St. Lawrence Railway. George Gilbert of Carthage received a charter to build from Carthage to the Oswegatchie River in Harrisville. Because of the expense of iron, the railroad was built with maple wood rails and was completed as far as Natural Bridge. By 1882, it was no longer in operation. In 1883, the Carthage & Adirondack Railway was chartered to finish the line, re-laying it with iron rails not only to Harrisville, but extending to a small mining community at Jayville owned by Magnetic Iron Ore Company. Jayville and Kalurah were reached in 1886, followed by Aldrich, Oswegatchie, and Little River (Benson Mines) in 1889. In 1892, the C&A was purchased by William Vanderbilt and added to his New York Central & Hudson River Railroad, which pushed the line to Newton Falls in 1896. Industry followed, building short railroad lines off the C&A into the wilderness to harvest timber or remove mineral products. Mecca Lumber ran a line south from Kalurah from 1903 to 1910; Newton Falls Paper Company operated a line out of Aldrich from 1915 to 1922; Post & Henderson Company ran a logging line south of Benson Mines from 1905 to 1908; Rich Lumber operated a freight and passenger line, the Cranberry Lake Railroad, from Benson Mines to Wanakena between 1903 and 1914; the Robert W. Higbie Lumber Company built the Newton Falls & Northern Railroad from Newton Falls to New Bridge, operating from 1906 to 1919. In 1941, Hanna Ore Company re-laid track on the old Newton Falls & Northern grade and extended it two miles into Clifton Mines.

The Carthage & Adirondack branch of the New York Central Railroad, and its spur lines, reached the Cranberry Lake region from the south and west. By the early 1900s, lands north and east of the lake were not yet serviced by either a main railroad line or spurs; the closest approach was the New York Central's depot at Childwold Station, 16 miles east of Cranberry Lake. This would change when William L. Sykes, president of Emporium Lumber Company and veteran railroad logger, set his sights on New York hardwood. Over 30 years of Pennsylvania logging was coming to an end, along with the timber, so Emporium began purchasing land in the Adirondacks in 1905. Around 150,000 acres were acquired to support another 40 years of company operations. A small logging site 10 miles west of Tupper Lake became Emporium's new sawmill and residential village, Conifer, in 1911. In 1913, Emporium built the Grasse River Railroad, connecting first with the New York Central at Childwold Station a mile east of Conifer, then heading west to Cranberry Lake. Like Rich Lumber's Cranberry Lake Railroad, the Grasse River Railroad also became a common carrier, with passenger traffic an important part of the logging company's revenue. These industrial railroads helped transform the Cranberry Lake region, greatly facilitating the influx of tourists, summer residents, and sportsmen into the most remote and inaccessible part of New York State.

The Carthage & Adirondack Railway and its branches, along with the Grasse River Railroad, did more than serve industry and the tourist trade. Residents of larger villages and isolated hamlets were all now part of a social community linked by rails. Loggers, mill workers, miners, farmers, businessmen, and their families took advantage of economical rail travel that was accessible to all. Railroads enhanced employment opportunities; jobs followed the tracks. Miners starting with Magnetic Iron Ore Company at Jayville in the 1880s moved with their employer to Benson Mines in the 1890s. Sawmill workers might be hired at Kalurah by Mecca Lumber Company or by the Post & Henderson mill at Jayville and then move on to Post & Henderson's mills at Benson Mines. They might have found new employment with Rich Lumber at Wanakena, Higbie Lumber at New Bridge, or with Emporium Lumber at Conifer and Cranberry Lake. Jobbers—contractors hired to keep mills supplied with logs—depended on rail lines and spurs to transport crews and set up and supply remote camps. In the off-season, the same rails returned lumber industry workers to their farms and homes in towns. But mass production of automobiles soon made them affordable by the average person, and the state subsidized development of paved roads. Between 1900 and 1920, Americans went from owning 8,000 cars to eight million. The efficient passenger rail system fell victim to the lure of independent travel and the freedom of the open road. Whether this loss was worth it—for individuals and society—is an argument beyond the scope of this book. Its purpose is to offer an informative look at life in the Cranberry Lake region during the heyday of rail.

One

Kalurah, Jayville, and Aldrich

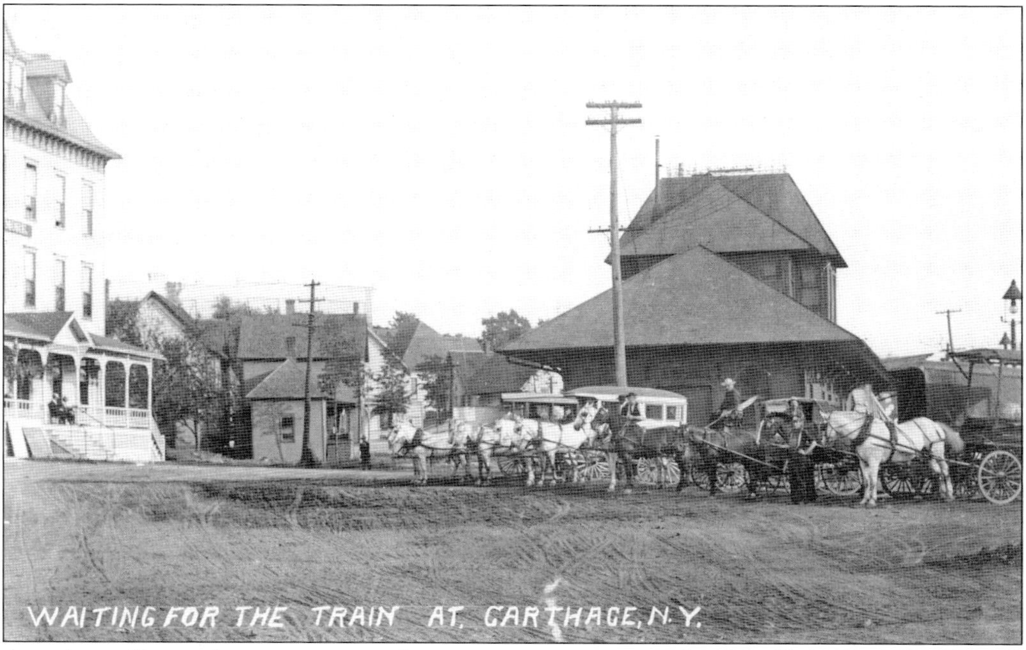

A variety of horse-drawn wagons and carriages are waiting at the New York Central's depot at Carthage, across from the Kenmore Hotel. Travelers could head into the Cranberry Lake region here via the Adirondack Branch, also known as the Carthage & Adirondack Railway. It acquired other colorful nicknames over the years, including "Lumber Jack Line" and "Gum Picker's Special." The 1880s and 1890s saw loggers and miners as the line's main passengers; they were later joined by sportsmen and tourists. Although passenger service on the C&A ended by 1944, freight service continued for many years.

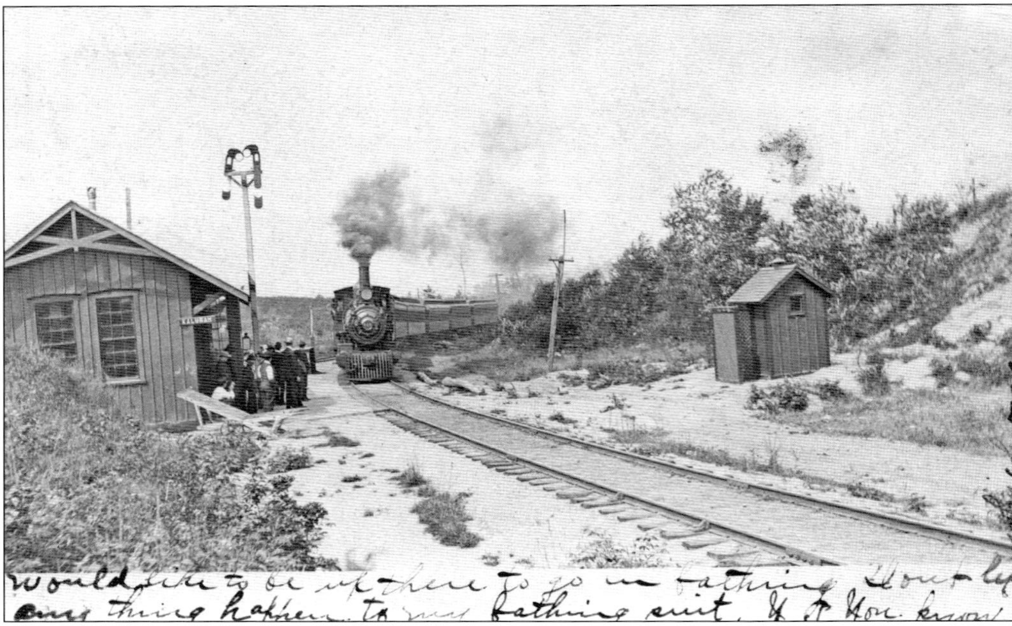

The C&A reached Kalurah—called Little Mill until 1903—before the end of 1886. These two postcards picture the Kalurah depot. The card above was postmarked in Kalurah on September 18, 1906, and shows a locomotive pulling five passenger and baggage cars. Kalurah may have been a regular station at this point; within a few years, it became a flag stop. The card below, postmarked in Carthage in 1908, pictures a group at the depot, with children wearing their Sunday best, perhaps on an outing. The men in both cards may have been employees of Mecca Lumber Company, which in 1903 built a sawmill at Kalurah and a logging railroad four miles south, operating until 1910. Mecca owned over 7,000 acres in the town of Fine and marketed pulpwood, hemlock bark, soft and hardwood lumber, and railroad ties, all loaded onto cars on the C&A. After Mecca moved to New Hampshire, the sawmill was operated by Alfred Kilbourne until Mecca sold its logged land to New York State in 1920.

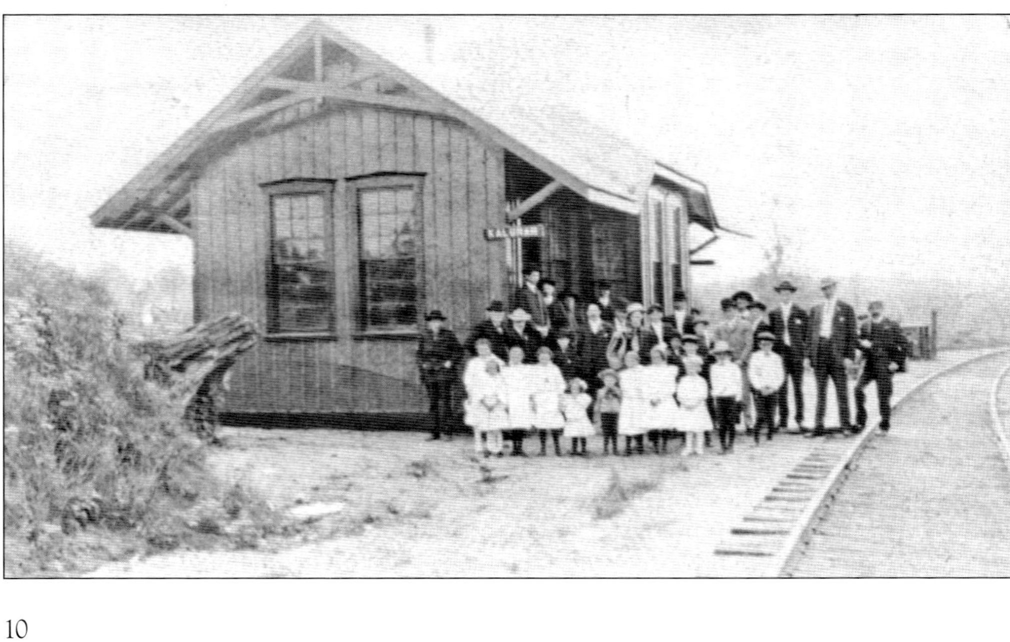

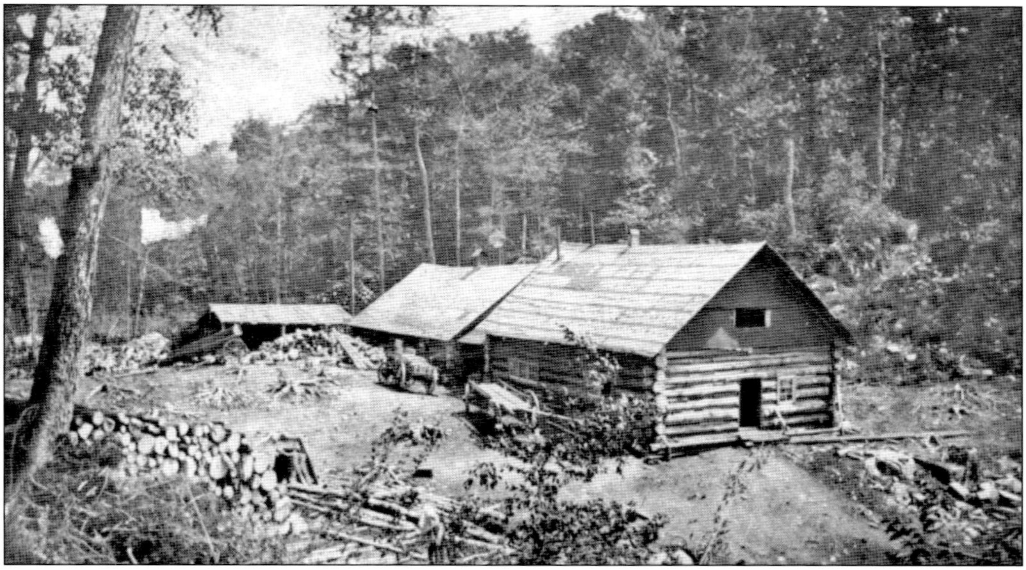

This card, postmarked at Kalurah on September 12, 1907, was sent to Harrisville. The sender, who may have worked at the lumber camp, wrote, "I don't think I will be down any more Saturdays." The solid log buildings included a men's camp, cook's camp, and a stable. Mecca Lumber built a camp at the southern end of its logging railroad at the Scuttle Hole Jackworks on the St. Lawrence–Lewis County line. Jackworks were conveyor belts that hauled logs out of the water and onto railroad cars.

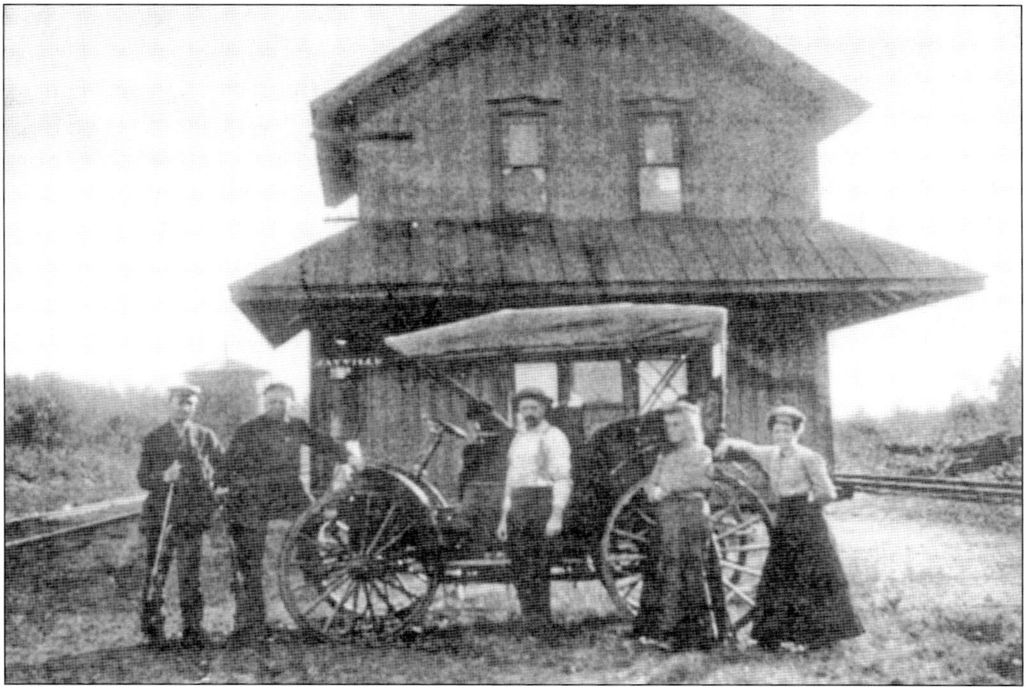

Jayville Depot was the final stop on the C&A from late 1886 until 1888. In this c. 1910 photograph, a high-wheeler automobile has been driven to the depot. The main line is left of the station; tracks on the right served the mines. Byron Benson, a Pennsylvania oil baron, organized both the C&A and Magnetic Iron Ore Company, which planned to mine at Jayville. The town boomed from 1886 to 1889, with around 200 tons of ore extracted daily and shipped to furnaces in Pennsylvania.

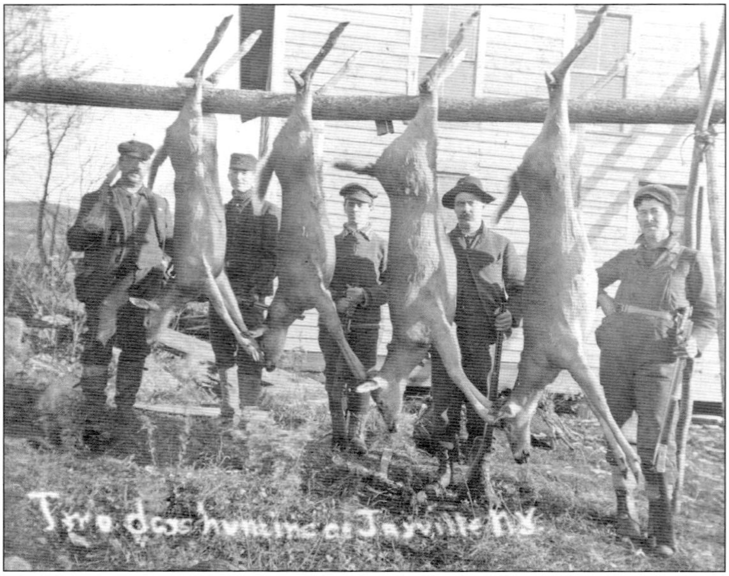

This card, postmarked November 7, 1906, is labeled "Two days hunting at Jayville NY." In 1889, Jayville was abandoned by Magnetic Iron Ore, which moved 13 miles east to the new terminus of the C&A at Little River or Benson Mines. Jayville had grown into a substantial settlement. In the 1890s, it was the site of Post & Henderson's first Adirondack sawmill; later, hunting, fishing, and tourism kept Jayville alive through the 1920s.

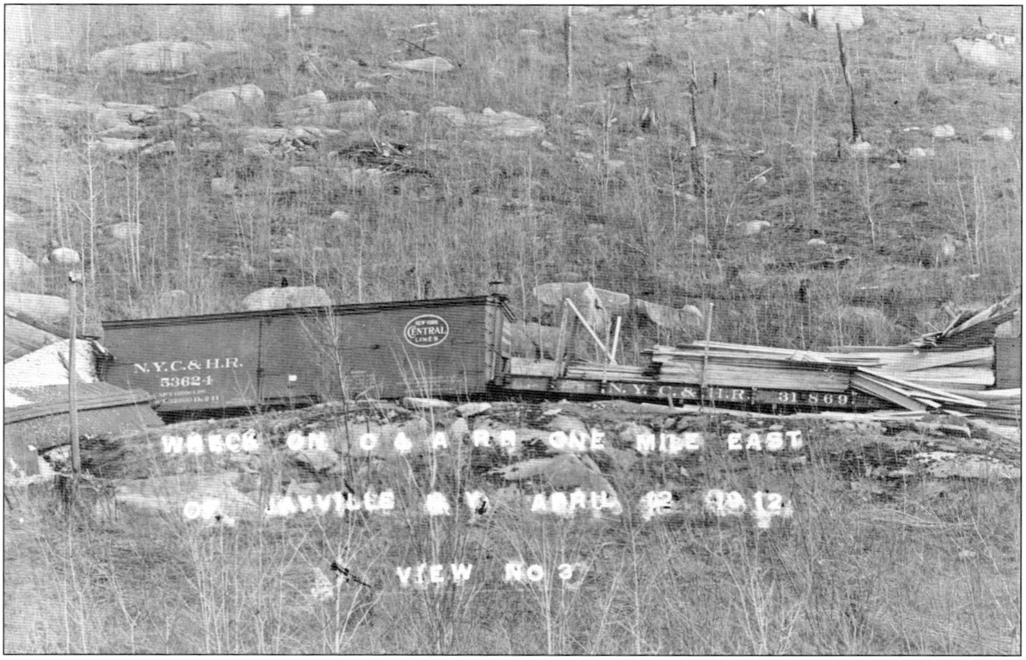

This card is the third in a set of six images of a "Wreck on C&A RR One Mile East of Jayville N.Y., April 12 1912." There was a grade ascending east from Jayville of over two percent that may have contributed to the derailment. Several cars loaded with lumber overturned. Postcards like these were sold by local photographers, who rushed to the site of a disaster—train wreck, fire, flood, explosion, tornado, or other catastrophes. The cards were often made in sets and were quite popular.

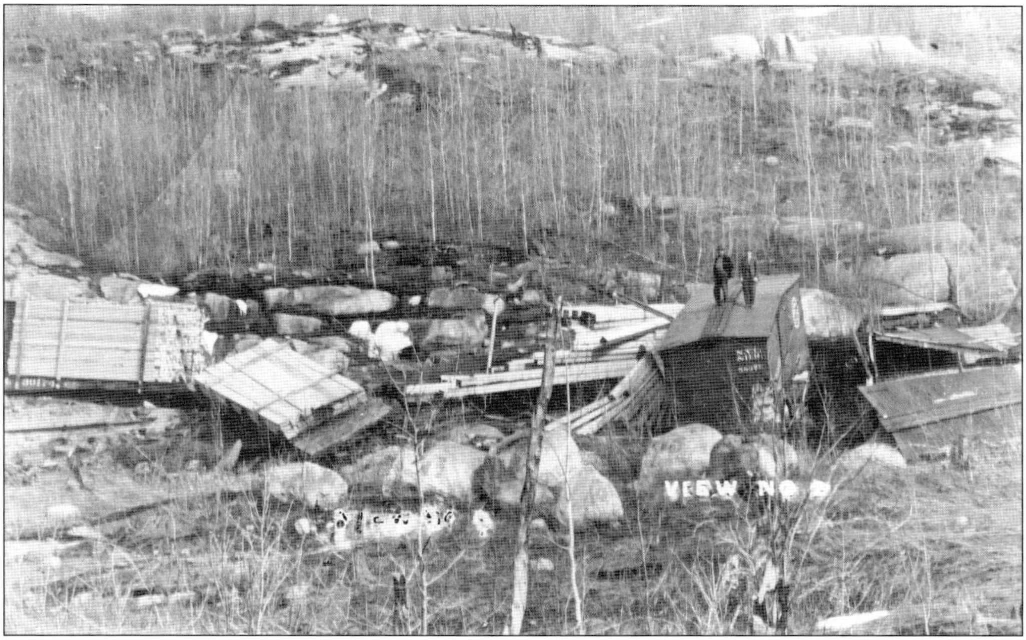

The card above shows more smashed cars. Two men are standing on top of one of the semi-intact boxcars, a risky move possibly inspired by the photographer to add a little color. The card below shows a rail crane attempting to right overturned cars. Cranes could run on either steam or gasoline; some were powerful enough to lift an entire locomotive. A New York Central work car is on the tracks behind the crane. This set of cards confirms early accounts of the Jayville landscape: a "denuded bedrock hill about 2,000 feet long and 100 feet high." Jayville village was located on the lowlands at the foot of the hill, "surrounded by swamps and tree stumps." However, east of Jayville was a prime area for berry picking. Passengers on the C&A would get off the up-bound morning train to pick blueberries and huckleberries and be picked up by the down-bound train in the late afternoon.

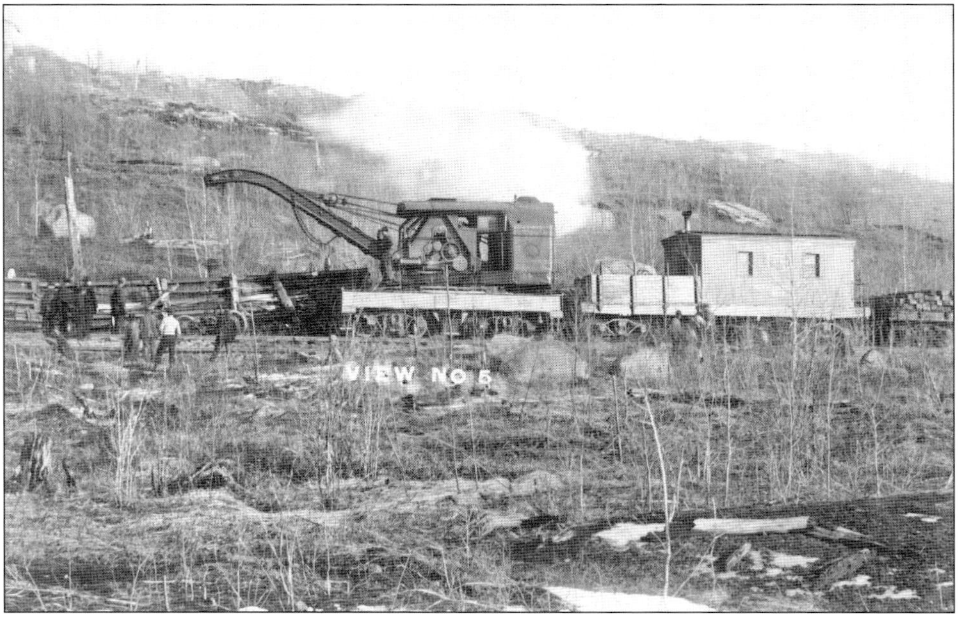

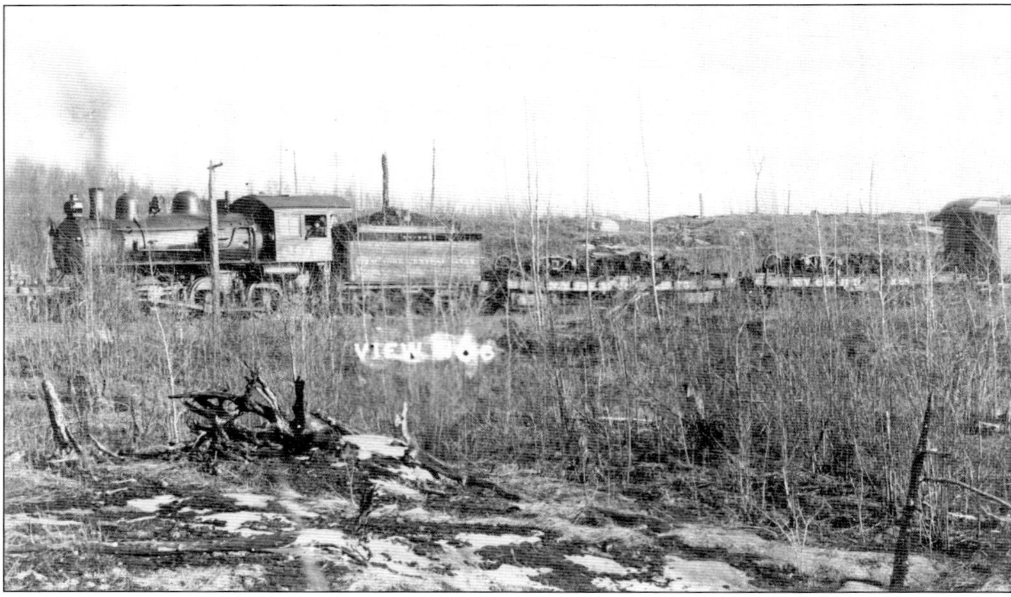

The final card in the Jayville wreck series shows New York Central engine No. 1693 pulling two flatcars loaded with trucks, wheels, and axles. The *Ogdensburg Journal* on April 15, 1912, described the wreck, noting that the C&A was tied up nearly 24 hours. A freight train was coming down the Jayville grade "at a pretty good clip" when 10 cars jumped the track and tore up the roadbed for a long way. "The wrecking train was sent to the scene immediately." No one was injured.

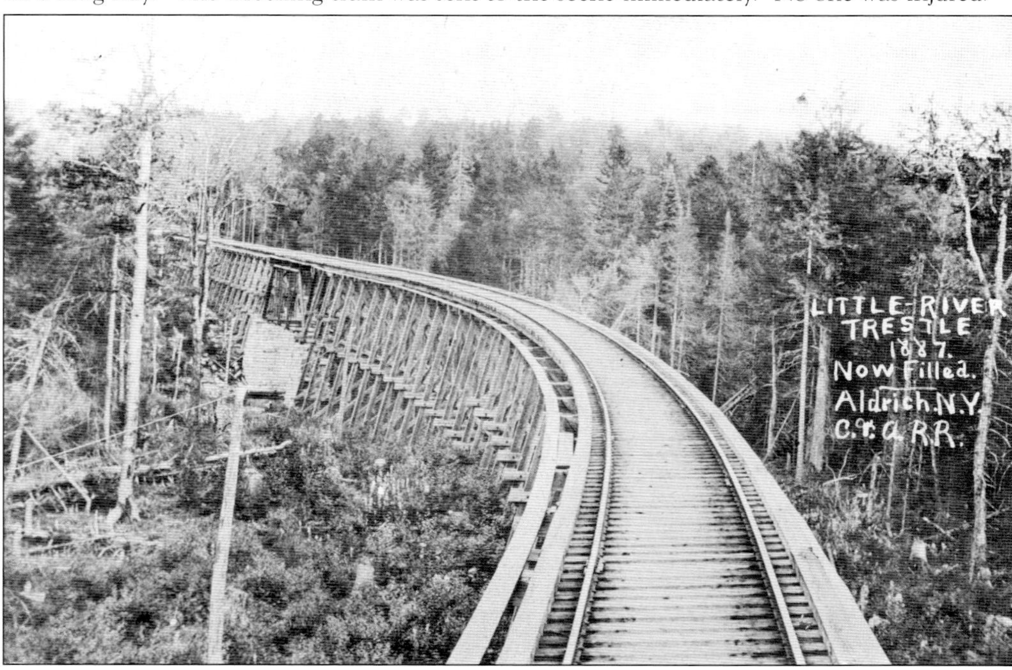

In 1887, the C&A began its Little River Extension from Jayville to reach the site of Magnetic Iron Ore Company's new venture at Benson Mines. In the summer of 1888, the railway reached Aldrich, named after one of the builders of the first sawmill. This postcard of the impressive trestle at Aldrich was originally a photograph by Henry Beach. Beach often used his older images to create new postcards. The c. 1907 card notes that the open trestle is "now filled."

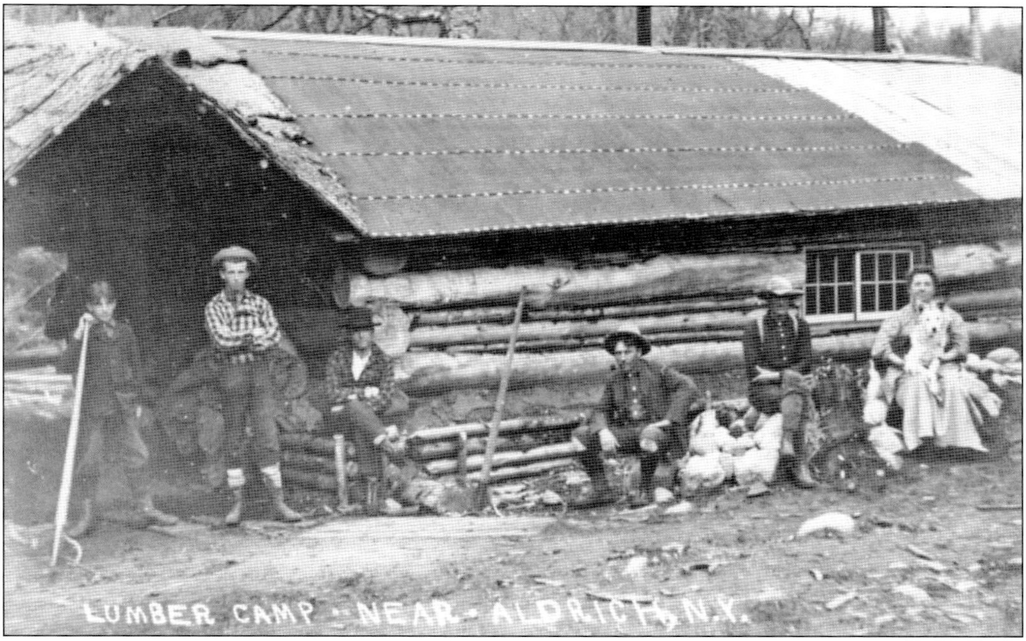

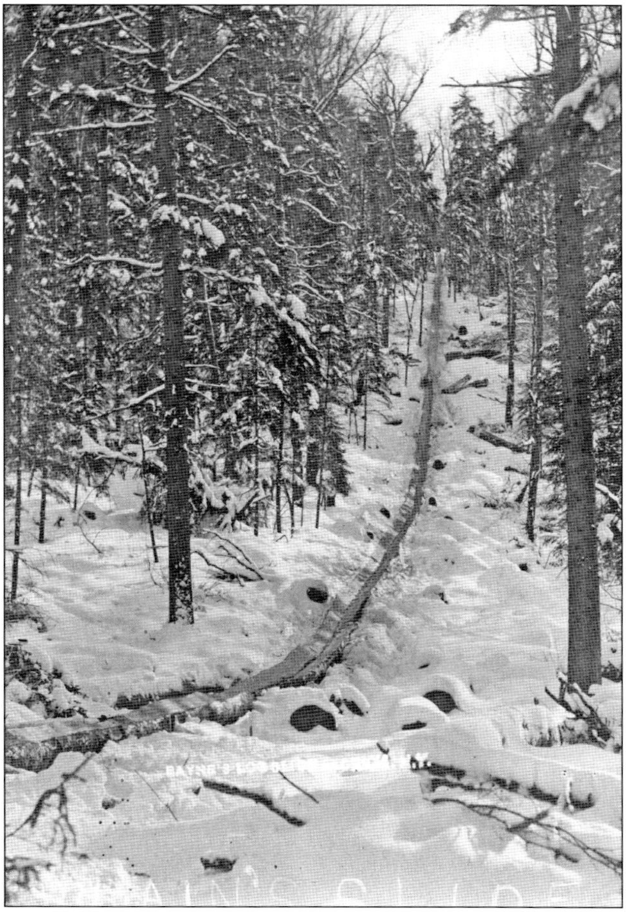

By 1902, a village of 25 families had grown up around two Aldrich sawmills. Camps like the one pictured in the card above would keep these mills supplied with logs, to be sawn into lumber and shipped out on the C&A. A block mill was also built, to cut pulpwood for shipment to paper mills. The men are holding the tools of their trade—peaveys, axes, and pike poles—while the woman with a dog in her lap was probably a cook. The cabin is rough, but served a purpose: it only needed to last until the surrounding forest was cleared. Peter Yousey was the best-known jobber—or contract logger—in the Aldrich area and also operated one of the sawmills until 1912. The card at right, postmarked October 16, 1907, at Aldrich, shows "Bayne's Log Slide Aldrich NY." Log slides were widely improvised; this one is made of logs joined end to end, squared on one side, and lined with a ribbon of steel. The top would be greased, and logs were pulled along the slide by a team of horses.

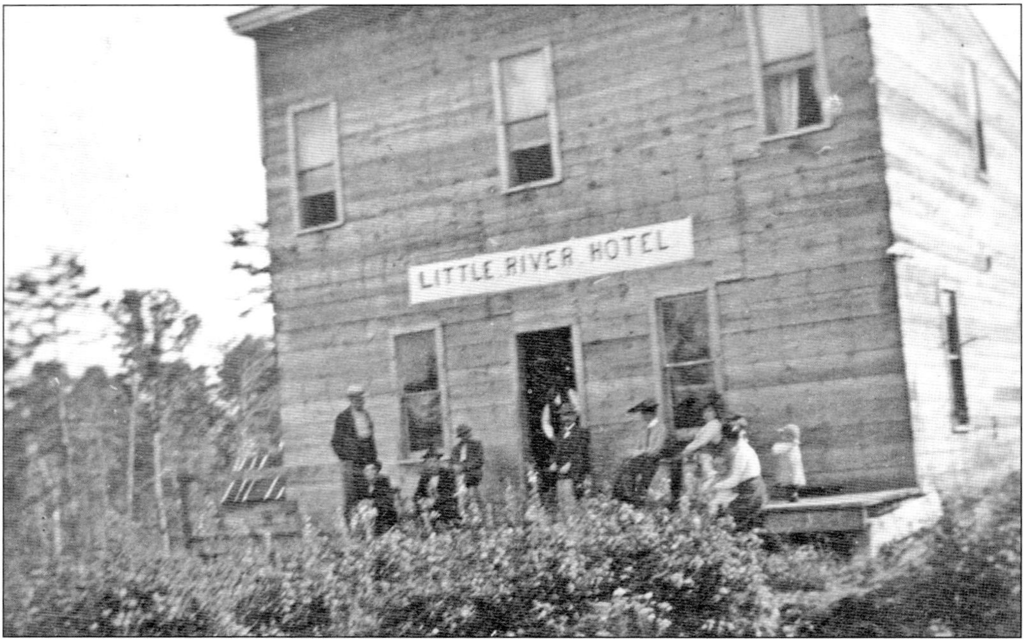

Not everyone working or visiting at Aldrich expected to stay in a log lumber camp. Mill officials, railroad employees, sportsmen, tourists, and their families preferred to lodge at a boardinghouse or hotel. The first was built in Aldrich in the mid-1890s and is pictured in this cabinet card. The "Little River Hotel" looks newly constructed; its raw pine board walls have not yet been given a coat of paint. The three women and several children in the group on the porch were probably relatives of local workers.

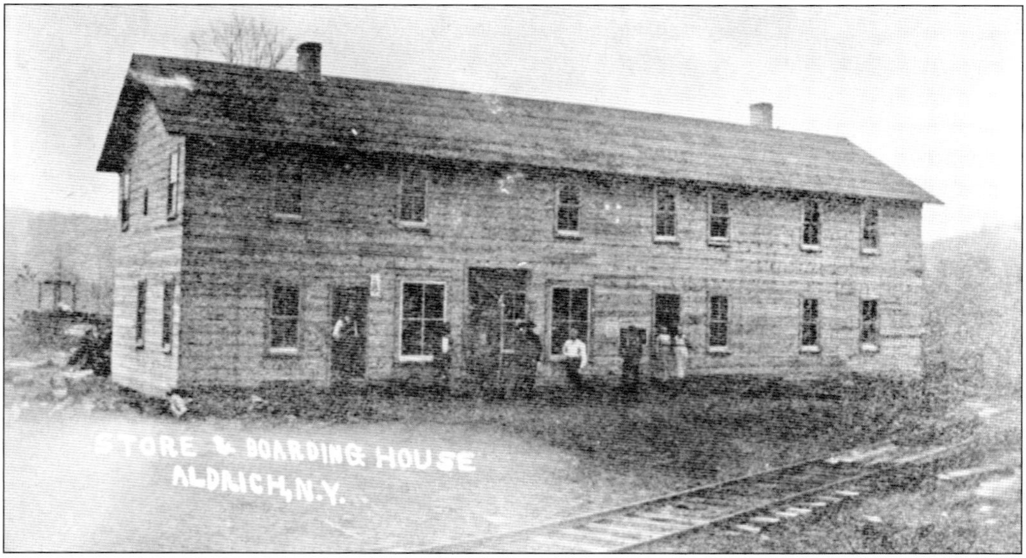

This postcard shows another Aldrich boardinghouse, constructed in 1902 by Peter Yousey's Aldrich Lumber Company. It was located next to the tracks and included a post office, general store, and public telephone. On October 11, 1906, a fire started in Yousey's dry kiln that quickly engulfed the sawmill, lumber yards, several freight cars, and most of the village, including this boardinghouse. The *Ogdensburg Journal* reported that the sawmill was supposed to have been fireproof, a dubious claim. Insurance covered part of the loss, and Yousey's sawmill was rebuilt.

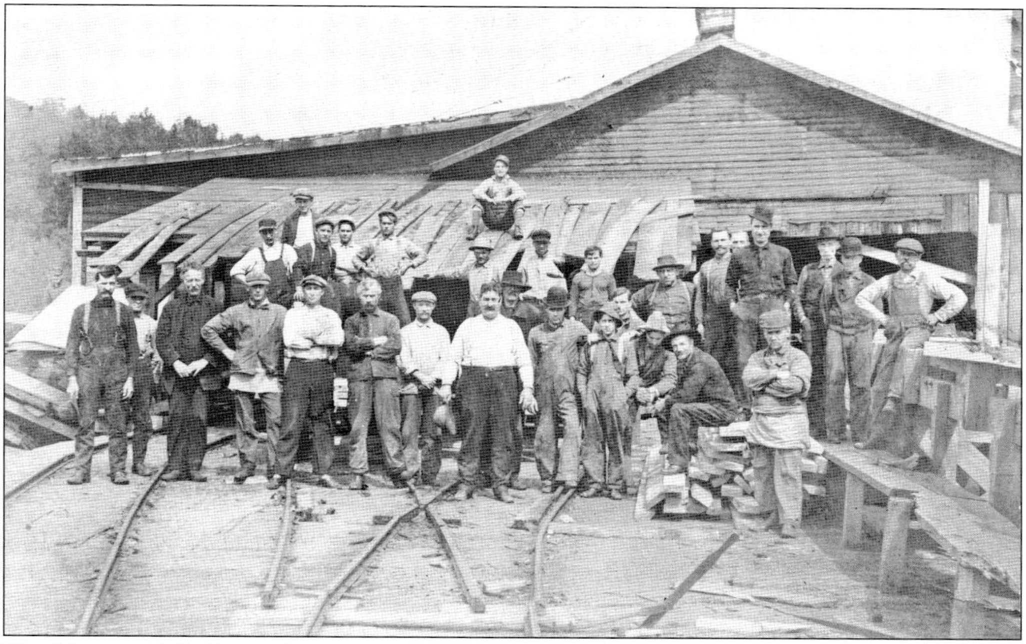

The Newton Falls Paper Company established a pulp and paper mill in Newton Falls in 1894. Much of its pulpwood was cut around Cranberry Lake and sent down the Oswegatchie River to the mill. In 1914, the company purchased 7,000 acres south of Aldrich and needed a railroad to transport logs to Aldrich. In 1915, construction began on the seven-and-a-half-mile line, with the new spur heading to Streeter Lake and then to Scanlon's Camp and jack works on the Middle Branch of the Oswegatchie River. The company purchased the existing block mill to cut up short lengths of pulpwood, which were sent to the paper mill at Newton Falls. Also purchased was one of the Aldrich sawmills; the card above shows this mill and 32 workers. Spruce logs were hauled to the sawmill and the lumber was loaded onto New York Central railroad cars, as seen in the card below, and taken to markets via the C&A Railway. The Newton Falls Paper Company ceased operations in the Aldrich area in 1922; the rails were pulled up in 1923.

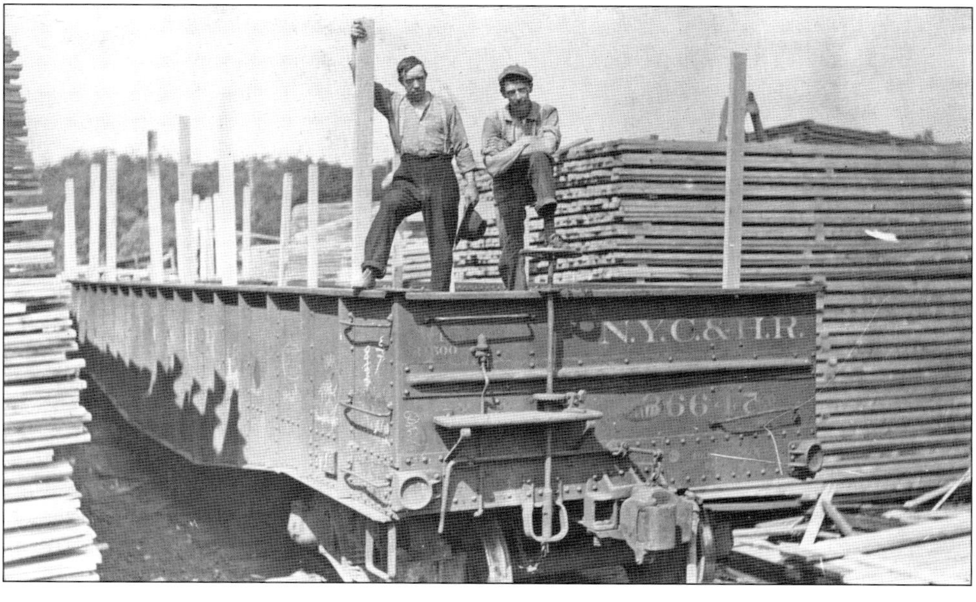

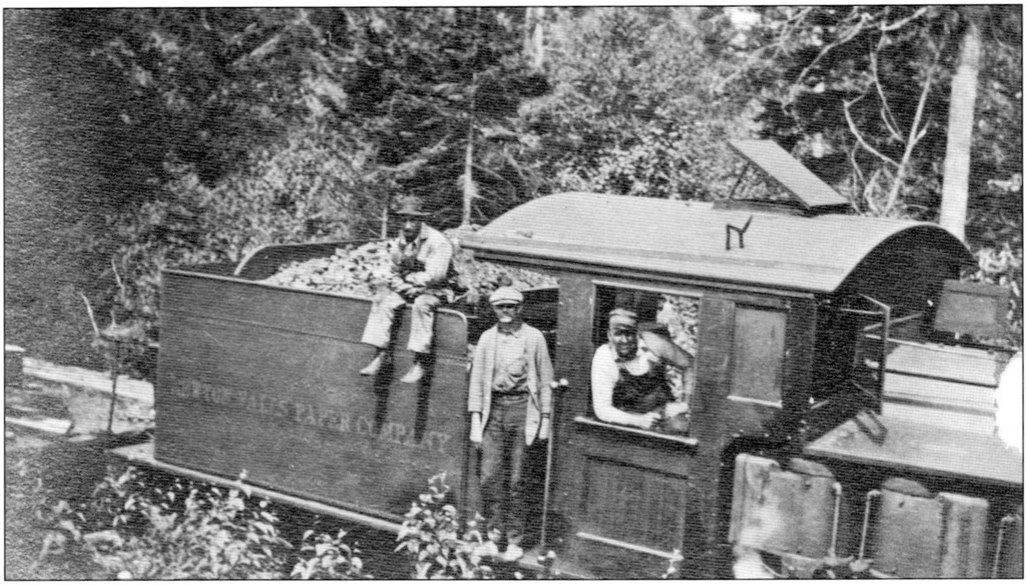

This photograph is labeled "Newton Falls Paper Company Train & Crew." The tender is lettered with the company name. The engineer leans from the window of the Shay locomotive, accompanied by a fireman and a general train or brakeman. Shays had two or three vertical cylinders on the right side of the engine; horizontal drive shafts extended to a gearbox on the outside of each wheel. In 1916, the paper company ordered a new Shay from the builder, Lima Locomotive Works. It was eventually sold to Emporium Forestry Company.

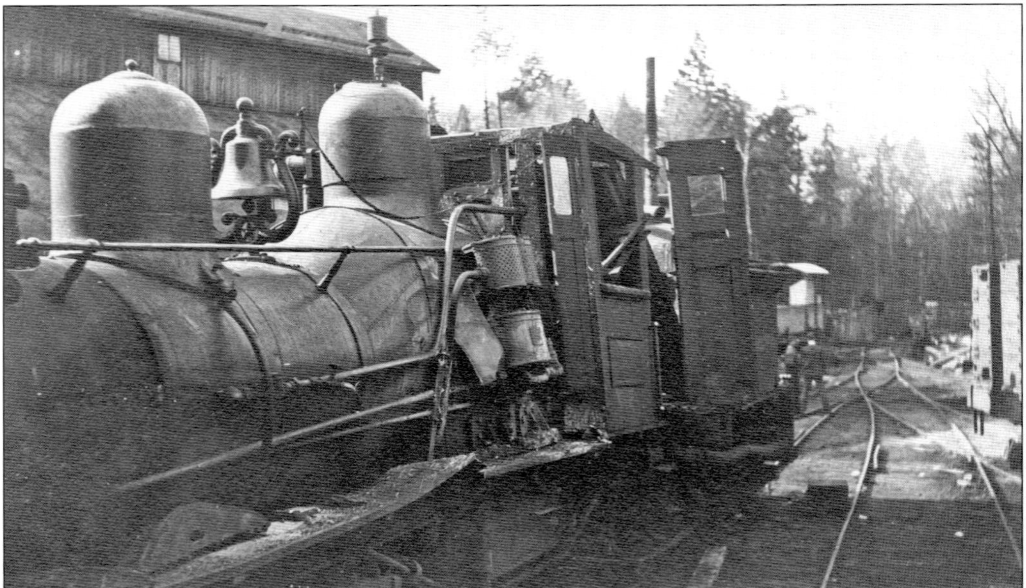

The reverse of this undated postcard notes that the engine met with a "mishap" near Aldrich. It is also a Shay, popular with logging railroads because of their ability to pull heavy loads over twisting track and steep grades. This locomotive is similar to the wreck of Rich Lumber's No. 2 Shay outside Wanakena in 1908 and may be the same engine. Low water caused the boiler to explode, killing a fireman and a traveling salesman. Train mishaps were common, often caused by careless dispatching, equipment failure, overworked crews, and alcohol.

Two

Oswegatchie and Browns Falls

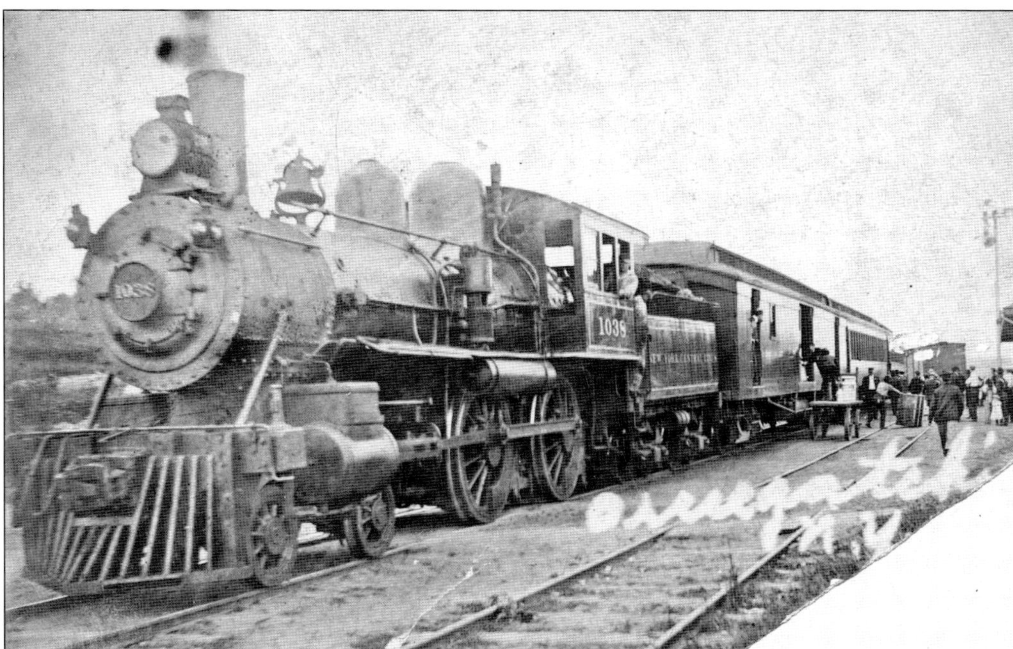

The C&A Railway reached Oswegatchie in February 1889. This c. 1907 postcard shows New York Central engine No. 1038 stopped at the station, heading toward Benson Mines and Newton Falls. Behind the coal tender is a milk car, with 10-gallon steel milk cans from local farms being loaded; these cars were insulated and packed with ice in summer. The new station at Oswegatchie started a boom in tourism at nearby Star Lake, and the hotel industry there flourished. Rail passengers were taken to Star Lake by stagecoach.

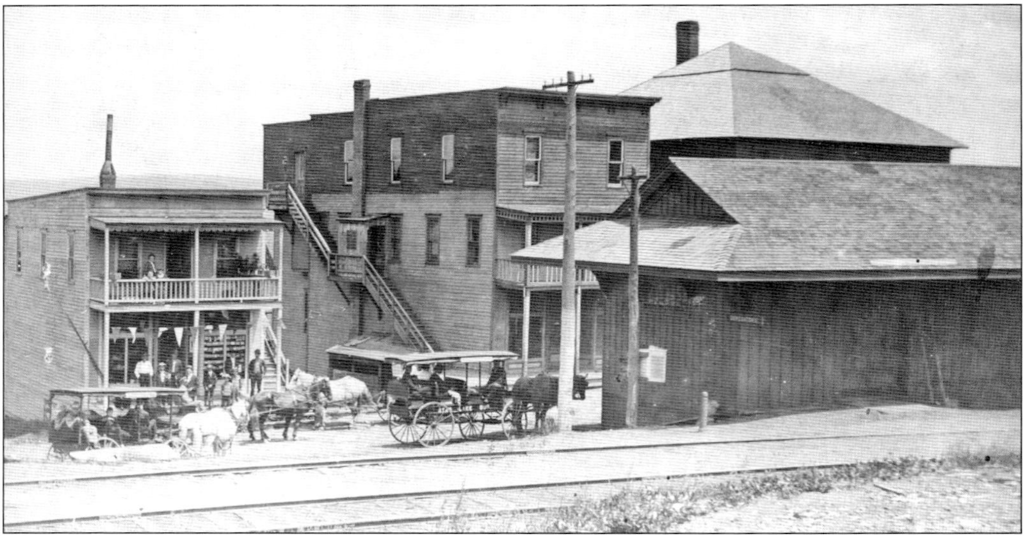

This card of the Oswegatchie depot and adjacent block is from around 1905. The building at upper right is the Forest House; the John Irvin building is in the middle, housing the post office and O.D. Collins store; at left is Harry Humble's general store. Horse-drawn wagons await the C&A train, including the "Star Lake Bus," owned by Winifred Backus, who charged passengers 25¢ per one-way trip from the station to Star Lake. Another carriage labeled "Sunnyside Inn" took passengers to that Star Lake hotel.

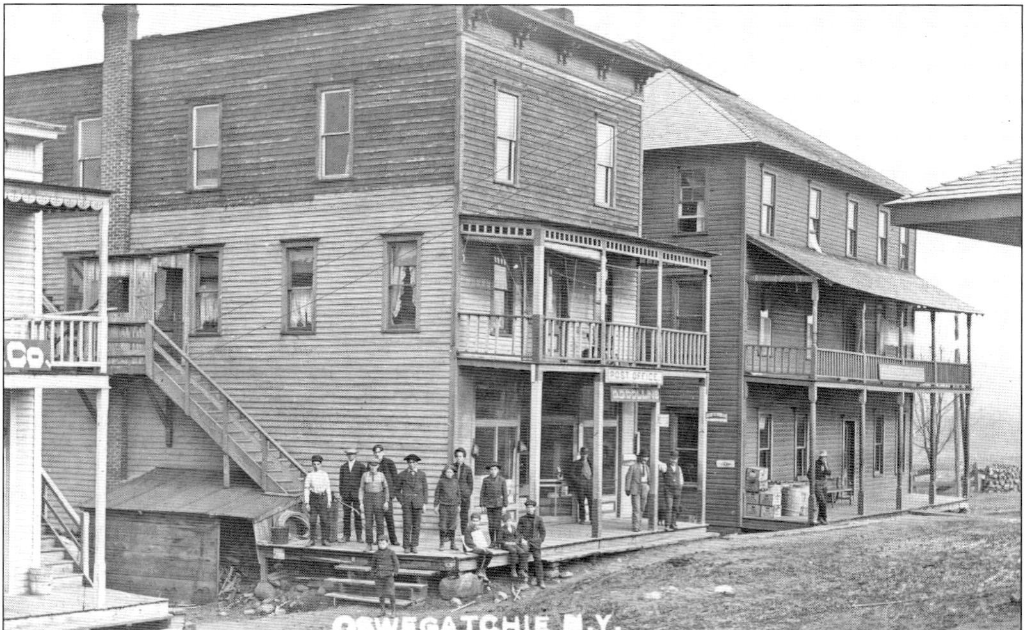

This image of the Forest House and the John Irvin building can be dated before February 20, 1911, when the town of Fine's worst fire swept through Upper Oswegatchie. The fire started at the Forest House, destroying three business blocks, two barns, and the railroad station. Firefighters had only a bucket brigade and resorted to shoveling snow onto nearby buildings to stop the flames. Total damage was estimated at $15,000. The Forest House was not rebuilt, but by April 1911, John Irvin's store and the rail station were under construction.

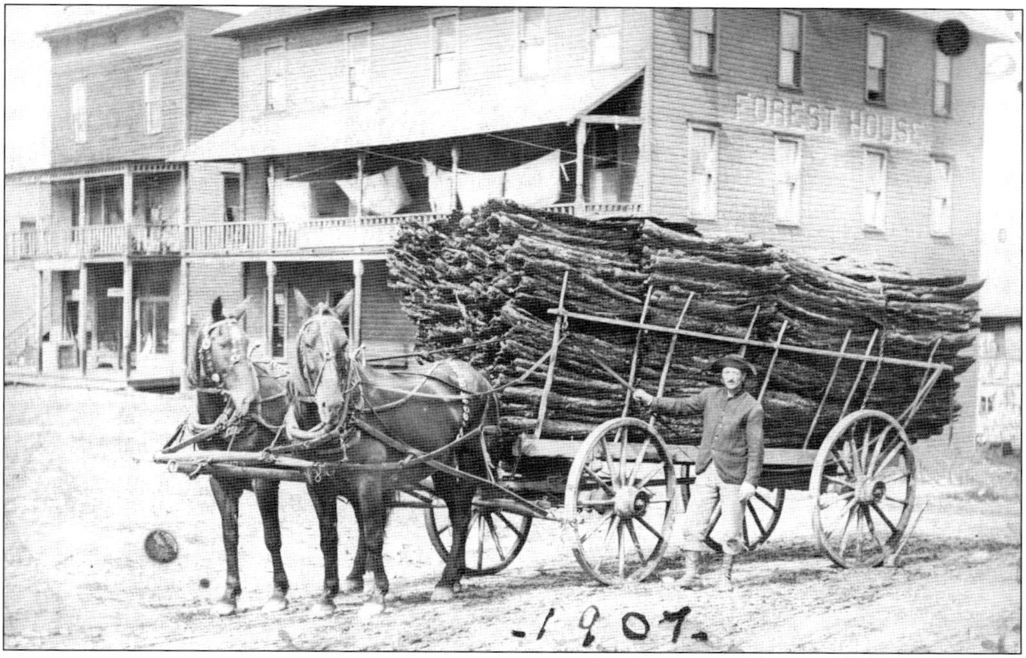

The Forest House and John Irvin building are in the background of this 1907 card. The Forest House advertised as the "Headquarters for Fishing and Hunting." Rates in 1907 were $1.00 to $1.50 a day for room and board. The card's reverse states that the man pictured is Ed Backus, with "the biggest load of bark to go up the crossing." The tannery in the village of Fine was the first real industry in the area and operated from about 1872 to 1910. Hides were tanned by tannic acid extracted from hemlock bark.

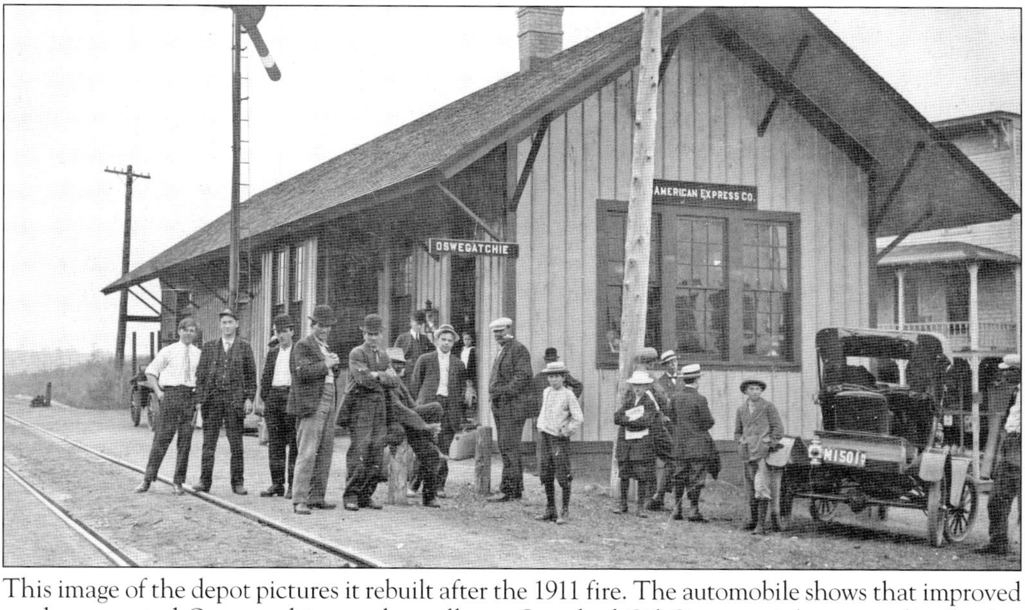

This image of the depot pictures it rebuilt after the 1911 fire. The automobile shows that improved roads connected Oswegatchie to other villages. Standard Oil Company's kerosene distribution center at Oswegatchie, owned by Ed Backus, also began delivering gasoline in 1910. The car may be a 1909–1912 Model T three-passenger roadster; the Model T was a success from its introduction in 1908. The middle class could now own a car, and even finance it.

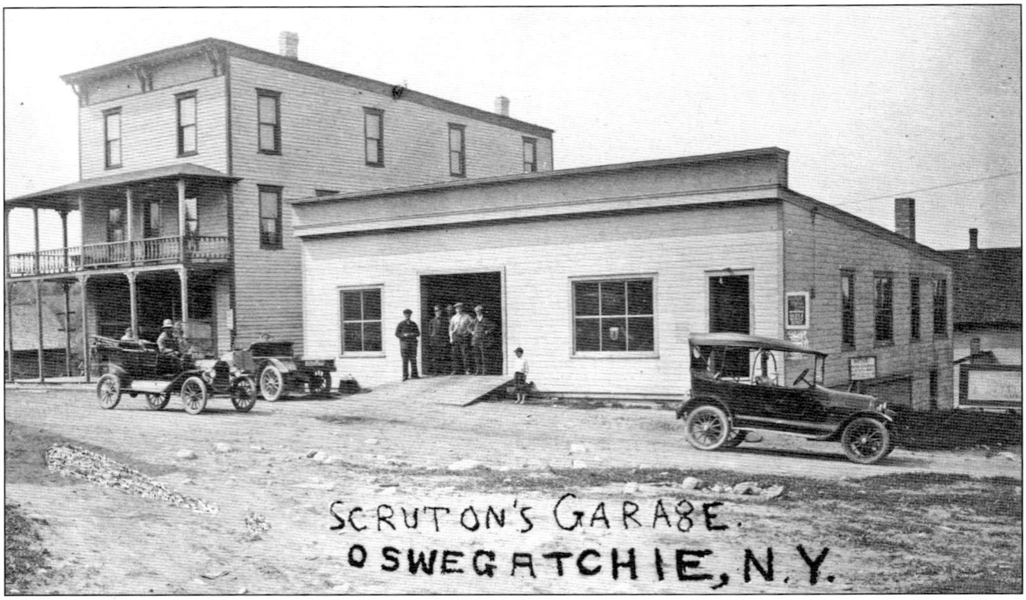

This view from the depot is also dated after the 1911 fire. The Forest House has been replaced by the first automobile garage in the town of Fine. Alton Scruton's service station was in the same building as his father, Thomas's, blacksmith shop. Two Model T touring cars are outside the garage, as well as an earlier two-seater with right-hand steering. There is an air-pump station; tires needed frequent patching due to the rough roads. Signs displayed include United States Tires Depot and Socony Gasoline.

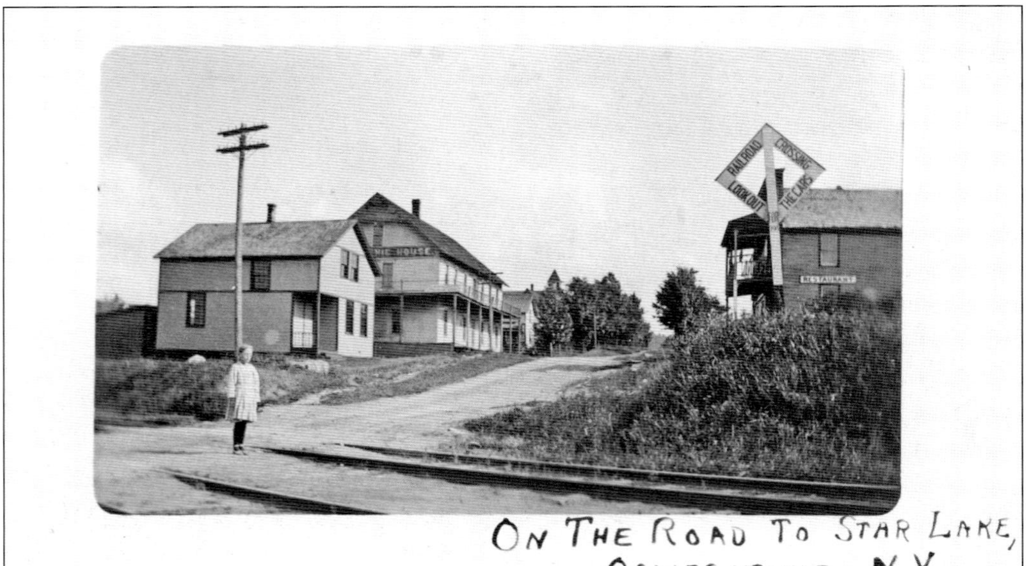

This card of the dirt road from Oswegatchie to Star Lake dates to before 1926. That year, a concrete state highway, Route 3, was completed from Fine to Cranberry Lake. At the intersection with the railroad, there is only a sign reading "Railroad Crossing Look Out for the Cars." The "Restaurant" at right also included a saloon, barbershop, and poolroom. The second building on the left is the Oswegatchie House; the spire of the Methodist church is in the distance. In 1957, a new Route 3 was constructed, bypassing Oswegatchie.

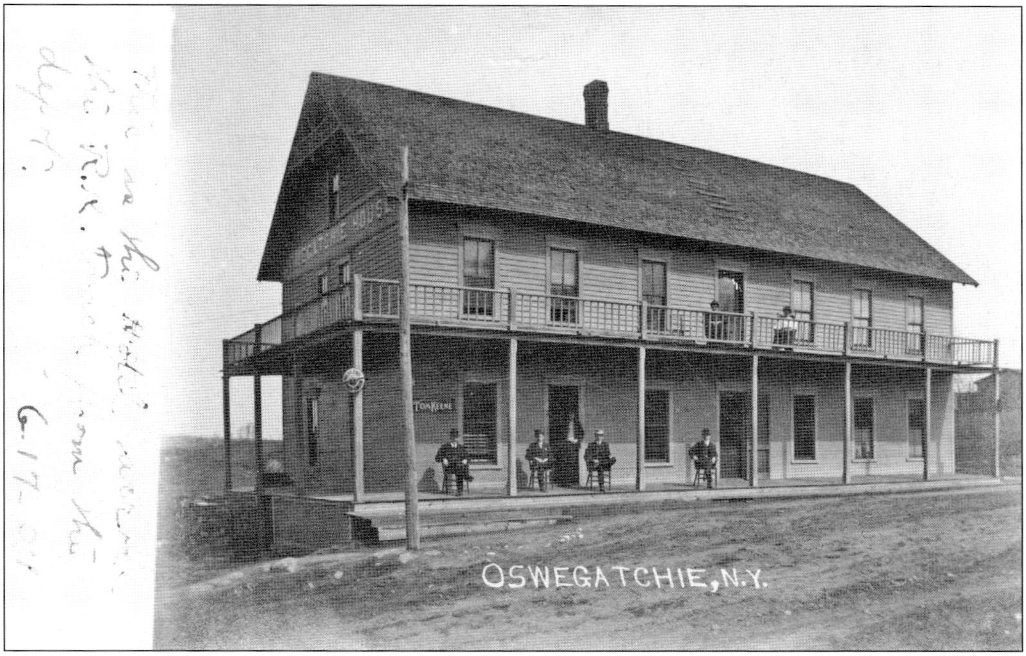

Oswegatchie House was built in 1874 by Charles Scott, 15 years before the C&A Railway reached the village. By then there were several farms, logging operations, and a sawmill. Oswegatchie House first boarded loggers and sportsmen journeying by wagon road to reach the wilderness. Business would have flourished after the rail line arrived. This card is dated June 17, 1907; the sender notes that "this is the hotel across the tracks from the depot." There are signs for Tom Keene cigars and West End Ales & Lager.

This card of the Methodist church was postmarked at Oswegatchie on May 8, 1907, and sent to Carthage. The first church in Oswegatchie was built in 1890 by both Baptists and Methodists as Union Church. In 1896, the Methodists built their own church in upper Oswegatchie. The Richardson Memorial Methodist Church was named after the family of the bride in the first marriage ceremony. The Star Lake IOF (Independent Order of Foresters), a leading fraternal benefit organization, also used this church as an assembly hall. It has been demolished.

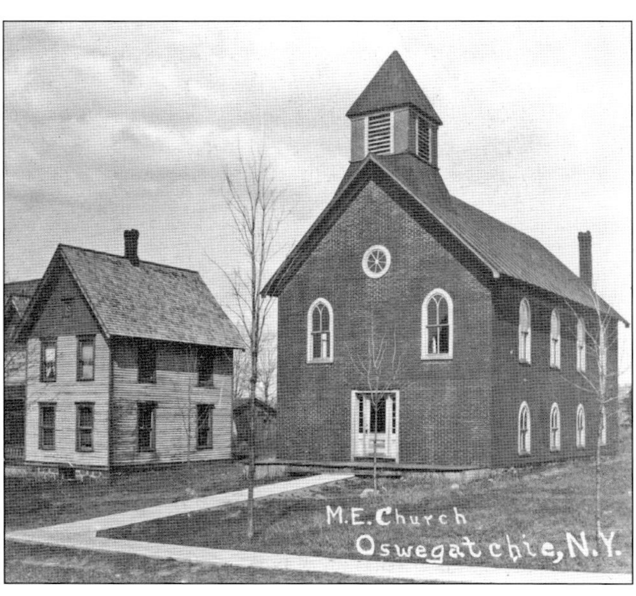

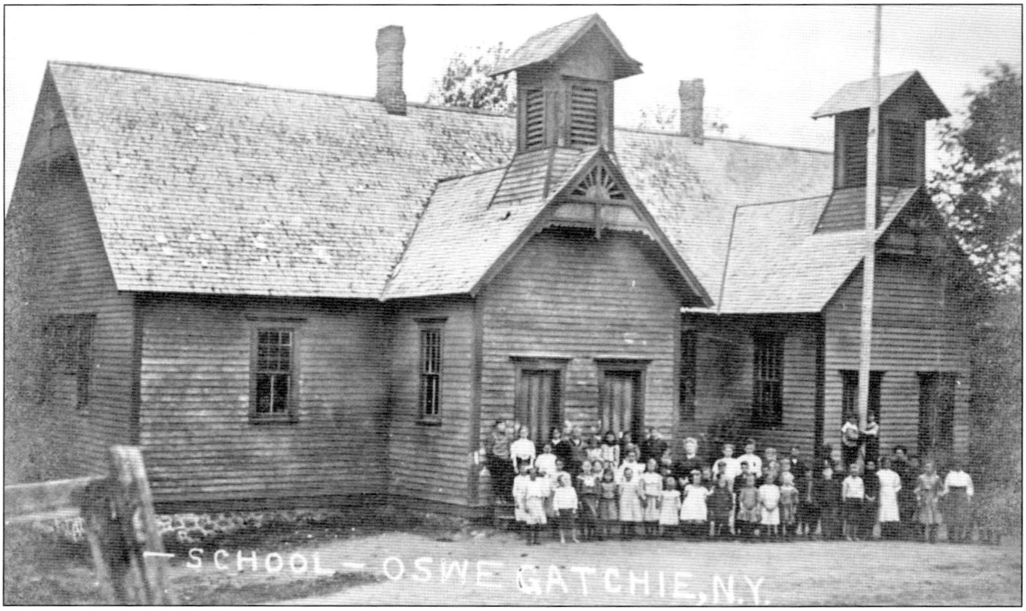

The Village of Oswegatchie was School District No. 2 in the town of Fine. The first school was built in 1892 and enlarged in 1894; before then, children attended schools in the Browns Falls area. This Union Free School was constructed between upper and lower Oswegatchie. It held classes through sixth grade. The card is un-mailed but is written "To Miss Vera Irvin—Forget me Not." Vera Irvin is listed as a pupil in an 1897 roster at the Oswegatchie School, under teacher Kate Griffin. Irvin later became a teacher.

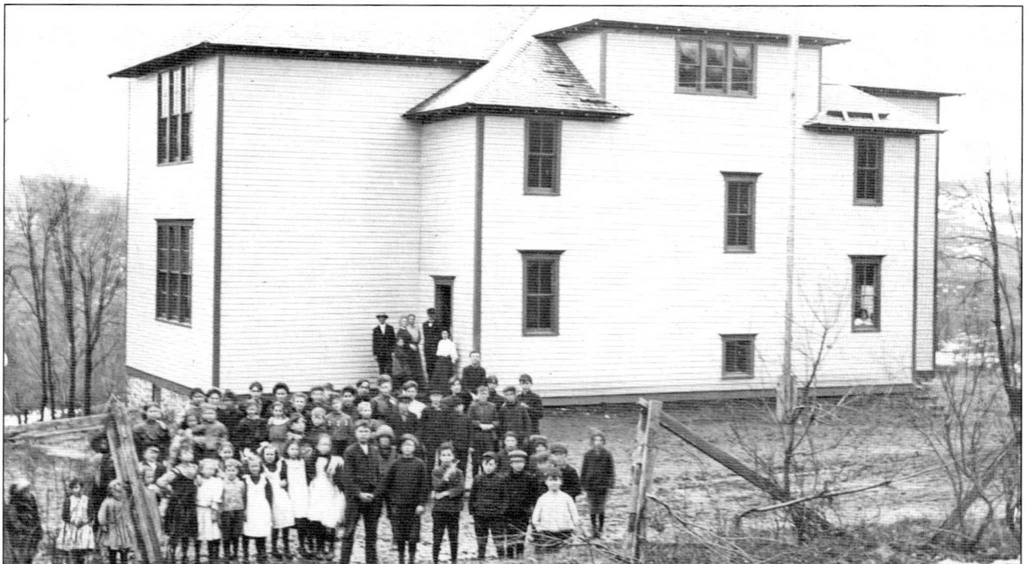

The first Union Free School was replaced by a larger school around 1905; it held two grade rooms downstairs and two junior high school rooms upstairs. Several teachers are standing in the doorway, with over 50 pupils from elementary to middle schoolers; this was as long as most students would attend. This school burned in 1922, and the town hall was used until a new school was built in 1924. This last school, along with all other district schools, was closed when the Clifton-Fine Central School was completed in 1952.

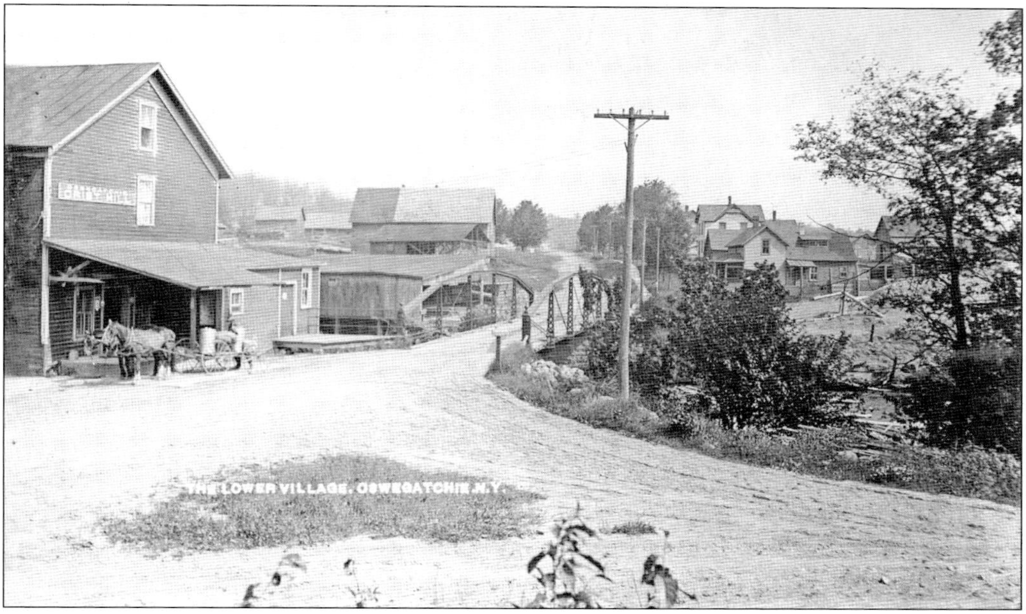

The card above of the Lower Village was sent on August 5, 1913; the message reads, "Out selling meat today. We have lamb and veal. Ed." Lower Oswegatchie, the area around Little River, was the first settled part of the village in 1870. That year, a crib dam and Charles Colby's up-and-down sawmill were built on the far side of the iron bridge. The sawmill was later equipped with a circular saw and eventually owned by Claude Colton. The gristmill on the near side of the bridge was built in 1895 by Claude's father, Ezra; by 1907, Claude also owned this mill. The below card, dated April 21, 1911, features a photograph taken below the Little River bridge looking up to the dam that powered Colton's mills. A horse-drawn wagon and a two-wheeled buggy are on the bridge. The iron bridge was replaced in 1926 by a concrete bridge when Route 3 was constructed. The saw and feed mills were sold in 1956 by Claude Colton's son Ellis to Winfred Trudo, owner of Trudo Lumber & Building Supply.

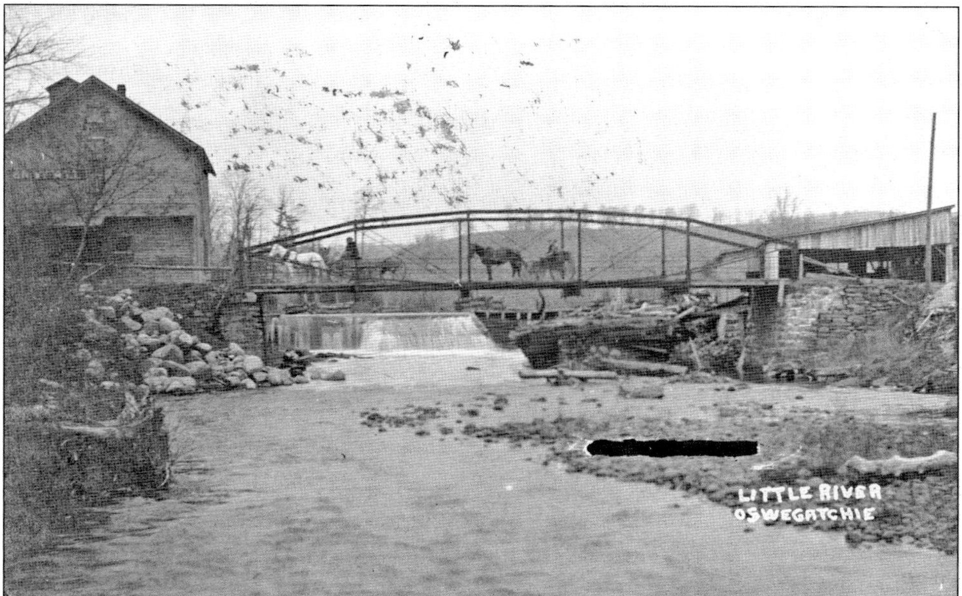

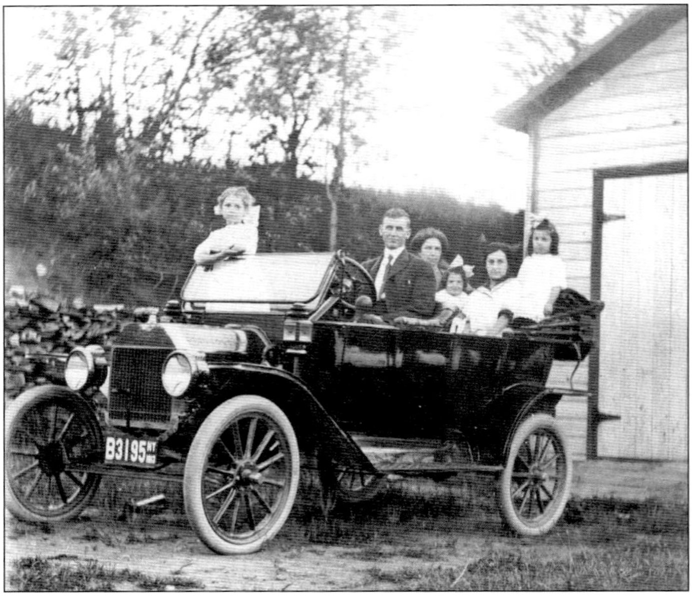

Prosperous businessmen in Oswegatchie were the first to acquire automobiles; Claude Colton purchased a Model T in 1908. Frank Kelly drove a Stanley Steamer; Kelly was a harness maker, and also sold bicycles and auto supplies at his store. The card notes, "Uncle Claude and Aunt Mary [Johnson] Colton and family at Oswegatchie." The license plate on their Model T reads 1913, the first year New York required plates to display their date of issue. A base Model T touring car in 1913 cost $600, equal to about $15,000 today.

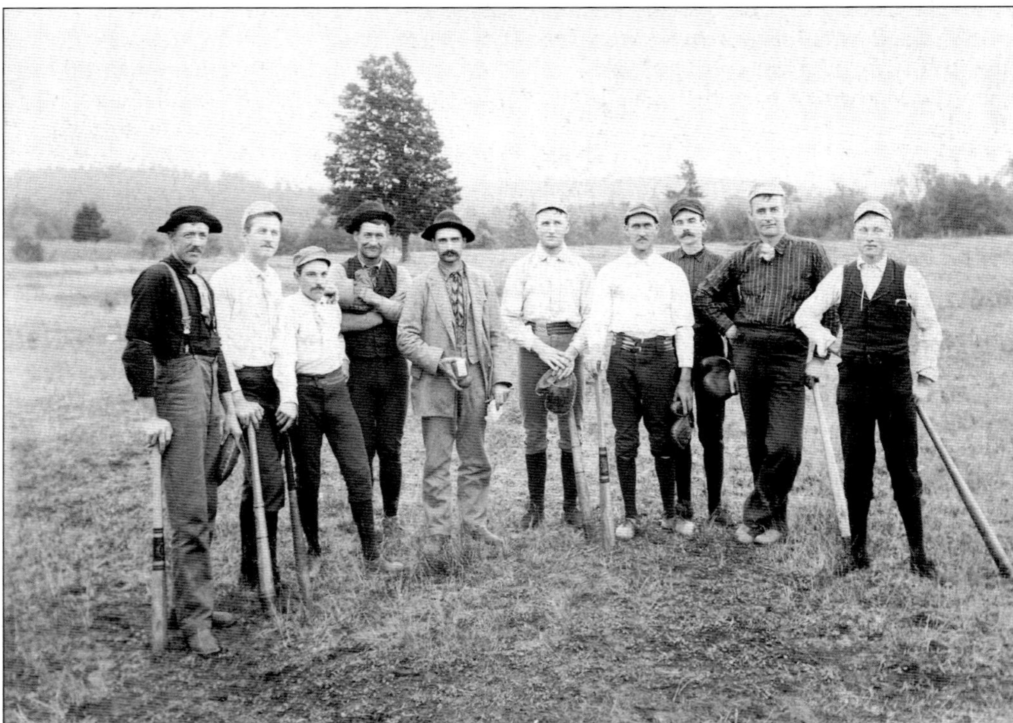

An Oswegatchie "base ball" nine is pictured in this photograph. From left to right are George Rice, Lee Caisy, Asa Hawley, George Brown, Mike Hayes (manager), Will O'Connell, Fred Waite, George Libby Jr., Den Carline, and Art Moore. In 1905, the *Ogdensburg Advance* reported that "Oswegatchie has some very fast players . . . fans are talking of hiring a crack pitcher." Trick pitches and inside strategy won low-scoring games during the early "dead ball" era. The grimy ball in the manager's hand would have been used for an entire game, becoming harder to see and unpredictable.

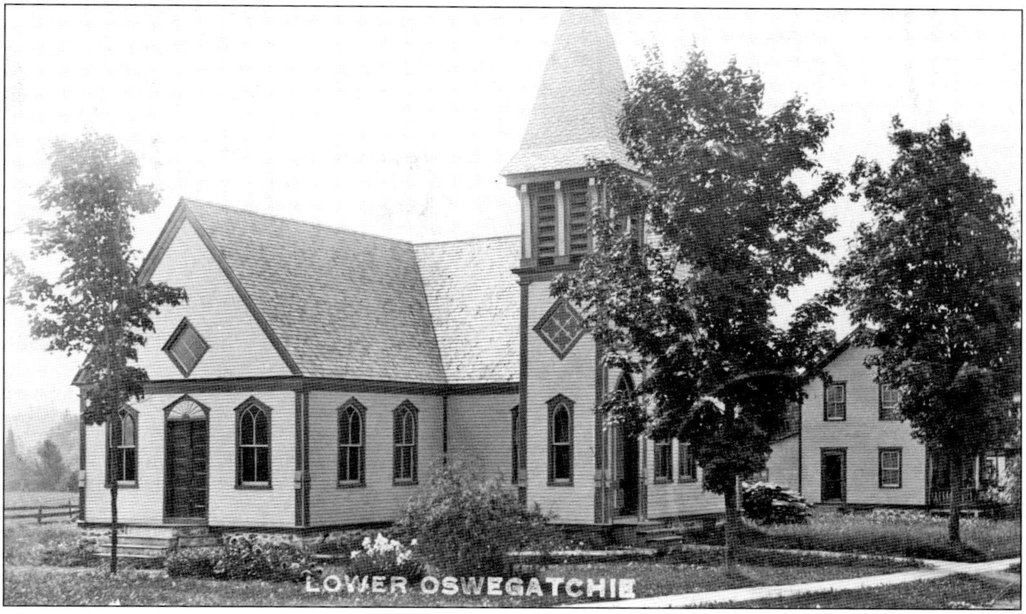

In 1874, the Baptists organized in Oswegatchie, with seven members. Their Union Church was built in 1890 in lower Oswegatchie. It served the Baptist and Methodist congregations until 1896, when the Methodists built their own church in Upper Oswegatchie. In 1898, Union Church officially became First Baptist Church under Rev. Clemons Shaw; founders included members of the Colton, Irvin, Ford, and Partlow families. Reverend Shaw received $5 per Sunday sermon. The church still conducts services year-round.

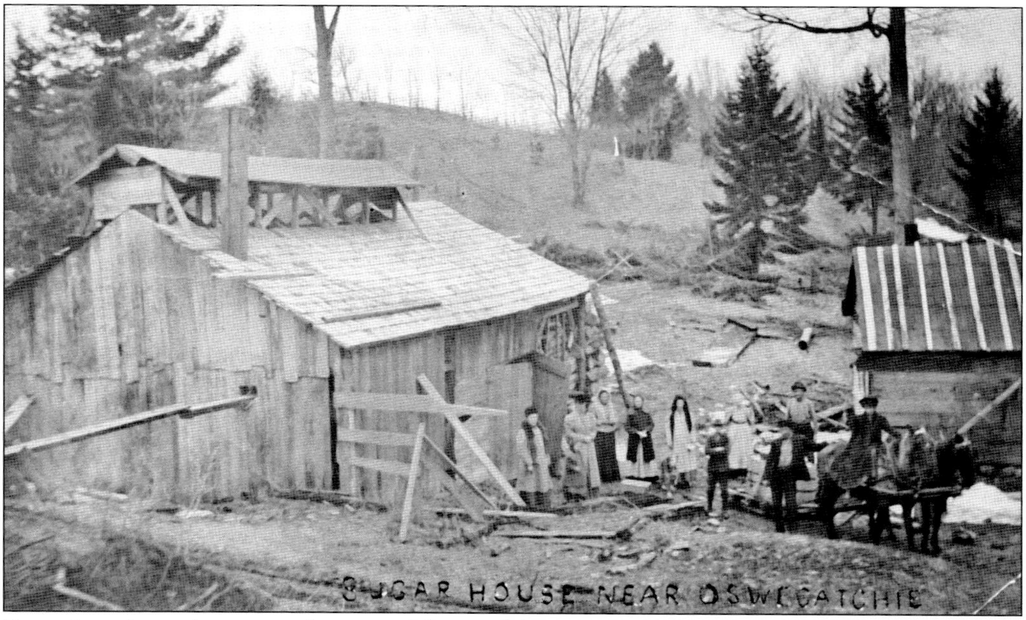

Farmers made maple syrup in the spring. This card shows a "Sugar House near Oswegatchie." At right, a team of horses is pulling a sled with a large tub. Sap was gathered in buckets, emptied into the tub, and drawn to the wood-fired evaporator. Often, the sap was boiled until it formed crystallized sugar; for the author's grandmother, growing up in Orford, New Hampshire, this was the rule. It stored indefinitely, could be used as sugar, or heated in a two-to-one ratio with water to make syrup.

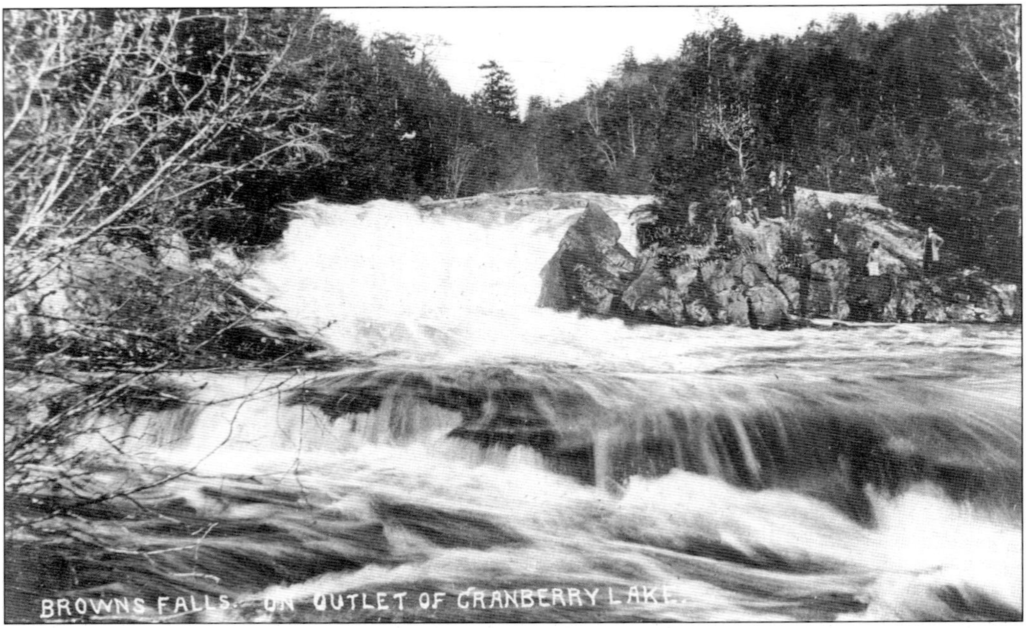

Browns Falls is on the east branch of the Oswegatchie River, flowing from Cranberry Lake. The first permanent home, a sawmill, and schoolhouse were built in 1834–1835 by Amasa Brown. By 1840, about 30 families had settled at Browns Falls. In 1844, the town of Fine was formed, named after Judge John Fine of Ogdensburg, landowner and sponsor of Amasa Brown, who became the first supervisor. This postcard of the falls by Henry Beach first appeared as a photograph in the August 10, 1890, edition of the *Illustrated Buffalo Express*.

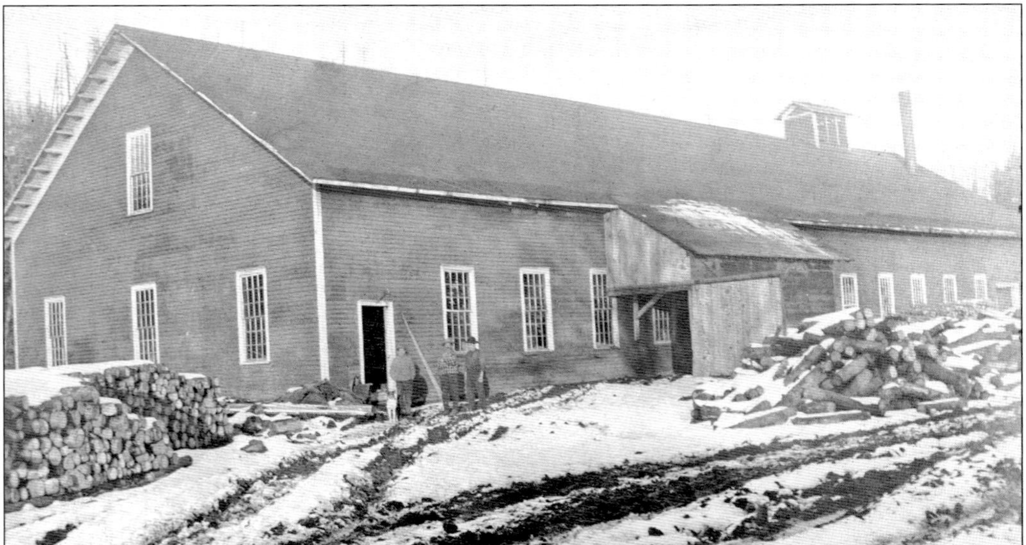

Ezra Jenne, born in Gouverneur, established the Standard Pulp Company at Browns Falls in 1892 and built a timber dam. The pulp mill on the south shore had a flume directing the water over eight wheels that drove the mill's machinery, supplied by Lowville Iron Works. Wood was sawn into four-foot lengths, debarked, and chopped. The sticks were sent to stone grinders to produce pulp, pressed into thick sheets, and then sent to Carthage paper mills, which leased the pulp mill in 1905. By 1910, it was closed and razed.

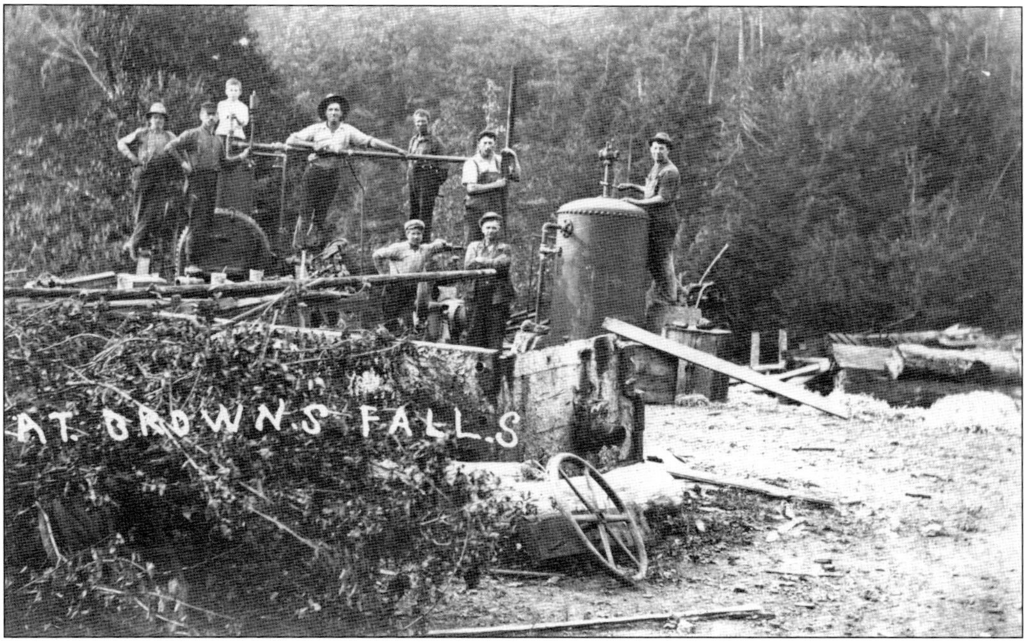

Operations at nearby Benson Mines needed a more reliable source of electricity. In 1912, the Benson Mines Company built a power plant at Browns Falls, about five miles away. The plant was downstream from the former pulp mill and used its log dam. The flume was fitted with a penstock, a 500-foot pipe that would allow for a greater drop and more generating power. The top card is one of a set showing construction work at Browns Falls from 1912 to 1914. The message on one card states, "Finished dam work 2 weeks ago Saturday. Finished getting out equipment 1 week ago Saturday. Now working for Benson Mines Co." Two generators were ordered for the power plant and sent by rail to the nearest depot, at Oswegatchie. The card below shows a team of 10 horses pulling one of the generators; the lower Oswegatchie iron bridge is in the background. The team is accompanied by at least a dozen men, probably to assist with control on the downhill run between the railroad station and the Browns Falls road.

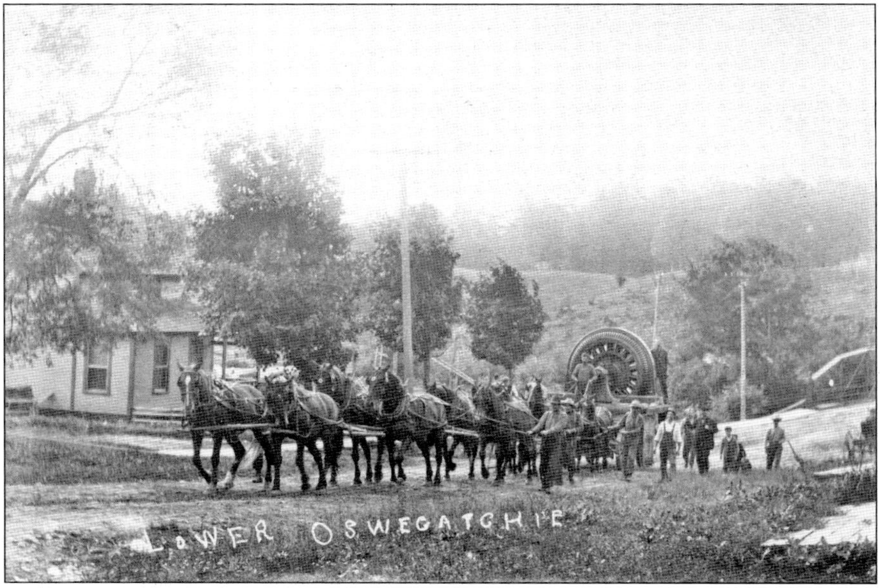

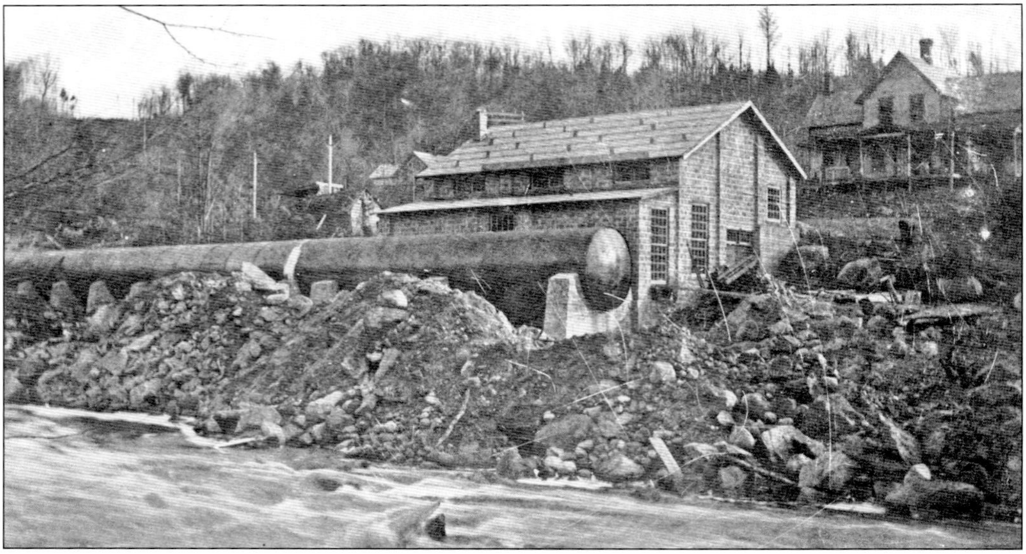

The 10-foot-diameter penstock was tapped at the power plant by two smaller pipes that descended through the floor and into the turbines. Each turbine turned a shaft connected to a generator on the first floor. Magnetic forces formed a current of electricity, carried to Benson Mines by wires on overhead towers. Water from the turbines flushed back to the river in a tailrace. This card was postmarked at Oswegatchie on September 10, 1913. Former pulp mill worker houses on the hill were also used during power plant construction.

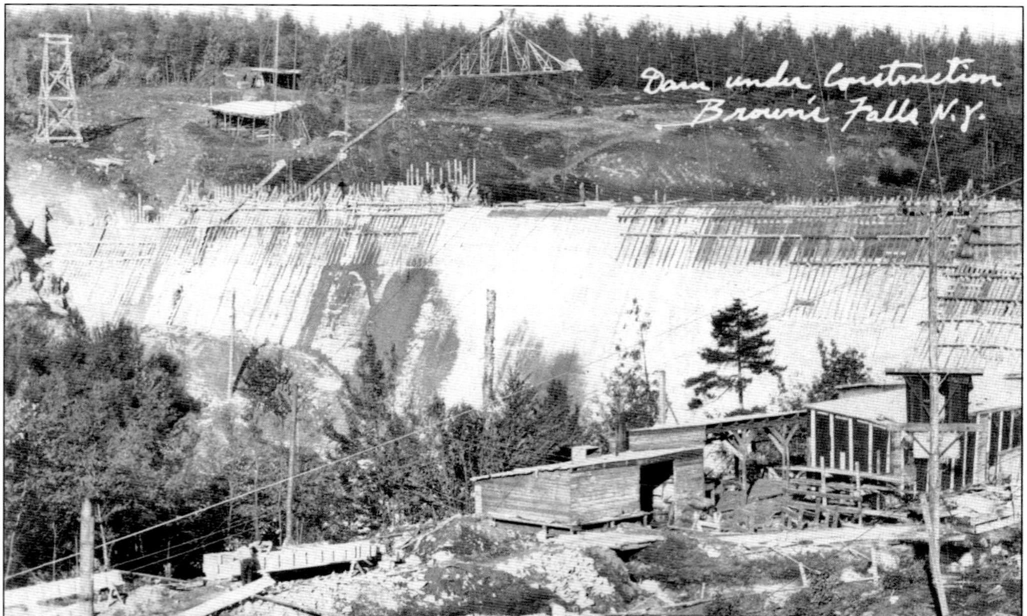

In 1914, Benson Mines Company built a concrete dam a half mile above the old dam, then ceased work. In 1919, Northern New York Utilities purchased the waterpower and enlarged the concrete dam to about 70 feet high and 800 feet long, as seen in this October 20, 1922, postmarked card. A 7,000-foot penstock was built leading to a new powerhouse, where two turbines each sent 12,500 horsepower to a generator. On May 15, 1923, the *Gouverneur Free Press* reported that the plant began sending current to Utica.

Three

Benson Mines

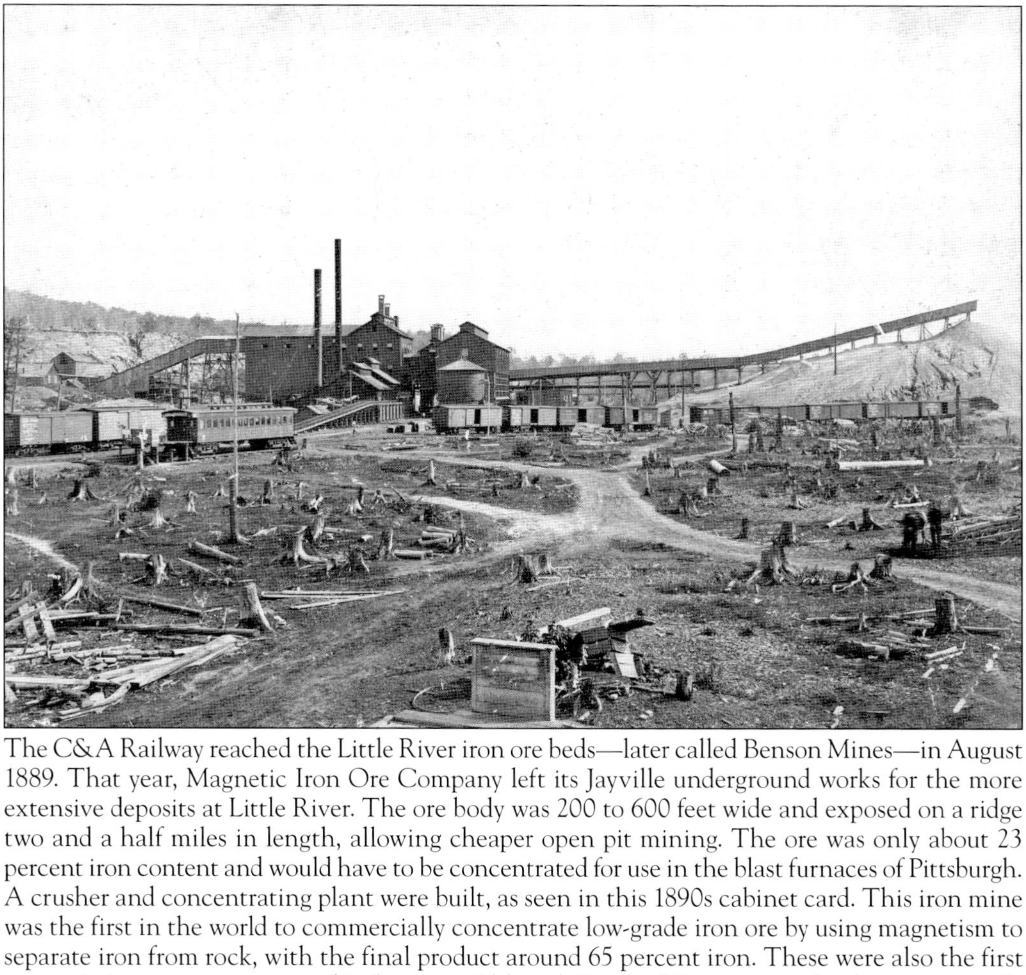

The C&A Railway reached the Little River iron ore beds—later called Benson Mines—in August 1889. That year, Magnetic Iron Ore Company left its Jayville underground works for the more extensive deposits at Little River. The ore body was 200 to 600 feet wide and exposed on a ridge two and a half miles in length, allowing cheaper open pit mining. The ore was only about 23 percent iron content and would have to be concentrated for use in the blast furnaces of Pittsburgh. A crusher and concentrating plant were built, as seen in this 1890s cabinet card. This iron mine was the first in the world to commercially concentrate low-grade iron ore by using magnetism to separate iron from rock, with the final product around 65 percent iron. These were also the first magnetic iron concentrates used in furnaces. Although Benson Mines operated only intermittently from 1889 to 1918, it was noted for its use of innovative technologies.

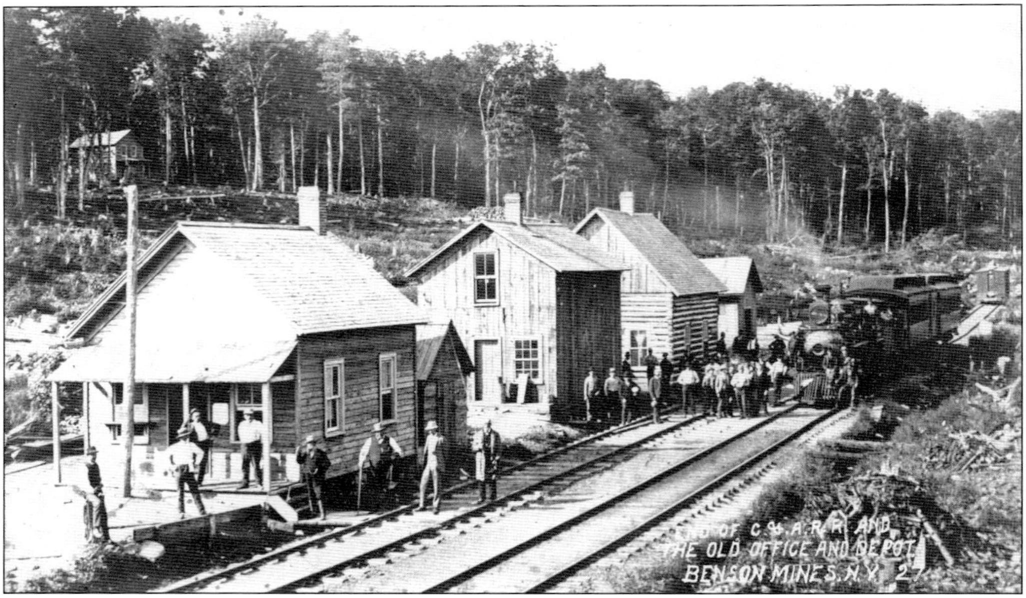

This postcard reprints an 1889 photograph by Henry Beach. It states, "End of C&A RR and the old Office and Depot, Benson Mines NY." The engine may be Carthage & Adirondack No. 1, *B.D. Benson*, purchased in 1886. In August 1888, Magnetic Iron Ore Company executed a mortgage for $600,000 with the Central Trust Company of New York; the loan was to fund equipment and build a plant at Benson Mines. Titles and rights to over 300,000 acres of northern New York land in four counties were pledged as collateral.

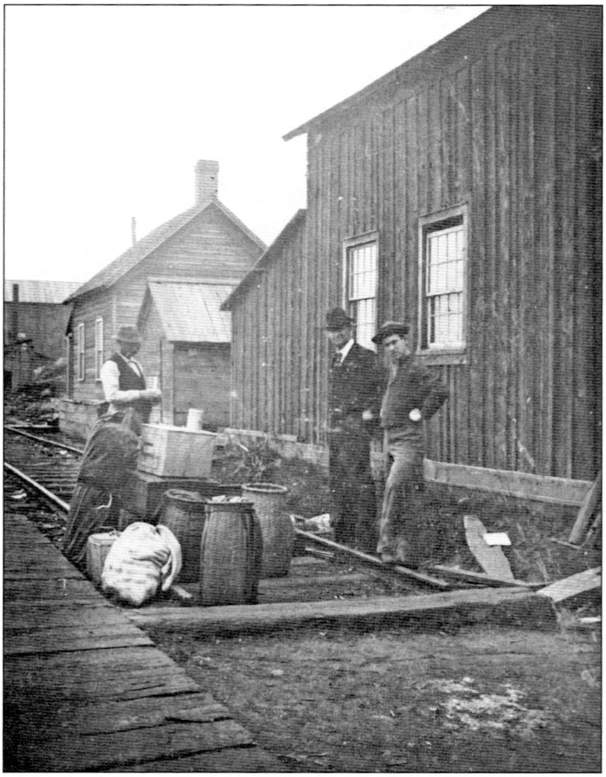

Benson Mines station was used by tourists to reach popular Star Lake. This cabinet card shows that sportsmen also took advantage of the new depot. The three men on the side track are equipped with rifles, pack baskets, a portable oven, and trunks. They are waiting for transport into the wilderness, possibly by stagecoach to Sternberg's Hotel, built in 1884 on the Inlet, three miles away. Guests could paddle up the Oswegatchie to world-famous trout fishing or carry boats two miles downstream to where the river flowed into Cranberry Lake.

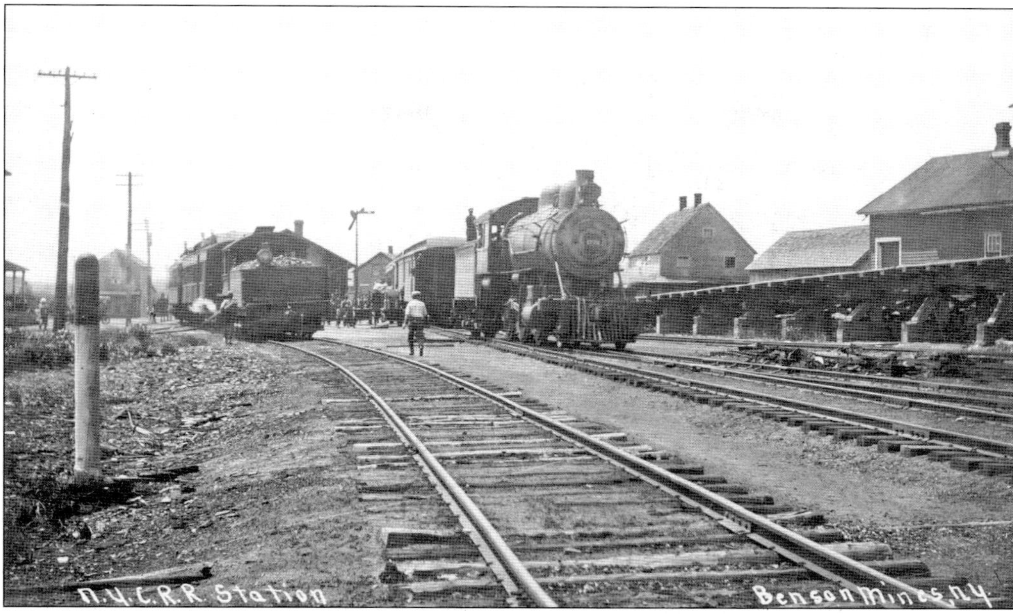

The new mining town was often featured in county newspapers. On August 22, 1891, the *Ogdensburg Journal* described a trip by rail from Carthage to Benson Mines, stating that "the company operating the mines intends to make it one of the largest in the country . . . although nearly 600 tons of the finest ore is taken from the mines every day, it is expected that by next year the output will be trebled." In December 1891, the *Journal* described how the freight train crew had a narrow escape when a large blast at the mines threw pieces of ore through the caboose. On February 7, 1900, the *Northern Tribune* informed readers that due to the heavy workload, a new (and younger) station agent had been assigned, and the depot was being enlarged. In 1902, it became a union station, with the chartering of the Cranberry Lake Railroad to Wanakena. All this meant that by the time of these 1907 cards, the Benson Mines railyard was crowded with the C&A main line, side tracks, and spurs.

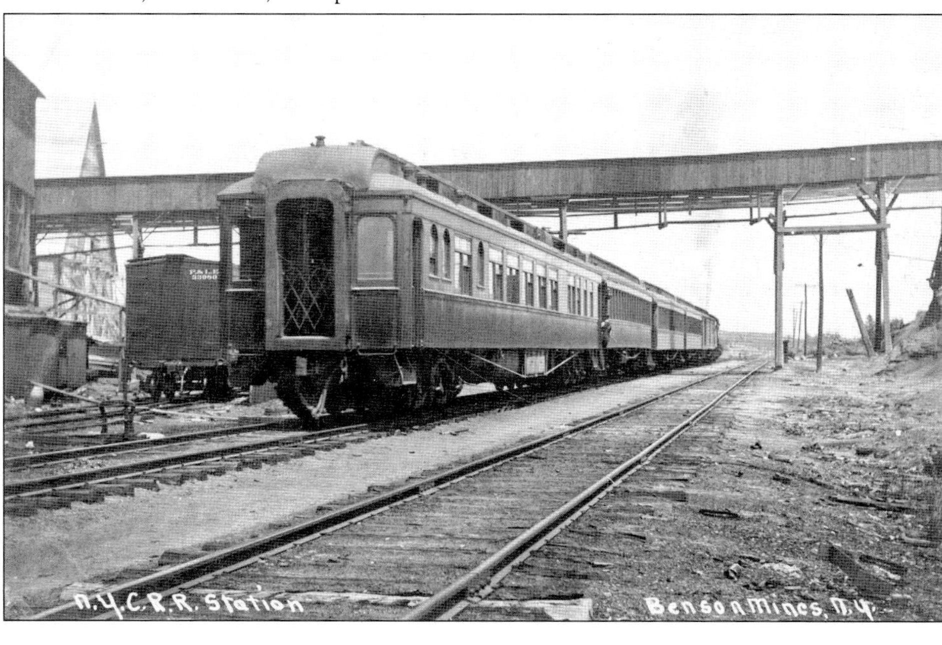

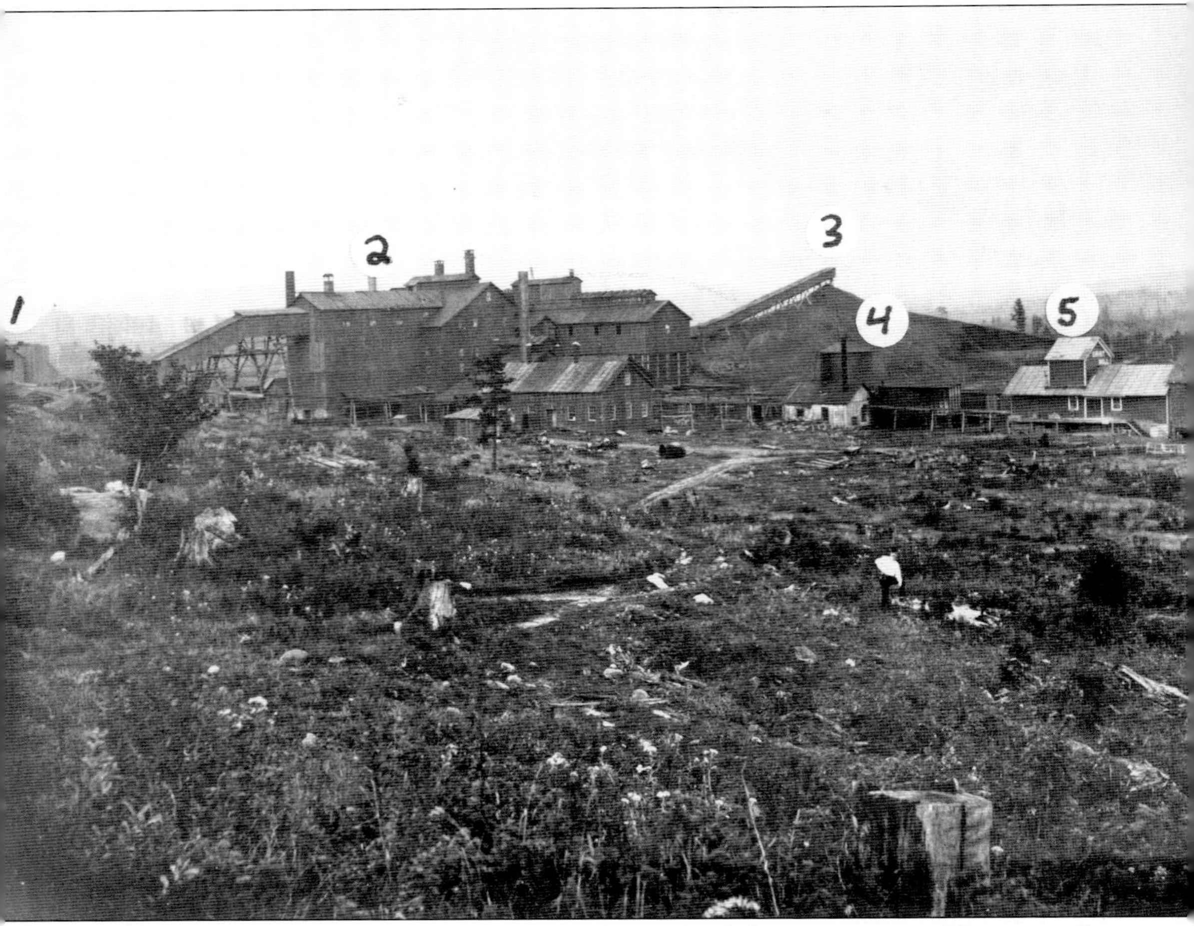

After 1889, Benson Mines grew into a substantial town, divided into two sections. The upper village held about 20 worker homes, a school, and two churches. The lower village included the depot, the Ellsworth hotel, the company store, a gristmill, and more homes, stores, and saloons lining the tracks. Until 1907, operations were sporadic, following cycles in the iron trade; the years 1889 to 1893 and 1900 to 1901 were the only periods at full capacity. By 1905, iron consumption was growing rapidly, and plans were made to improve and expand the concentrating plant at Benson Mines. An article in the *Massena Observer*, dated June 13, 1907, announced, "Benson Mines to Boom," due to the high price of iron ore; also, Magnetic Iron Ore's property was now leased to the

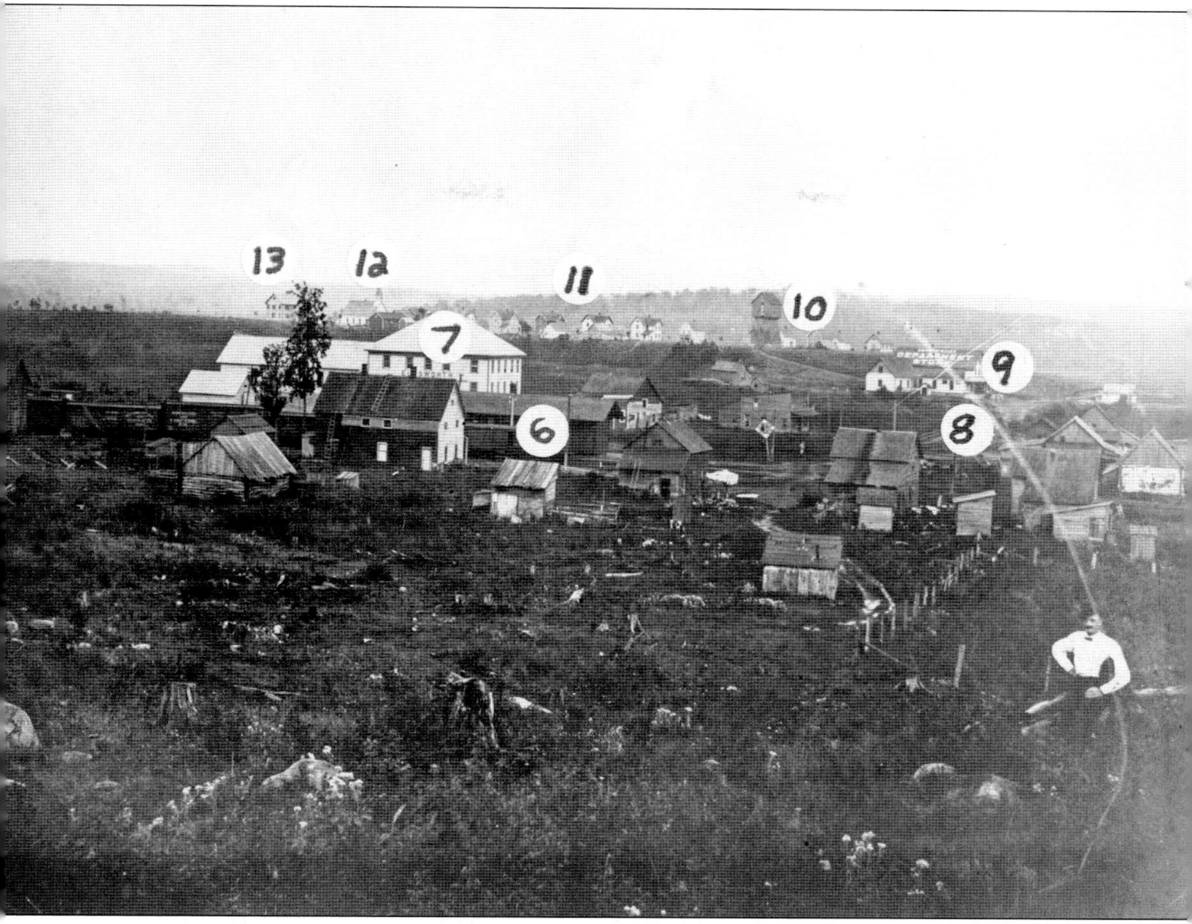

Benson Mines Company. After spending $150,000 on new mining and milling equipment, full operations began in fall 1907. This panoramic photograph is from around 1902–1905; the view is southeast from the lower to the upper village. The open-pit mine (out of view) was cut into a ridge northeast from the concentrating plant. The numbers on the image identify: (1) crushers, (2) magnetic concentrating plant, (3) waste rock conveyor and tailings pile, (4) railroad water tank, (5) gristmill, (6) Carthage & Adirondack/New York Central depot, (7) Ellsworth Hotel and barn, (8) Little River bridge, (9) Benson Mines company store and office, (10) Upper Village water tank, (11) worker homes, (12) Roman Catholic church, and (13) public school.

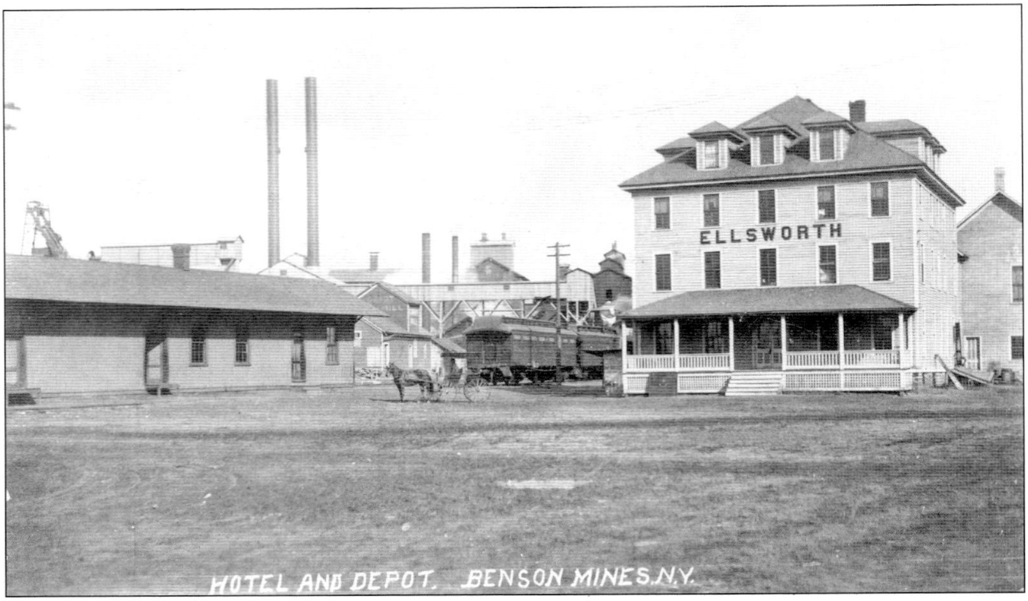

The Ellsworth Hotel was built in 1903 by master chef Sylvester "Sam" Spain. Spain's Parker House rolls and the Ellsworth's large bar made it the most popular hotel at Benson Mines. On September 21, 1908, an exhibition boxing match was presented between Bob Fitzsimmons, 46-year-old-former world heavyweight champion, and Jim Paul, champion lumberjack brawler. The *Watertown Times* reported that Spain sat ringside with a baseball bat, while the referee attempted to restrain Paul from kicking, biting, and gouging. Fitzsimmons ended the match decisively in the fourth round.

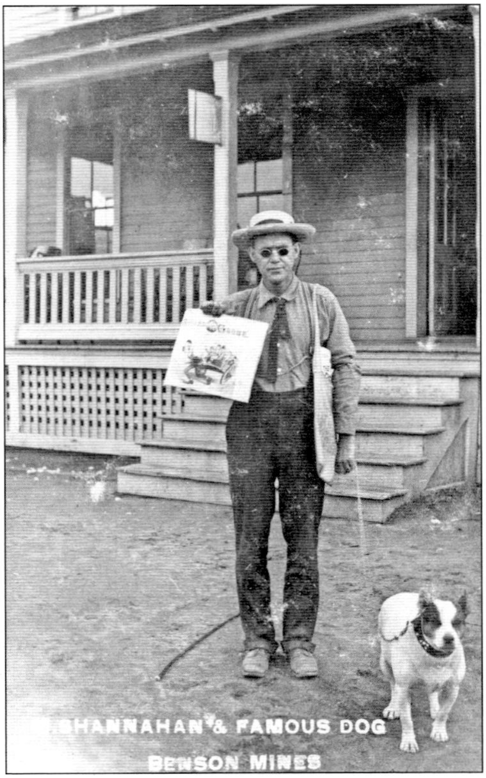

Mike Shanahan was born in Pennsylvania in 1865. On February 27, 1893, he lost his sight in an explosion while working on the Gouverneur & Oswegatchie Railroad. Shanahan was clearing a blasting hole of "ice;" it was actually dynamite. After his discharge from the Ogdensburg hospital, he attended a school for the blind and learned to use a guide dog; he then became a newspaper and magazine vendor. Shanahan is pictured in front of the Ellsworth Hotel with his "famous dog," holding a *Saturday Globe*. He had 14 guide dogs during his career.

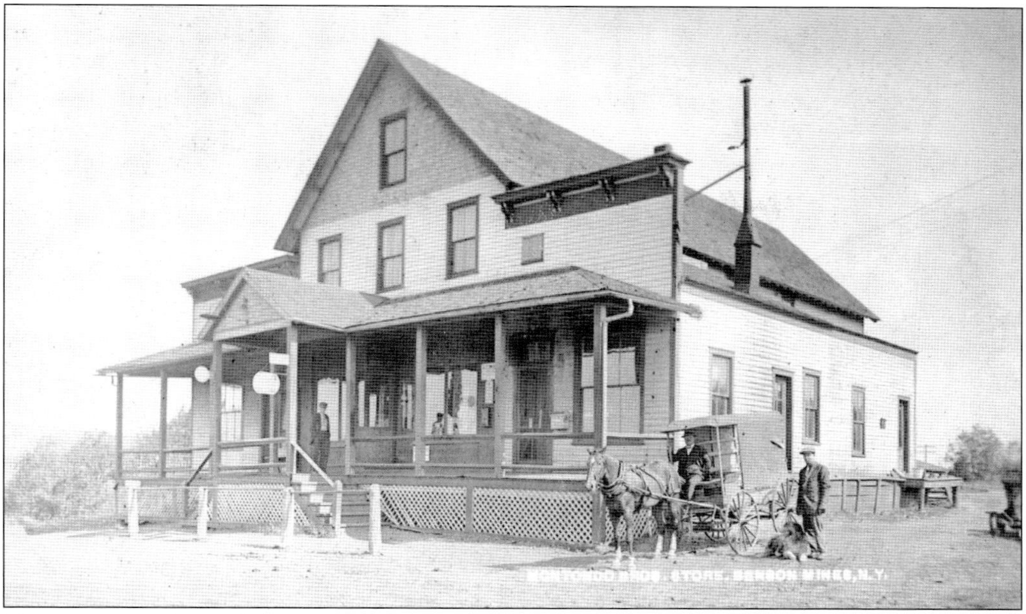

Magnetic Iron Ore built its company store in 1892 near the Little River bridge, between the upper and lower villages. The first floor housed the general store, post office, company office, laboratory, and a meat market. A dry goods and millinery department were on the second floor. Furniture, undertaking services, and automobile rentals were also offered by the Montando brothers, store proprietors at the time of this c. 1910 card. Local deliveries were made by the horse and wagon pictured. The store burned in February 1933.

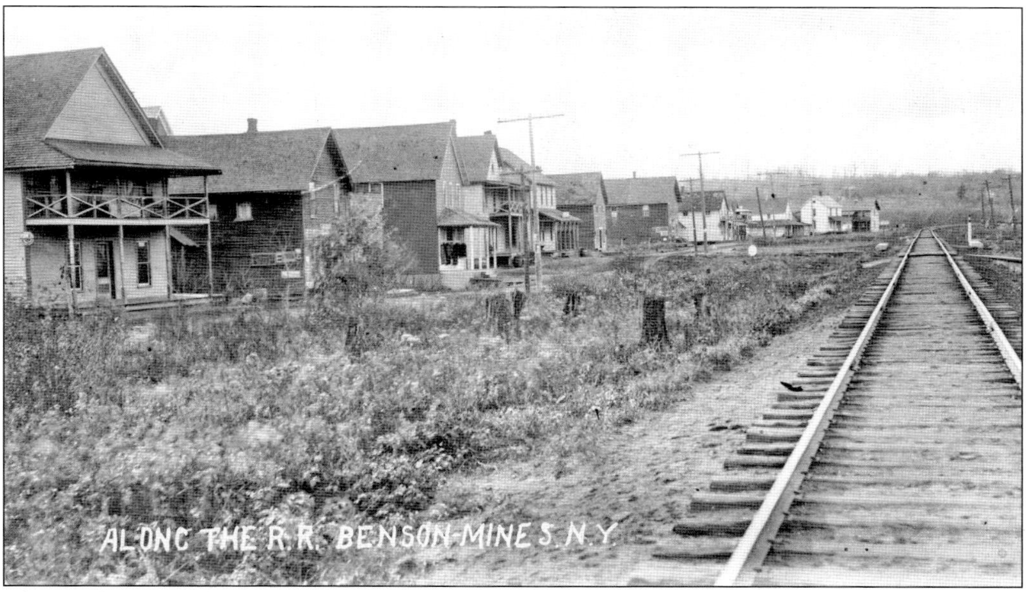

The "Midway" was located along the C&A tracks leading into Benson Mines. It held a few stores and small hotels and plenty of saloons. Patrons were miners, residents of nearby dry towns, and lumberjacks spending their season's pay by treating entire barrooms to drinks. From left to right are Bart Lyman's saloon (West End Ales & Lager), Brady's store (Helmar Turkish Cigarettes and American Navy Plug), O. Bauman & Sons Clothes, the Benson Mines Hotel, Berry's saloon, Cady's store, Roushorn's saloon, a boardinghouse, and two Burrell brothers saloons.

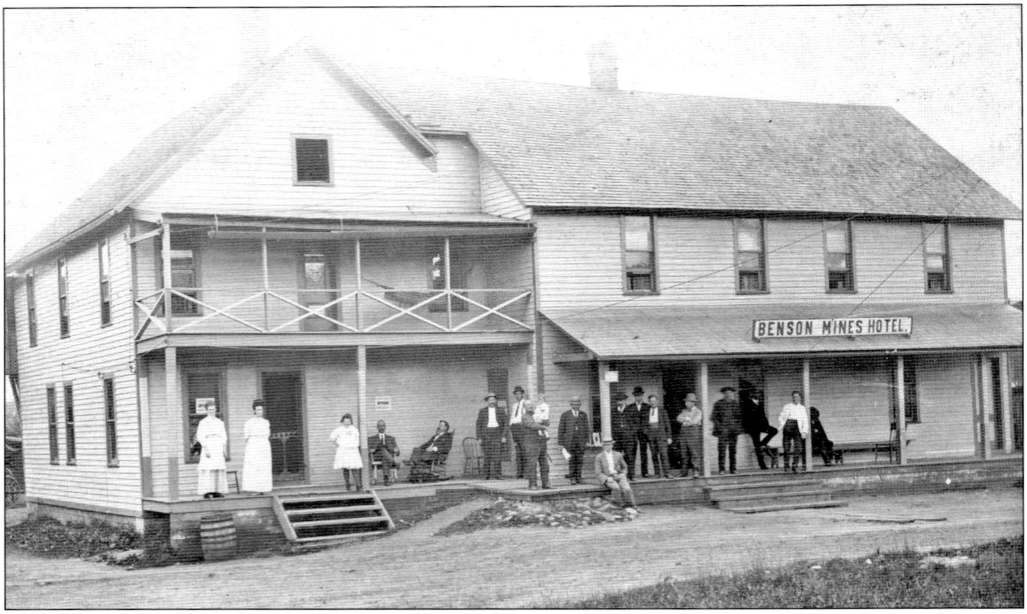

This card, postmarked at Benson Mines on August 14, 1907, shows the Benson Mines Hotel—the second-most patronized hotel after the Ellsworth. The sender notes that it had the only available room he could find; 1907 was an active year at Benson Mines, with ambitious plans and new construction. A sign reads, "Optician Here Today;" dangerous work and few safety precautions might have kept the optician busy. Accidents resulting from the proximity of the hotels and saloons in the Midway to the railroad tracks were also numerous.

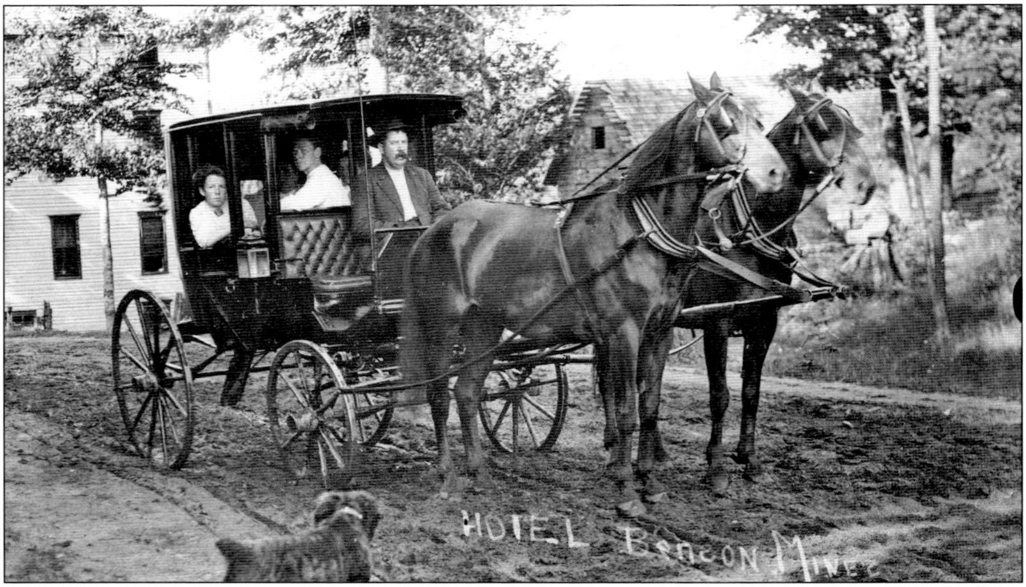

This unused card is labeled "Hotel Benson Mines." The carriage probably does not belong to the Ellsworth Hotel in the background, which was located next to the C&A depot. The Benson Mines Hotel is more likely, as it was located along the tracks a half mile west of the depot. This older, Rockaway style carriage is fancy (for Benson Mines), with diamond-pleated upholstery, roll-down curtains, and beveled glass and brass lanterns. The light horse team with its cigar-chomping driver looks set to deliver a fast ride around town.

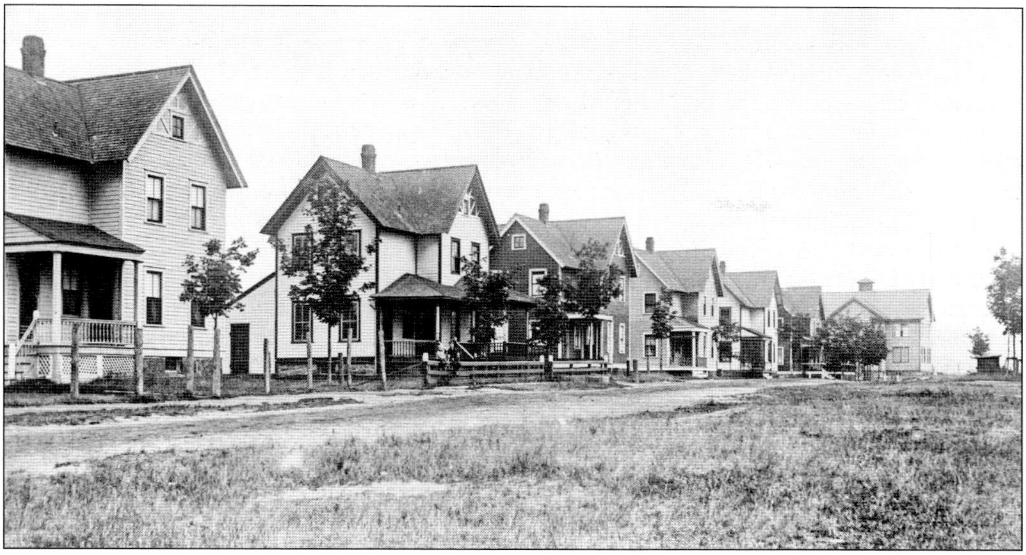

In June 1892, the *Northern Tribune* reported that Magnetic Iron Ore was building a school and 16 worker houses. The public school is at the far end of this line of residences. More homes were built across from these, at the southern end of Magnetic Iron Ore's property. They were for supervisors and workers with families. When Jones & Laughlin Steel took over operation of Benson Mines in the early 1940s, these houses were moved to Star Lake, grouped into the Woodhaven location, and assigned to managers and technical staff.

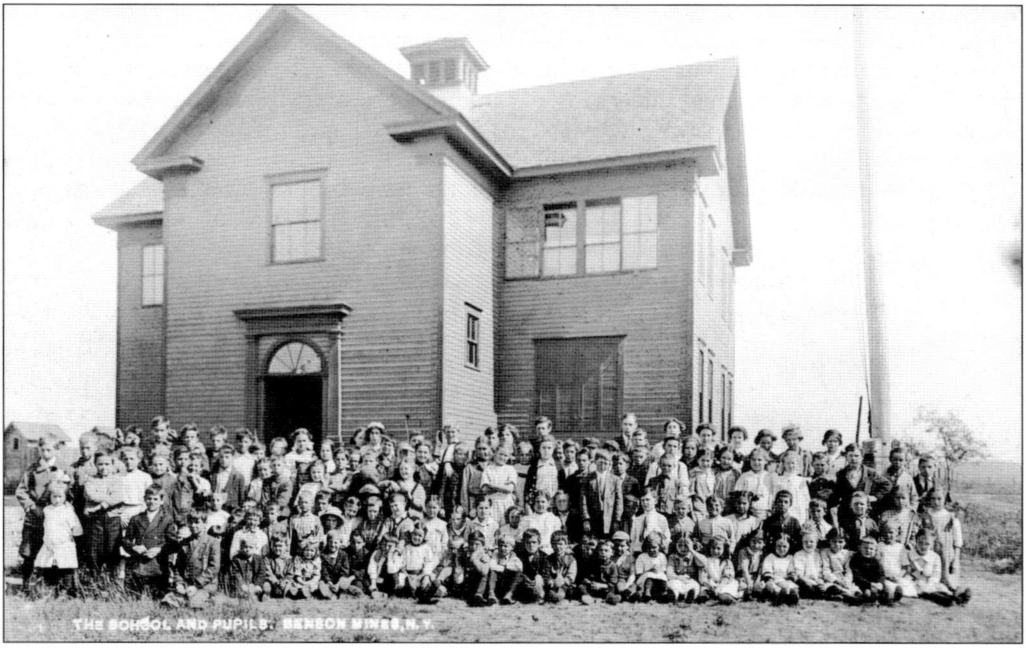

Many workers at Benson Mines were French-Canadians with large families. In this card postmarked on October 22, 1913, at least 115 students are pictured, plus six teachers and a principal. A 1904 article in the *Ogdensburg Journal* reported that the school held a well-attended ice-cream social for the benefit of its library and gym, netting $15. The school was not moved to Star Lake later by Jones & Laughlin. It served as the company office until mid-1951, when a new office building was completed, and the school was demolished.

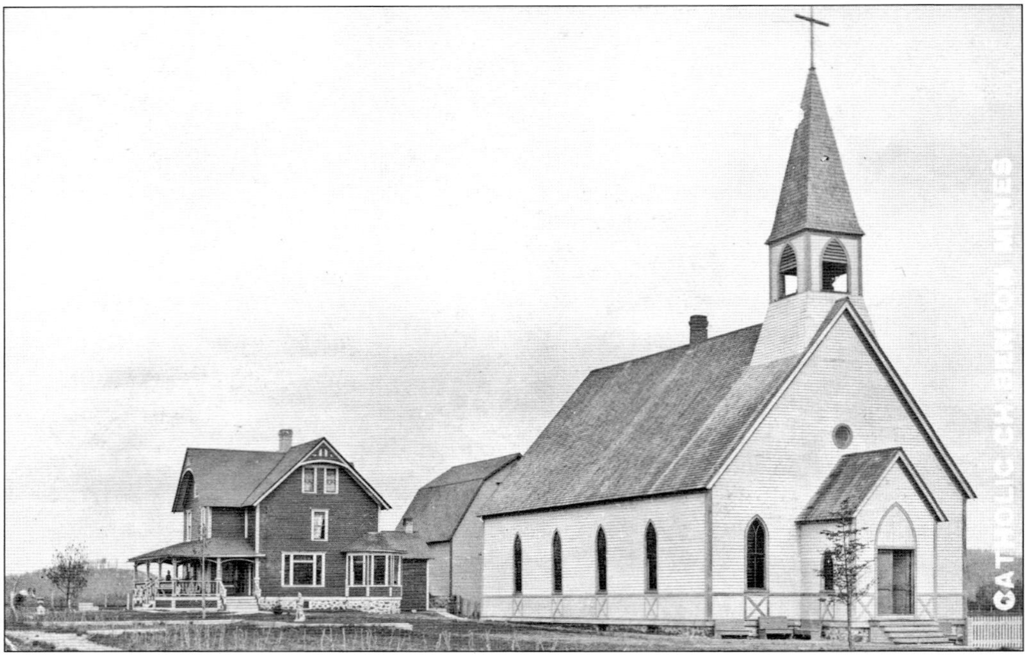

In 1892, Magnetic Iron Ore donated land across from the public school for a Catholic church. St. Hubert's Church—named for the patron saint of hunters—was dedicated on July 30, 1893. The rectory was built in 1906 by the Burrell brothers, owners of two raucous saloons. In 1942, both church and rectory were moved one mile west on Route 3 to Star Lake. The church served until a new complex was built, combining church, school, and rectory. The new St. Hubert's was consecrated on July 20, 1980.

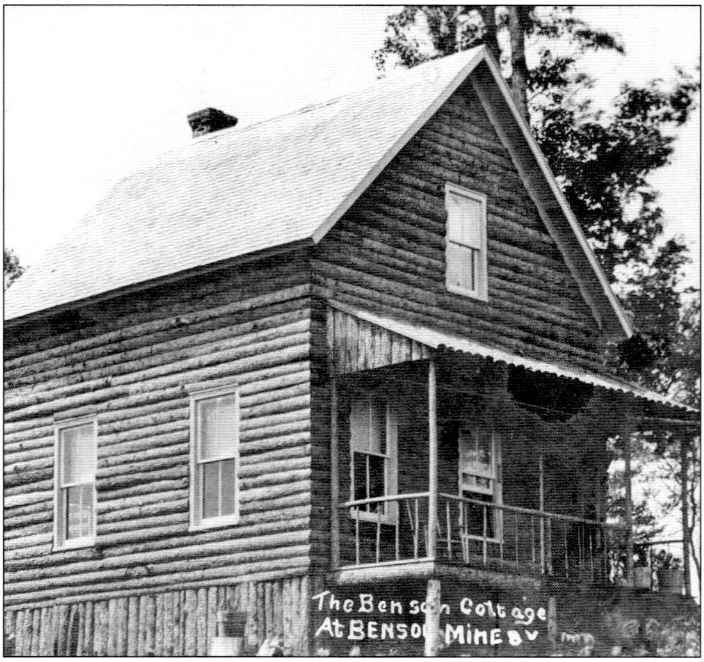

In March 1883, Magnetic Iron Ore was incorporated, and the Carthage & Adirondack Railway was chartered. Magnetic Iron Ore was controlled by Byron Benson, a native of Fabius, New York; his friends dubbed him "Little Napoleon." Benson was also president of the C&A Railway. After his death in 1888 it was left to his sons, William and Robert Benson, and another relative, Cadwell Benson, to oversee the move from Jayville to the Little River iron ore beds. This card of the family cottage is postmarked October 15, 1909.

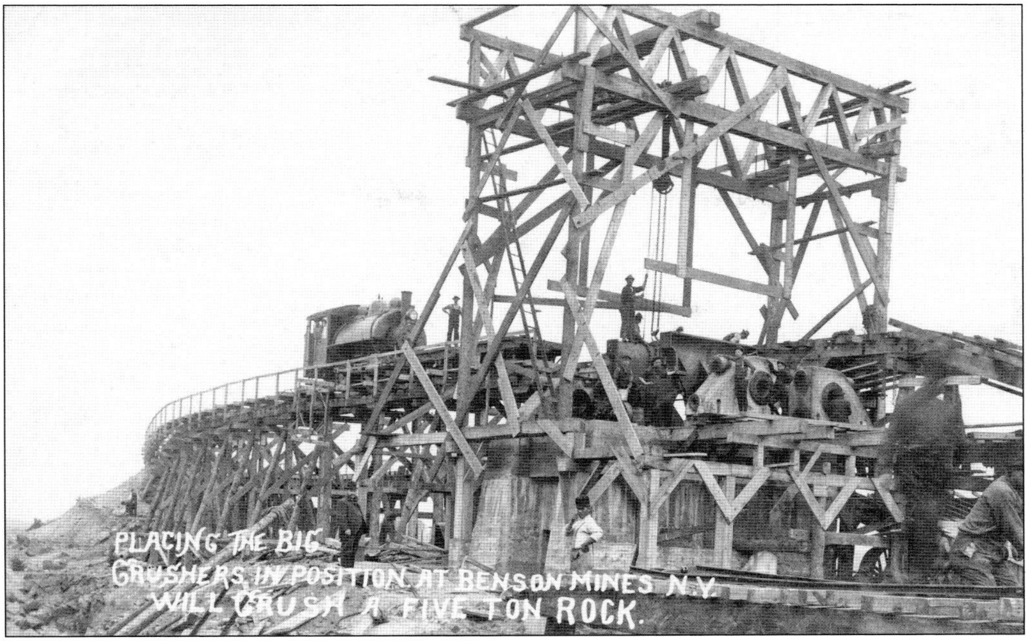

In December 1906, Benson Mines Company was incorporated in New York "to operate mines and quarries;" in 1907, the company leased Magnetic Iron Ore's property. Benson Mines Company's first project was to replace the mine's original jaw crushers with more efficient roller crushers. The card above by Henry Beach is titled "Placing The Big Crushers In Position At Benson Mines N.Y. Will Crush A Five Ton Rock." It shows a trestle leading from the mines to the new crusher building under construction. The small mining engine on the trestle pushed loaded ore cars to the primary six-foot Edison roller crushers, capable of handling five-ton rocks. The ore was then crushed by secondary rollers. The Beach card below shows the completed crusher building and states, "Where the Ore is Crushed, Largest Roller in the World." The ore had to be finely crushed before it was sent to the magnetic separators in the complex to the left of the crusher building. At full capacity, the crushers could process about 1,000 tons of ore daily.

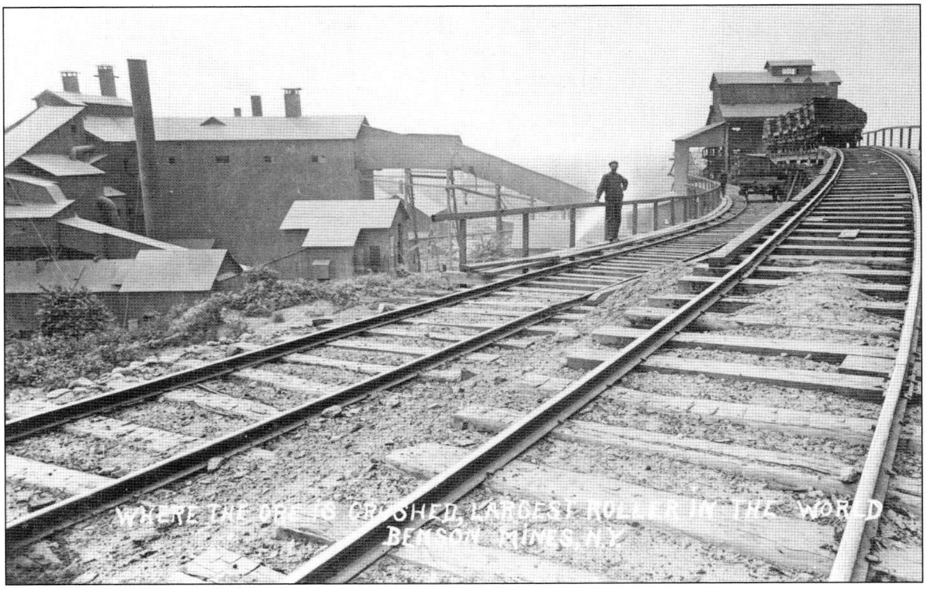

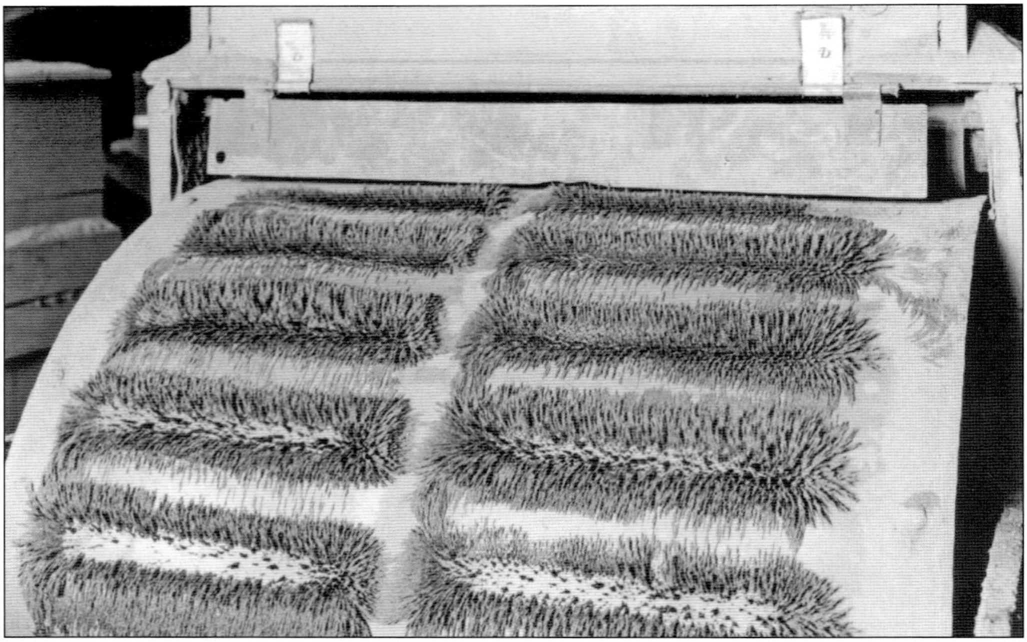

This magic lantern slide is titled "Ball-Norton Magnetic Separator, Showing Iron Adhering to Drum and Lines of Force. Benson Mines, NY, 1913." Magnetic Iron Ore initially installed three; they were replaced with improved models in 1911. The separator has stationary magnets, alternating in polarity, within a revolving brass drum. Crushed ore is deposited on a belt at the drum's top. Non-magnetic tailings are flung away; magnetite is carried to where the belt leaves the drum and magnetic field and drops into a bin. Drum separators could process 20 tons of ore hourly.

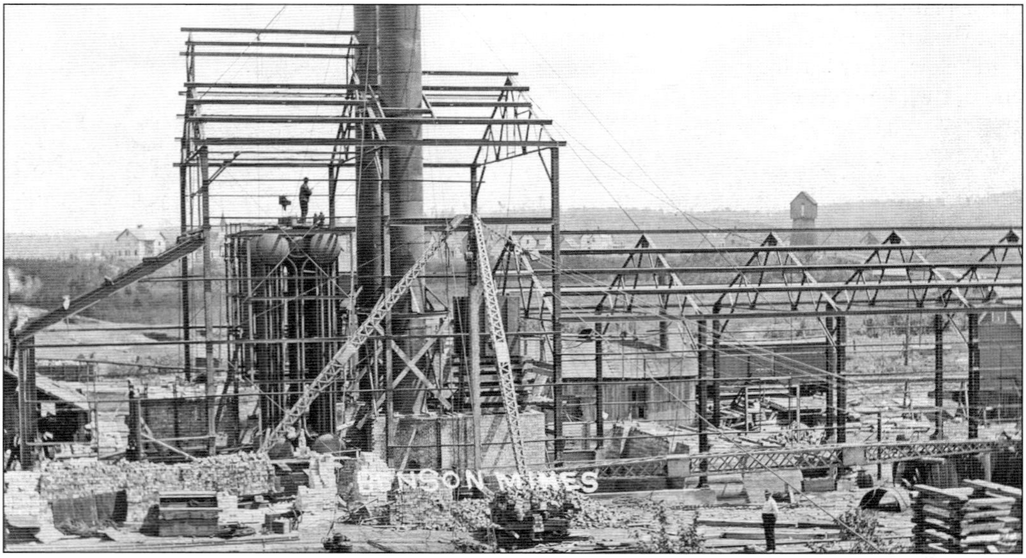

Concentrates from magnetic separators were too fine for use in a blast furnace. Benson Mines Company adopted a state-of-the-art treatment used by Northern Iron Company of Port Henry, New York. Construction of the nodulizing plant was followed by the magazine *Iron Trade Review*, reporting on promising new technology; the *Ogdensburg Journal's* articles emphasized potential jobs. Construction began in April 1909 and finished in November; the plant measured 50 by 225 feet. This view of the boiler room notes "it only shows one end of the new building."

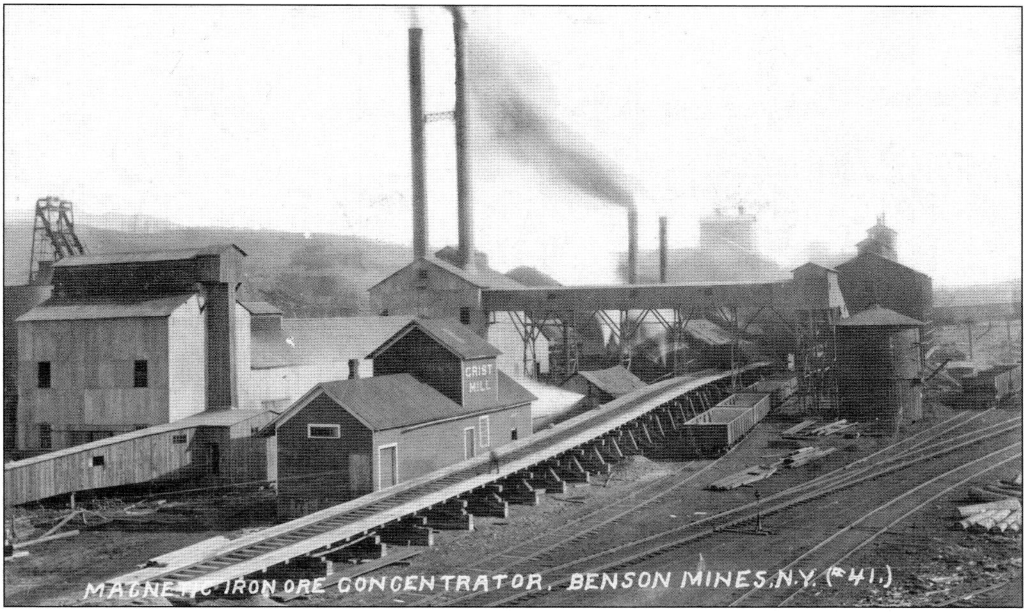

The card above shows the completed nodulizing plant next to the gristmill. The process started with magnetite from the concentrators mixed with powdered coal. This was fed into the upper end of a 100-foot-long inclined rotary kiln lined with firebrick. The coal ignited, generating high temperatures and causing the ore particles to partially fuse. The rotary action kept the ore from forming a solid mass; it agglomerated in small nodules. By the time the ore reached the lower end of the kiln, the coal was burned out, and the ore was nodulized. After cooling, the ore was stored in bins, ready to ship to furnaces. Benson Mines had two kilns, located in the long midsection of the plant. The building at the near end housed four coal-fired Westinghouse gas producers to heat the kilns. The base of two of the producers, with their water cooling jackets, is seen in the card below. After leaving the kilns, the hot exhaust gas was driven through the boilers at the far end of the plant, generating steam to power machinery.

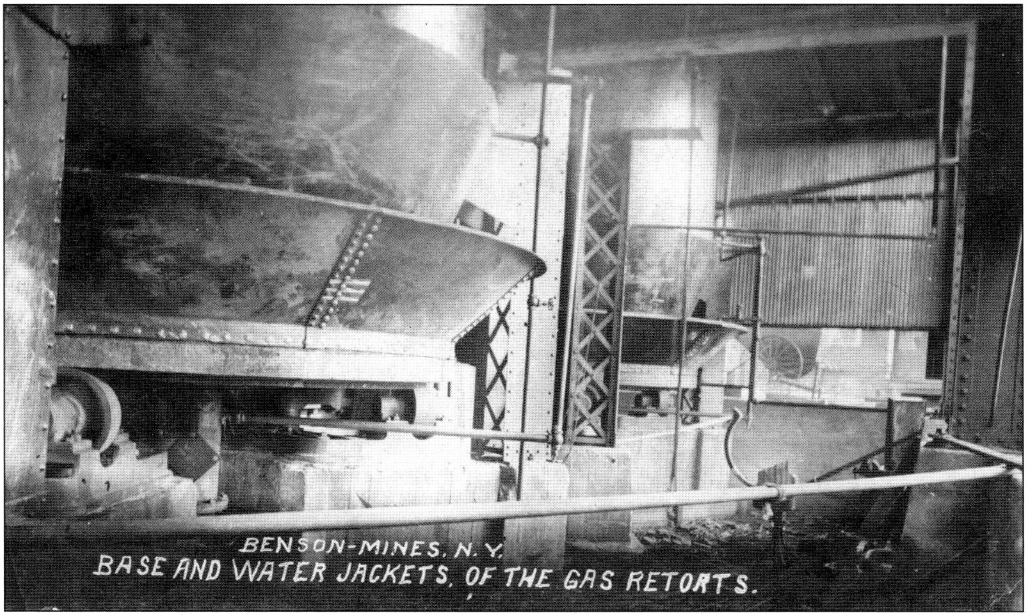

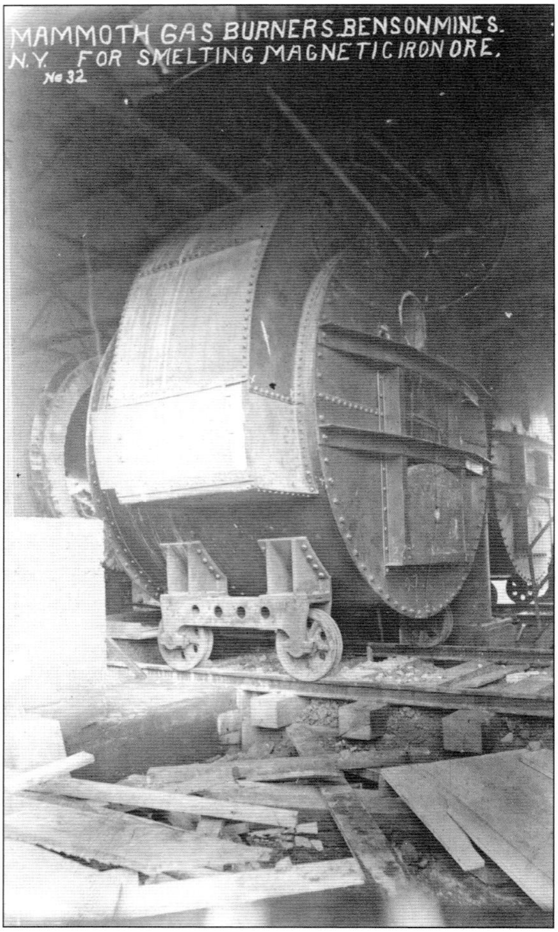

News articles estimated the cost of the nodulizing plant at $100,000; its capacity was 400 tons of ore daily. The *Ogdensburg Journal* on July 16, 1909, reported that the first of the 100-foot kilns had left Syracuse on a Friday night on three railcars, reached Carthage early on Sunday, and then took four hours to reach the mines. To get the kiln faced for unloading, the cars were run to Newton Falls, turned around on the wye, and returned to Benson Mines. On October 1, 1909, the *Journal* hailed a "Big Improvement at Benson Mines," with a three-column article on the plant startup. It noted that Benson Mines had the largest of the three nodulizing plants operating in the United States. It also described the plant's "fireproof" construction, with a steel frame and corrugated steel siding. Ten carloads of concrete were used in the foundation. These two 1911 cards show the massive doors at the upper end of the kilns and a view of the rotating kilns; the worker at the far end gives the scale.

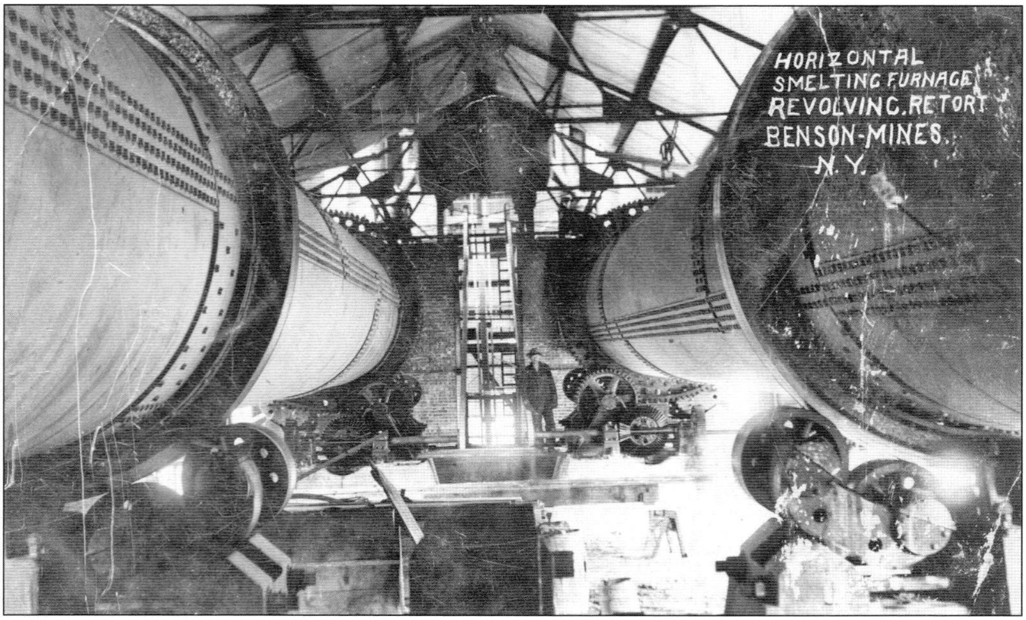

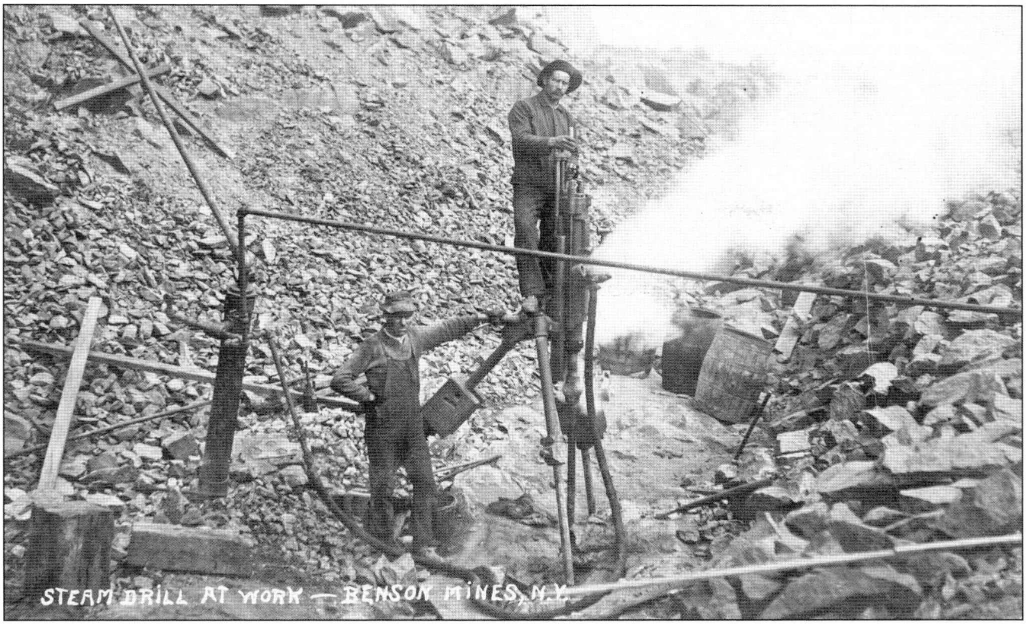

Early mining of iron ore was labor intensive and dangerous, even in open pit mines. In the 1890s, workers at Benson Mines used shovels and wagons to remove the topsoil; small steam drills bored holes into the bedrock (above), and the holes were packed with dynamite. Large chunks of rock were blasted from the face of the mine, and men with picks broke up large blocks, loaded the ore into cars, and pushed them on railways (below). The cars were pushed to the crushers by a mining locomotive. Accidents involving the use of dynamite by inexperienced workers were common; on August 15, 1908, the *New York Times* reported a calamity. Several drill holes had each been filled with 200 pounds of powdered dynamite (instead of sticks) and were being tamped with iron bars (state law required wood). A spark caused an explosion in one of the holes, which set off blasts in two adjacent holes. The detonation was heard in Star Lake. The result was the death of four men, several serious injuries, four widows, and 14 fatherless children.

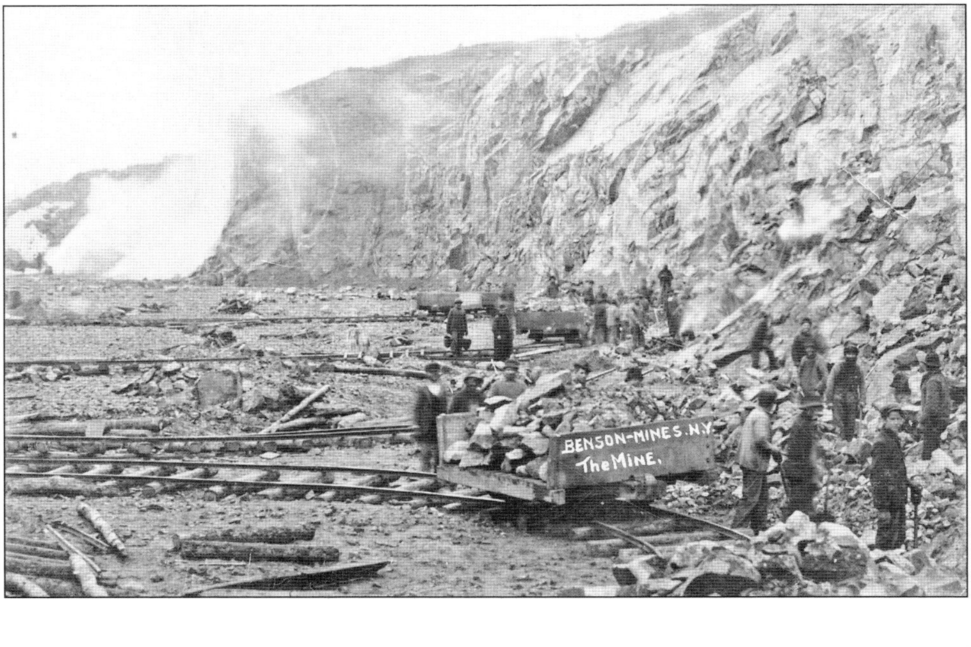

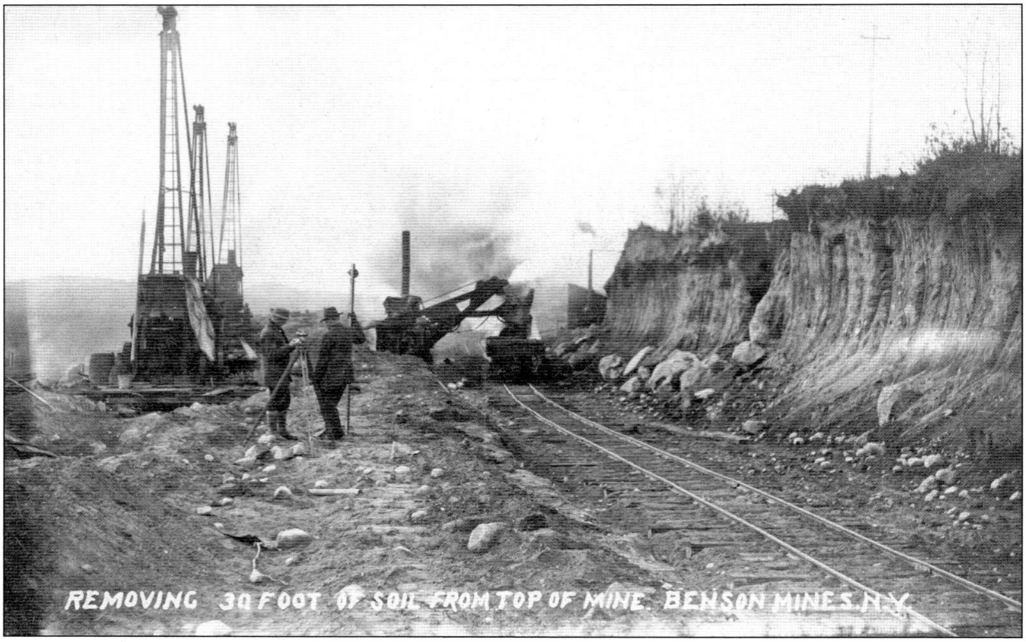

Between 1907 and 1911, Benson Mines Company replaced its steam hammer drills with more efficient churn drills. A churn drill used a heavy chisel-point drill bit connected to a cable; the bit was raised and dropped to break up rock. Liquid or compressed air flushed drill cuttings out of the hole. The card above shows steam churn drills and a steam shovel; the shovel is "Removing 30 Foot of Soil from Top of Mine." Once bedrock was reached, three churn drills—the largest available—were lined up on the edge of the pit, as seen below. They drilled a row of holes 50 feet deep and four to six inches in diameter. Powder from broken sticks of dynamite was poured into the holes and packed with a tamping bar, then electrically detonated. Henry Beach's estimate of 3.5 tons of "dinamite" is overstated; the average blast involved two to four filled holes and a total of 400 to 800 pounds of dynamite. Up to 1,000 tons of rock would be blasted into the pit.

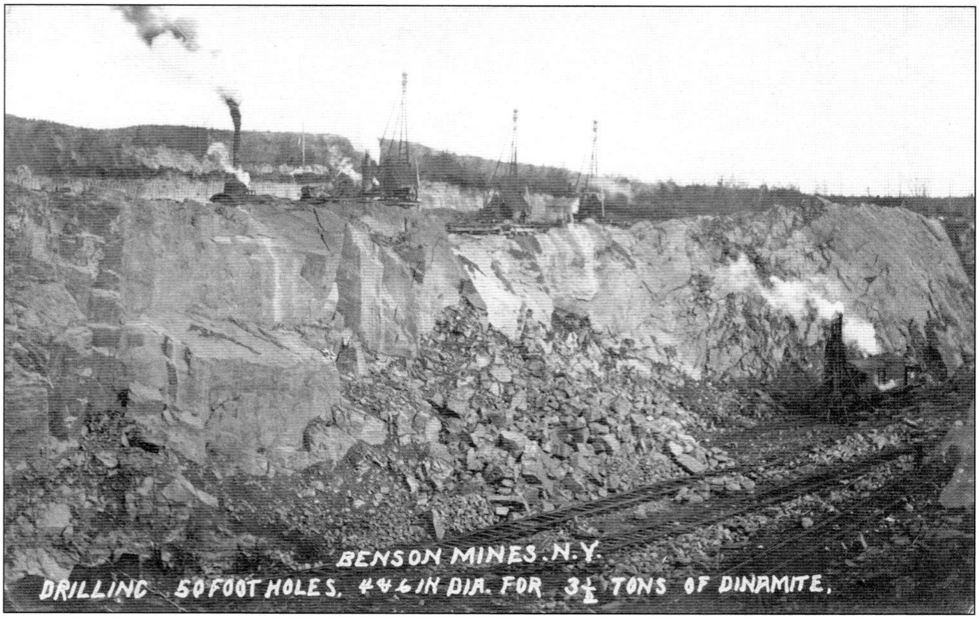

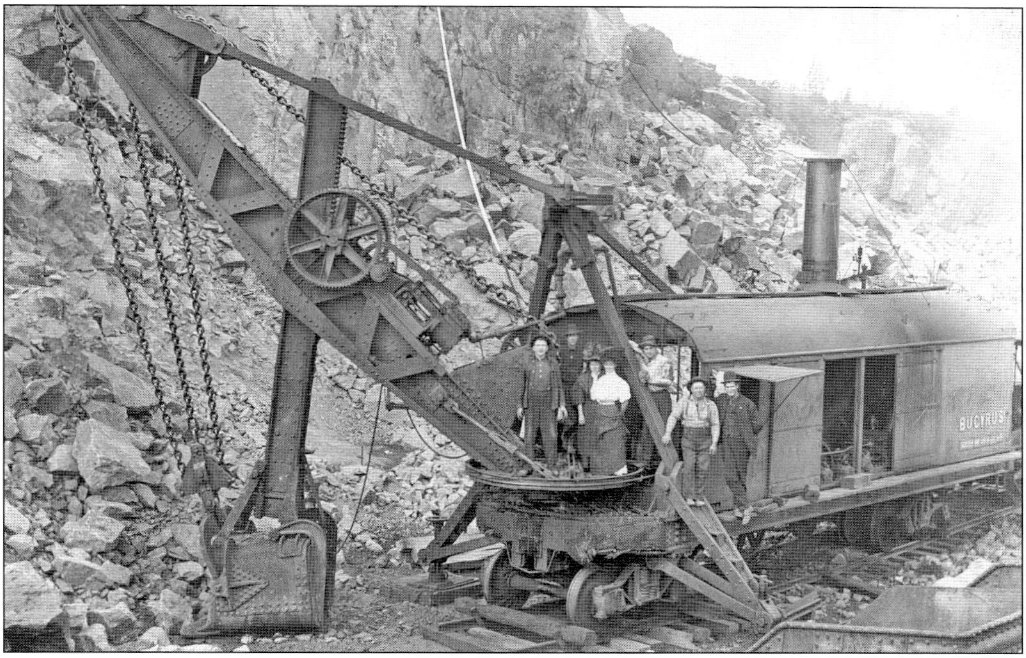

The 1910 book *Ore Mining Methods* by Walter Crane summarizes the pros and cons of steam shovels. Advantages included that they cover a large amount of work, require low operating cost, load railcars directly, and perform cheap topsoil removal. Disadvantages were the high purchase cost, high rate of depreciation, and the skilled labor needed. Benson Mines Company acquired two 60-ton standard, or railroad car frame Bucyrus shovels; the reduction in overall labor costs justified the purchase price. The lower end of the boom rests on a swing-circle, and both revolve together in a partial arc. The boiler is located over the rear trucks and generates steam for three engines controlling shovel movements and propulsion. The shovel crew consisted of an engineer, two firemen who kept the firebox supplied with coal and the boiler with water, and a "craneman" who rigged the boom's chains and cables. The above card shows two women posing with the shovel crew; below, a shovel loads ore into hoppers in front of a mining locomotive. The ground support crew is repositioning temporary tracks; they also set the shovel's outriggers.

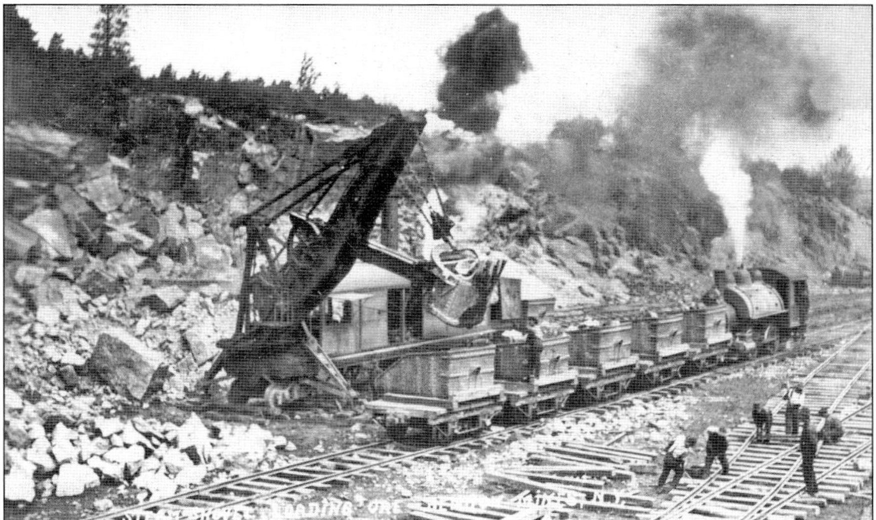

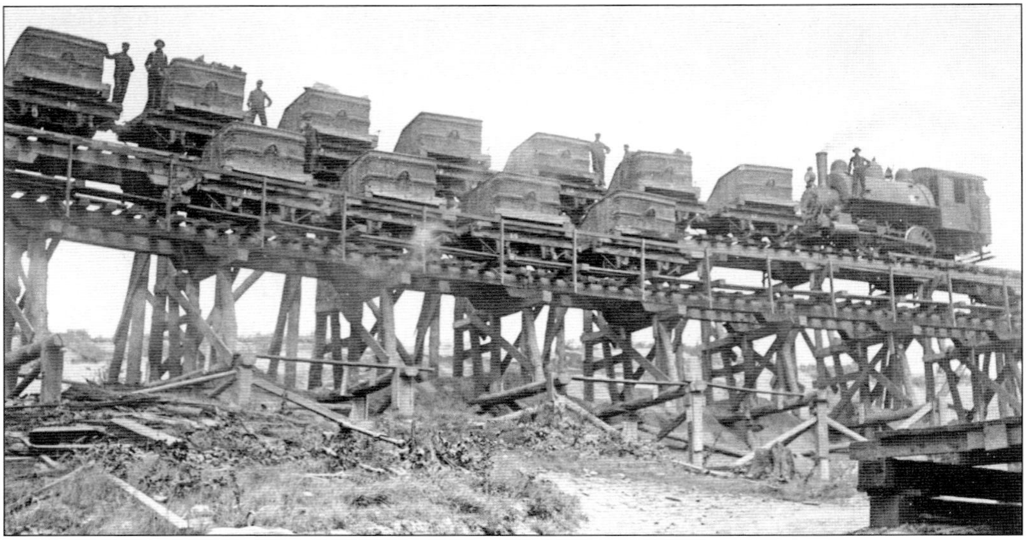

This card, labeled "Ore Train of Dump Cars" shows a Dinky engine pushing ore cars on the elevated rails near the crusher. Dinkies were compact but powerful and often carried water in a saddle tank mounted on top of the engine for increased traction. Henry Beach's photographs of Benson Mines between 1889 and 1919 appealed to the public, who proudly sent postcards of the dust-choked mine to friends and relatives. With no social safety net, each worker might be supporting immediate and extended family; new industry brought jobs and hope for further development.

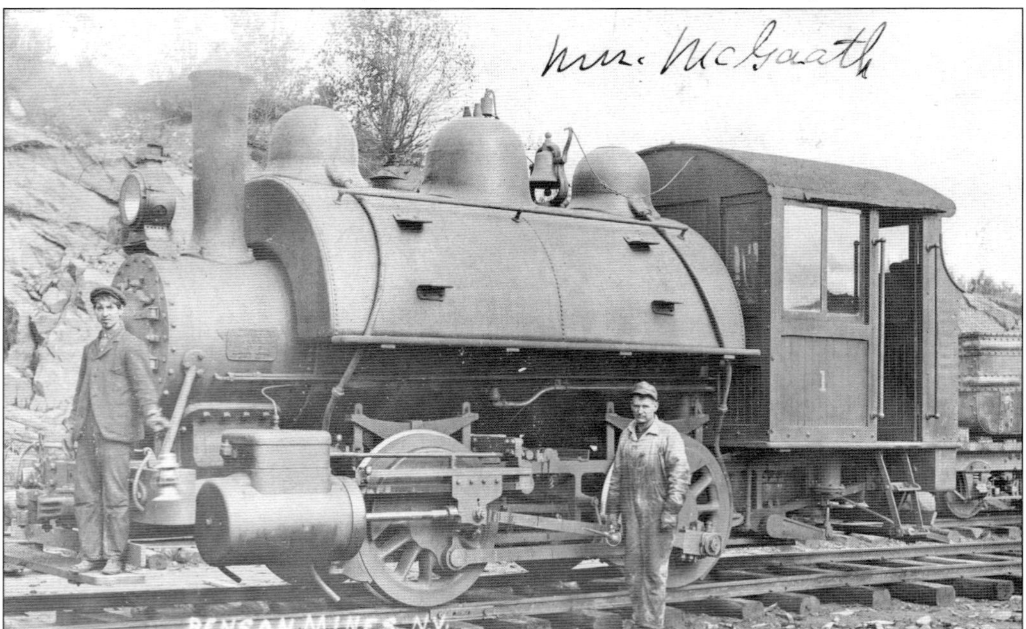

This image shows Dinky No. 1. By 1915, Benson Mines was at a disadvantage; new mines around Lake Superior could ship richer ores without concentration. Demand for iron during World War I allowed Benson Mines to run at full capacity from 1916 to 1918 on a contract with Bethlehem Steel. By 1919, the war was over; in June 1923, Benson Mines Company was declared bankrupt. Northern New York Utilities—purchaser of the Browns Falls electric plant—promptly cut off power to the village. Mine buildings were dismantled, and all equipment was removed.

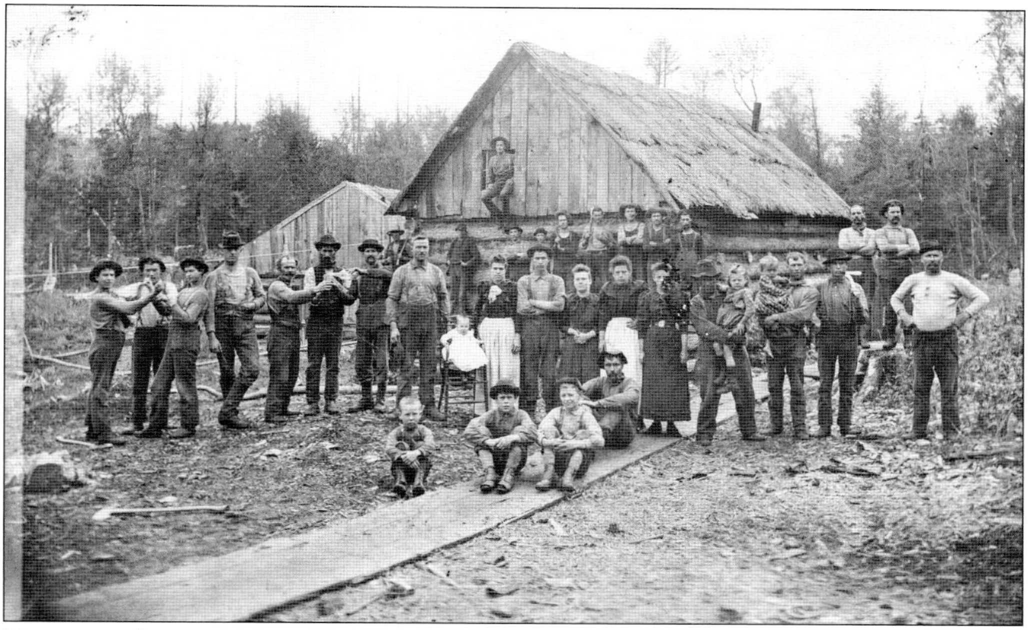

Mining was the main activity at Benson Mines, but the logging industry also sustained the economy. The image above is an 1890s cabinet card of a logging camp at Benson Mines. Lumberjacks with families are at center. The loggers are the usual diverse crew, ranging in age from early teens to elderly. Men at either extreme probably did not fell trees, but did the cooking, sharpening of tools, or other chores. Many of the loggers hold double bit axes; several are pretending to box; others pass a bottle of liquor—prohibited at most camps. The postcard below was produced at the Runions Studio in Star Lake around 1907 and shows a load of logs at Jim Weston's camp. Weston, a larger-than-life character known for his tireless work ethic and beer drinking, was the best-known jobber in the area. The team of draft mules needed less feed than horses and were surer-footed, but tended to object if they felt overworked. The logs might be headed to the nearest large sawmill—the Post & Henderson mill in Benson Mines.

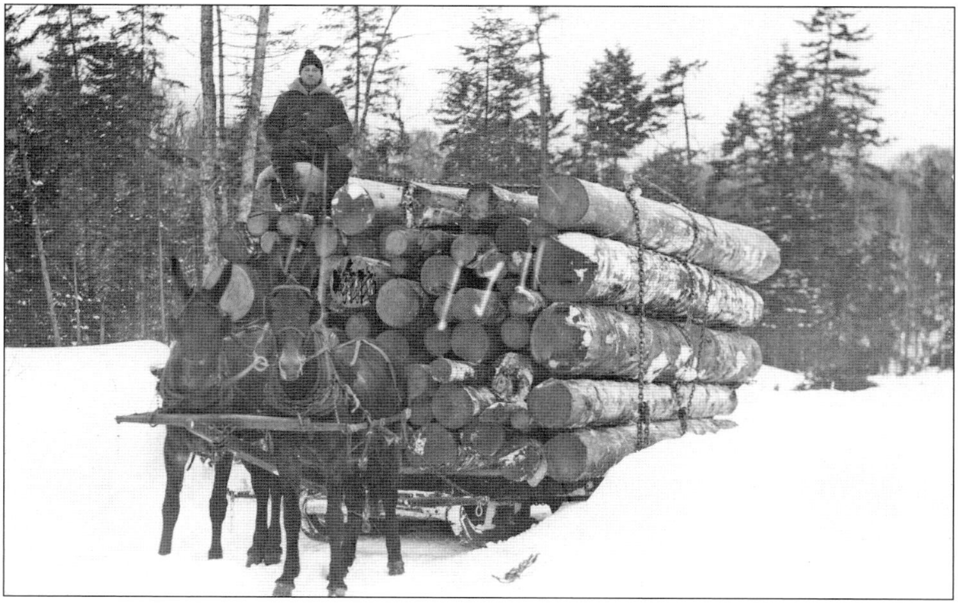

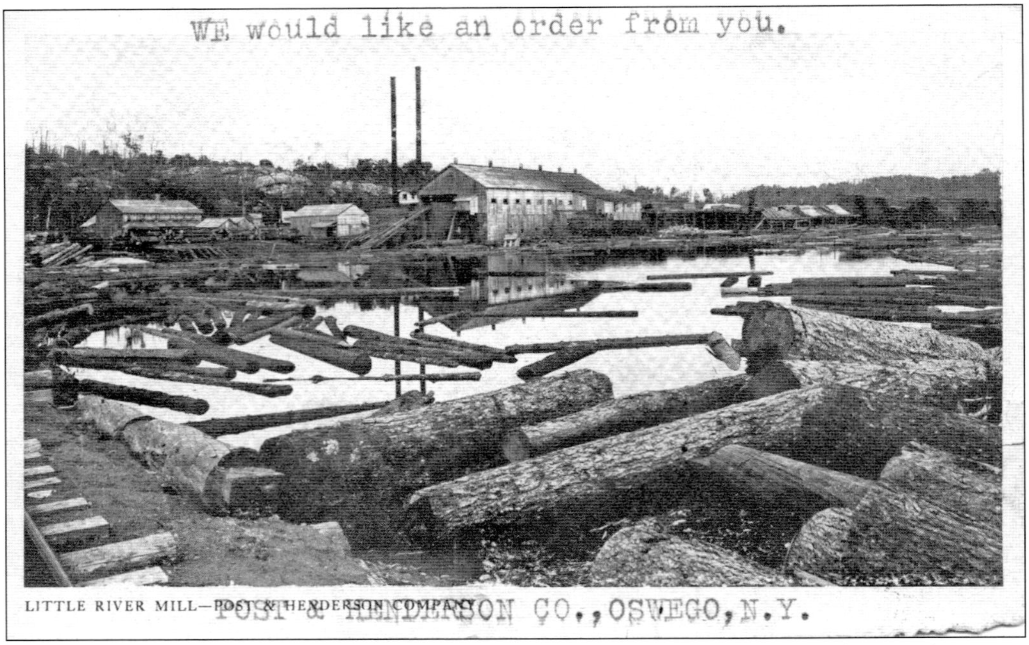

Post & Henderson Company was founded by Robert Post and Washington Henderson of Oswego. In 1889, the partners built a sawmill at Jayville; in 1891, Ryther & Pringle, Carthage machinists, built an engine and cars with flanged wheels to run on the mill's pole railroad. In 1898, Post & Henderson moved to Benson Mines, purchasing 6,600 acres of timberland and a small sawmill built in 1894 by Bench Lumber Company of Auburn; it was also using the Ryther & Pringle system. Post & Henderson constructed a larger sawmill along Little River, pictured in the upper advertising card. After the earlier sawmill burned in April 1900, the company built a conventional railroad eight miles south from the Little River mill, as seen below. In 1906, this mill cut 11 million board feet. Post & Henderson sold its land to the state in April 1908, and later that year sold the Little River mill to Peter Yousey. It closed in mid-1909. In October 1909, Emporium Lumber Company purchased the rails removed from Post & Henderson's railroad, and its Baldwin locomotive.

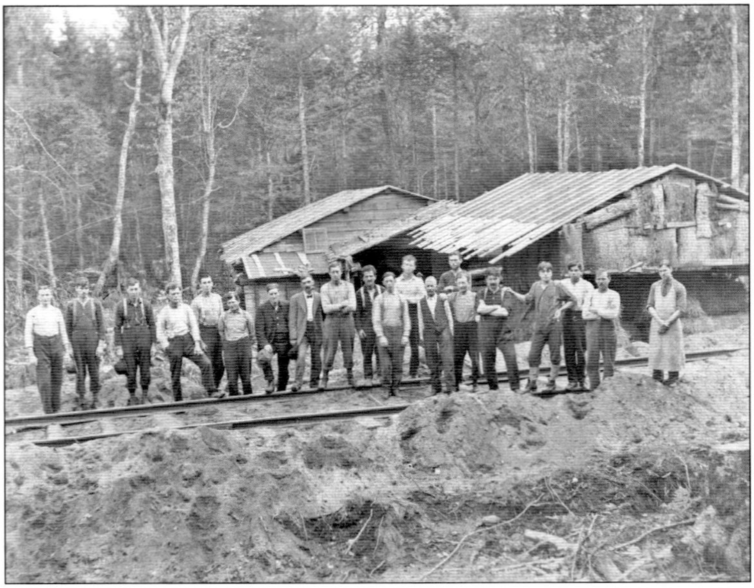

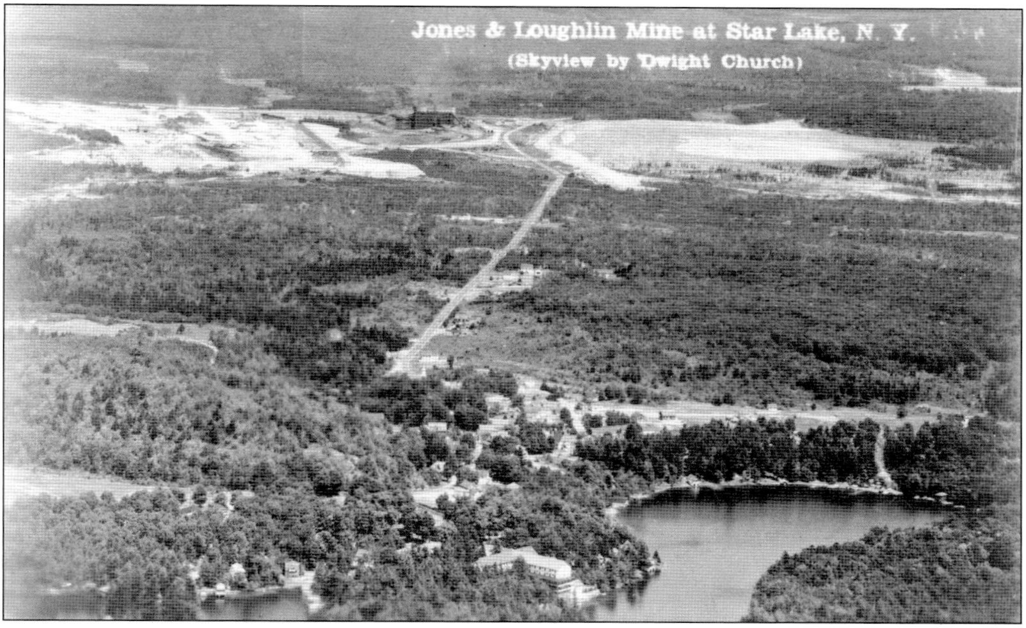

"Benson Mines Again to Do Bit for America," a Syracuse *Post-Standard* headline announced on August 2, 1941. On December 7, Pearl Harbor was attacked; by then, Jones & Laughlin (J&L) Steel Company of Pittsburgh had leased 3,200 acres from Benson Iron Company. J&L expected to spend $2.75 million on construction and equipment over the next 18 months. The above late 1940s "skyview" by Dwight Church shows Star Lake in the foreground, with Route 3 heading east. The tailings pile is at upper right; the J-shaped pit at upper left; concentrating and sintering plants are at center. Below is a view from the tailings pile. The building at left is the coal car thawing shed; the dark sinter plant is behind it; the concentrating complex is at center right. The original Benson Mines School is still in use as the company office, dating the card to before 1952. Compare the location of the school with its place in the early panoramic on pages 34–35. All visible buildings have been demolished or moved; the depot and tracks were relocated.

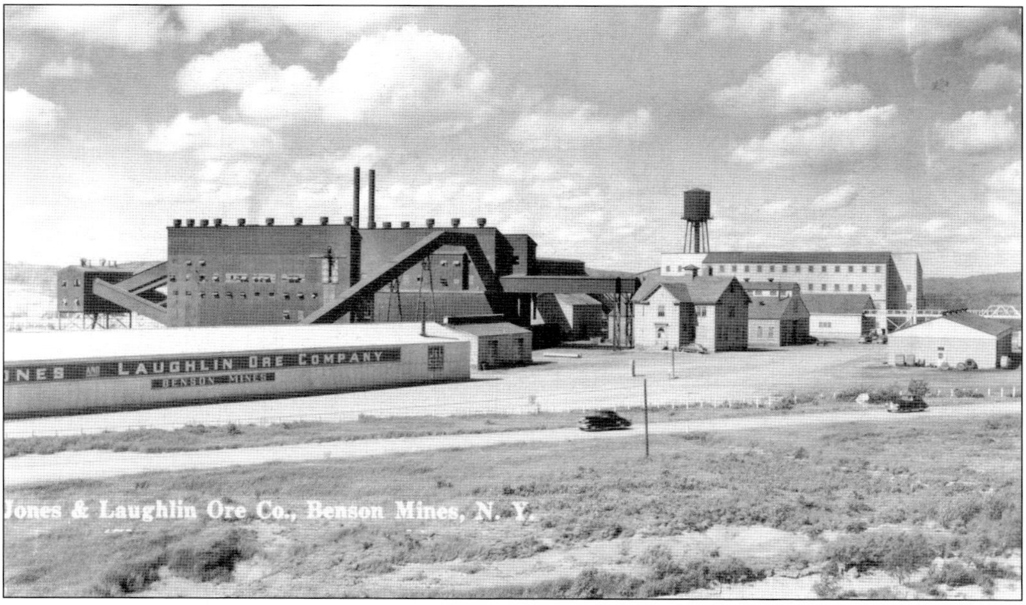

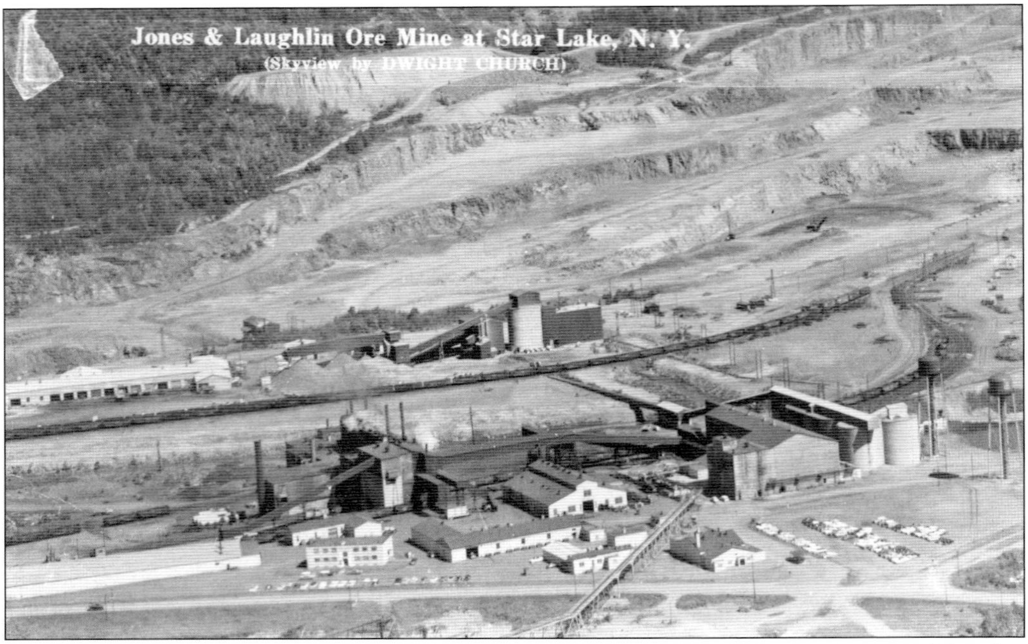

J&L borrowed $7 million from the Defense Plant Corporation to increase capacity and develop a wet concentration process—washing away non-magnetic tailings. In February 1944, the sinter plant began shipments to Pittsburgh furnaces. Three oil-fired sinter machines, 6 feet by 100–150 feet long, heated ore and coal on a moving grate, fusing particles of iron. J&L purchased the Defense Plant holdings in December 1946, and in 1952 became the New York Ore Division of J&L Steel. Around 1950, martite, a non-magnetic iron ore, was discovered; in 1952, a gravity plant was built using water and spiral separators to process it. In 1954, an Aerofall Mill was added, grinding ore in one step from large chunks to small particles. By 1960, all major construction was completed, 840 men were employed, and annual capacity was about 1.1 million tons of magnetic and 700,000 tons of martite concentrates. The card above looks north to the expanding pit; the one below looks south, with the sinter plant at center right, concentrators and storage bins at center left, and tailings at upper left.

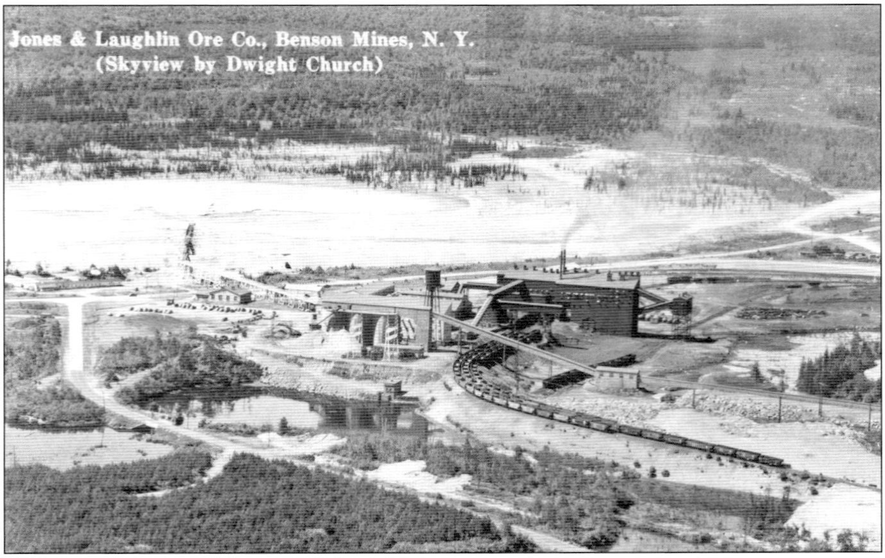

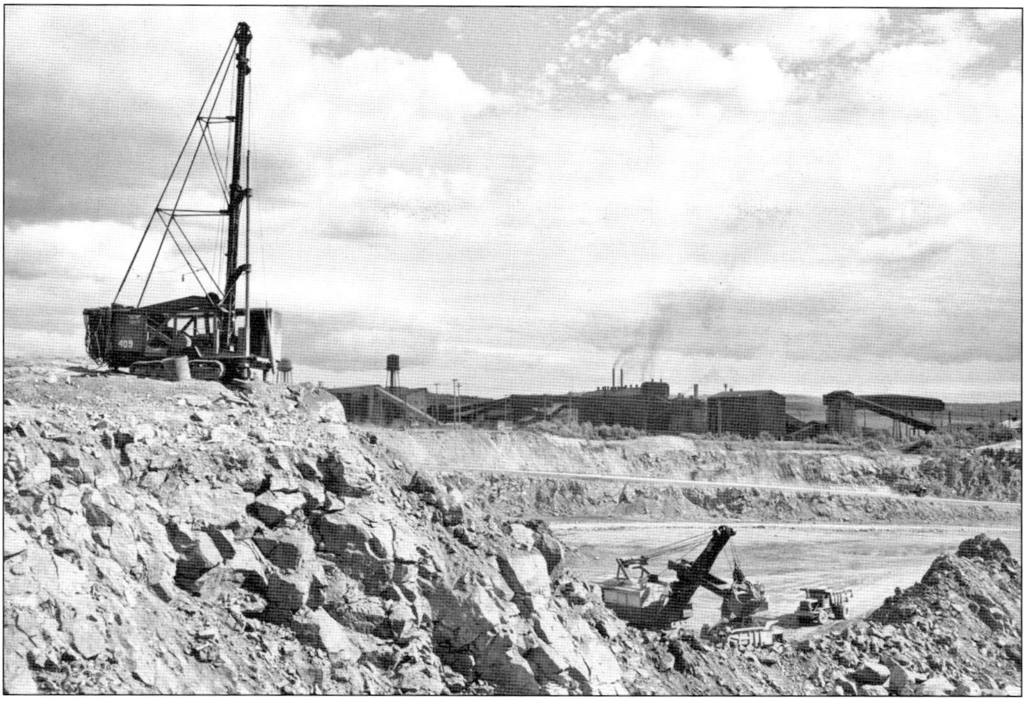

J&L's quarrying process replaced coal-fired steam with electricity, using power from the Browns Falls hydro plant and avoiding exhaust gases. The original mine was on an open ridge; J&L's was a deepening pit. The electric Bucyrus-Erie churn drill above used eight-inch bits to bore holes for explosives. Klaxons sounded before a blast. The Marion six-yard shovel and 85-ton-capacity Euclid dump trucks pictured are also electric. The tires on the Eukes are about eight feet tall. These Lectra Haul trucks dumped ore into an 8-by-50-foot hopper at the edge of the pit, which fed the 54-inch primary gyratory crusher. Large chunks of ore were broken first by a drop ball crane. Both primary and secondary crushers were underground; conveyors moved crushed ore to storage silos for the magnetic and martite concentrators. In the 1950s, Benson Mines was the largest open pit magnetite mine in the world. There were two eight-hour shifts daily, hauling a total of 15,000 tons of ore. The pit is now filled with water, creating Lake Benson.

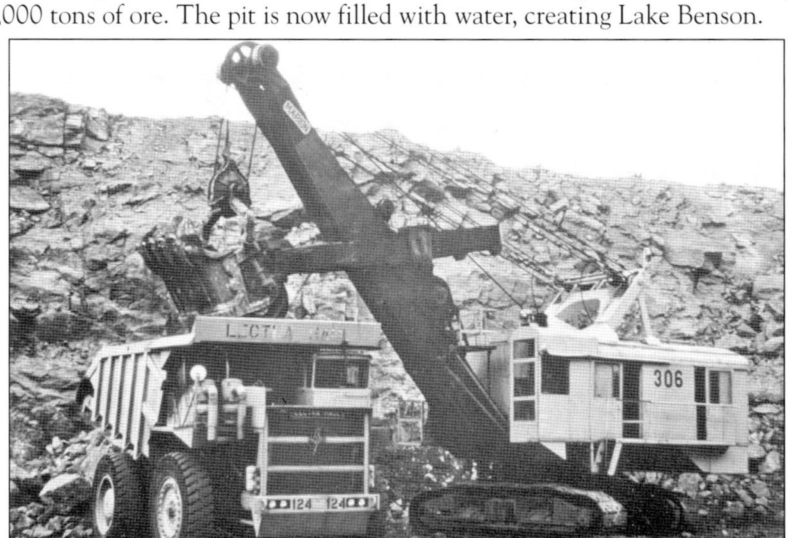

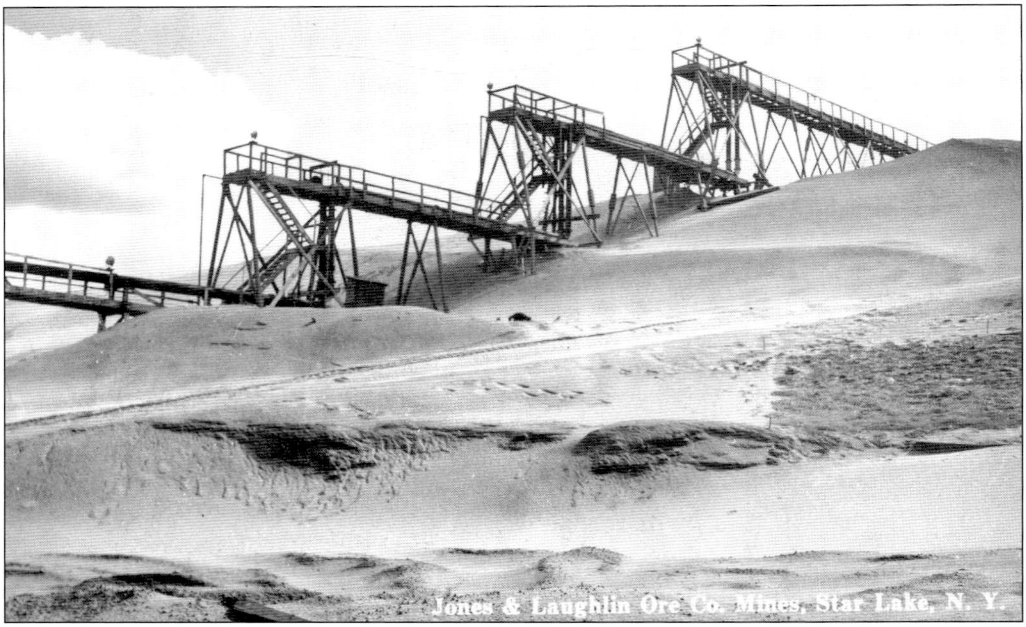

Tailings were non-magnetic waste from the concentrators—a slurry of water and rock sand. Tailings were carried in pipes over Route 3 and pumped to the disposal pile through stepped pipes laid on trestles, as seen in this 1954 card. Capacity was 6,000 tons daily, discharged into the center during winter and around the edges in summer. The mounds of gravel and rock visible now around the borders of the mine are not tailings but overburden—the non–ore bearing layer that had to be removed before mining could begin.

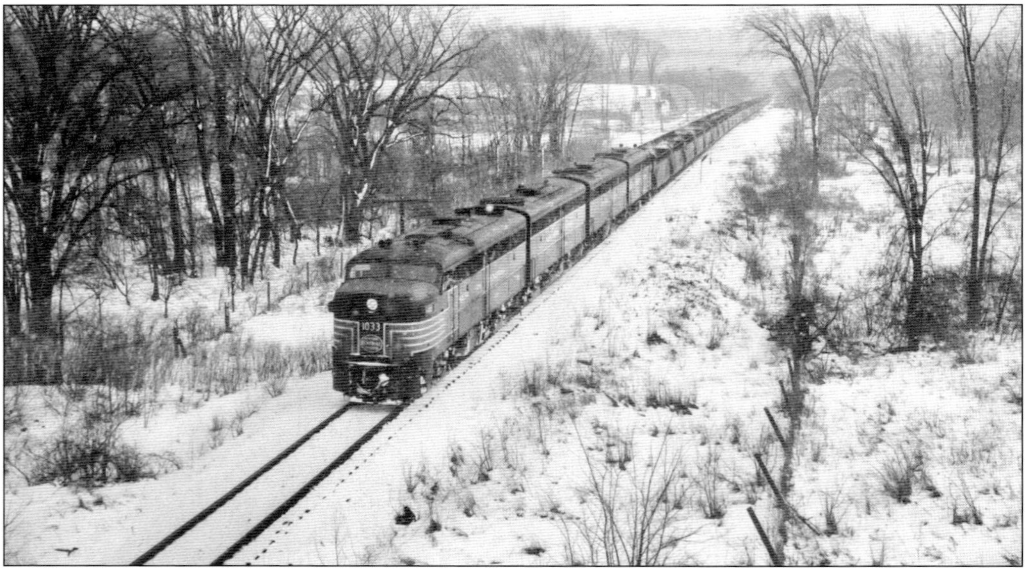

By 1941, a one-coach "doodlebug" was the only rail service to Benson Mines. With heavier traffic expected, the New York Central beefed up its C&A line. This photograph shows the "Ore Train Special" at Watertown on January 21, 1965. The engine is No. 1033, an Alco diesel-electric; with three added cabless boosters, 6,000 horsepower was developed. Benson Mines ended production in late 1977. Factors included cheaper foreign ores, labor disputes, and environmental regulations. A planned $20 million electric smelter—a steel producing furnace—was never built.

Four

WANAKENA

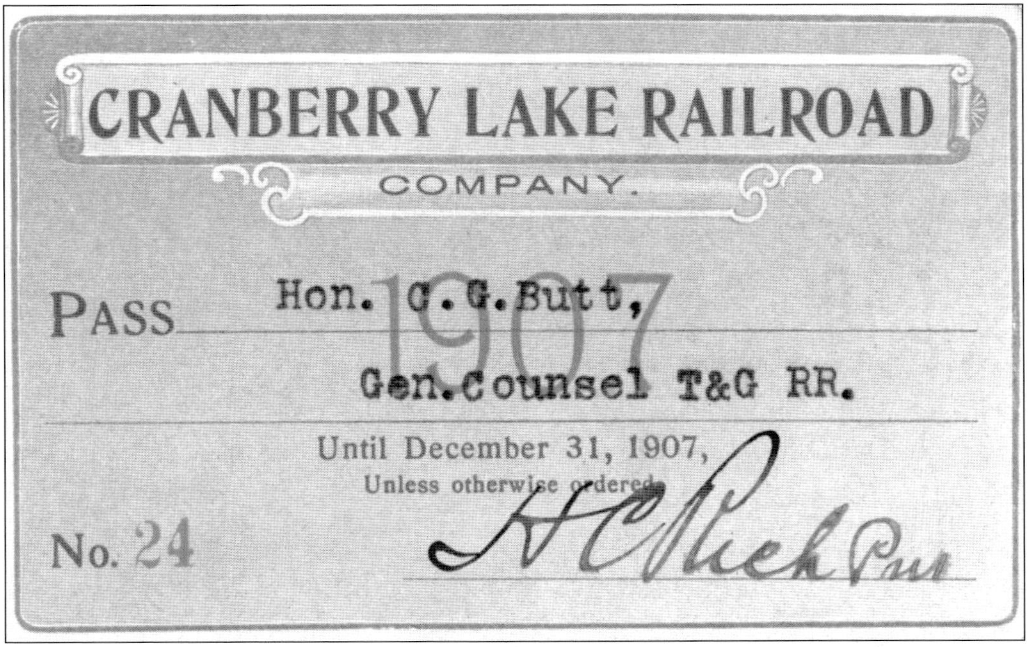

Rich Lumber Company, owned by cousins Herbert and Horace Rich, began operations in Pennsylvania in 1885. In 1901, with its woodlands cleared, 16,000 acres of virgin timber were purchased on the southwest side of Cranberry Lake. Access would be by railroad, running six miles from the C&A depot in Benson Mines to the new village of Wanakena. The Cranberry Lake Railroad was chartered on February 24, 1902, with a capital stock of $80,000, divided into 800 shares of $100 each. Subscribers included members of the Willson, Andrews, Keith, Ford, and Rich families; all would be active in Wanakena. This 1907 Cranberry Lake Railroad pass was signed by company president Herbert C. Rich and issued to C.G. Butt, general counsel for the Tonopah & Goldfield Railroad. The 100-mile line connected two gold and silver mining towns in Nevada.

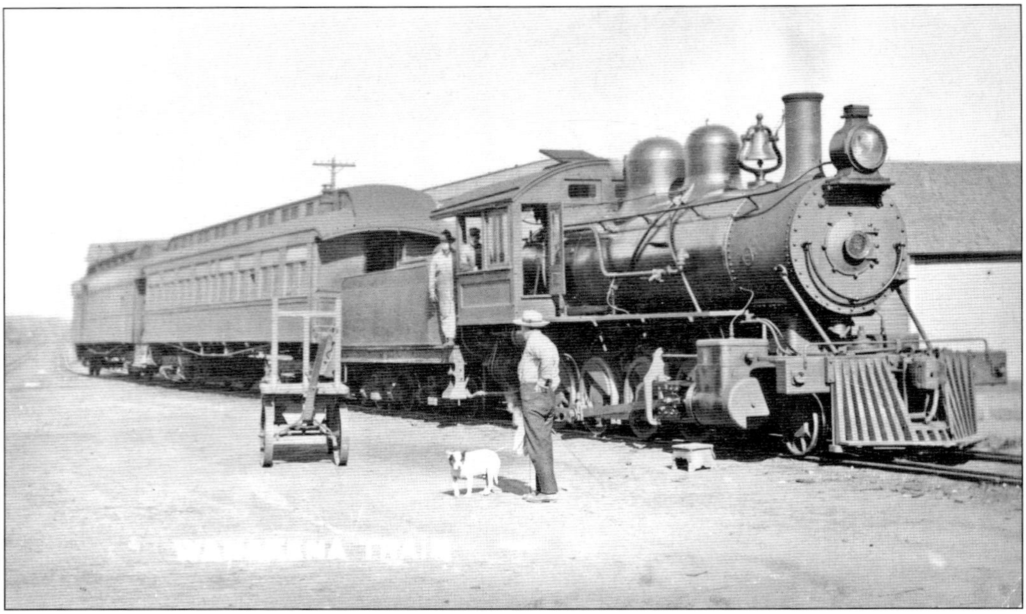

The Cranberry Lake Railroad was completed in September 1902. The line was first kept busy freighting building materials, dismantled homes, and employees and families from Rich's previous location at Granere, Pennsylvania. Rich Lumber planned for its captive railroad to be a freight line, transporting products from the mills of Wanakena, and supplies to the village. After the company realized Wanakena's potential as a gateway to Cranberry Lake, common carrier status was expedited. The route was straightened, sharp curves eliminated, and the track upgraded. For two years, Rich Lumber used Shay geared locomotives to move its passenger coach and baggage car between Benson Mines and Wanakena. Two 50-ton Shays were brought from Granere, Nos. 2 and 4. In 1905, the company bought a new 51-ton rod engine from Lima Locomotive Works to take over from the slow and noisy Shays. The card above shows Lima No. 5 at Benson Mines, with blind newsy Mike Shanahan and his dog. The card below shows a cogwheel drive Shay, an early view since the engine is still lettered "SBRR," for the South Branch Railroad at Granere.

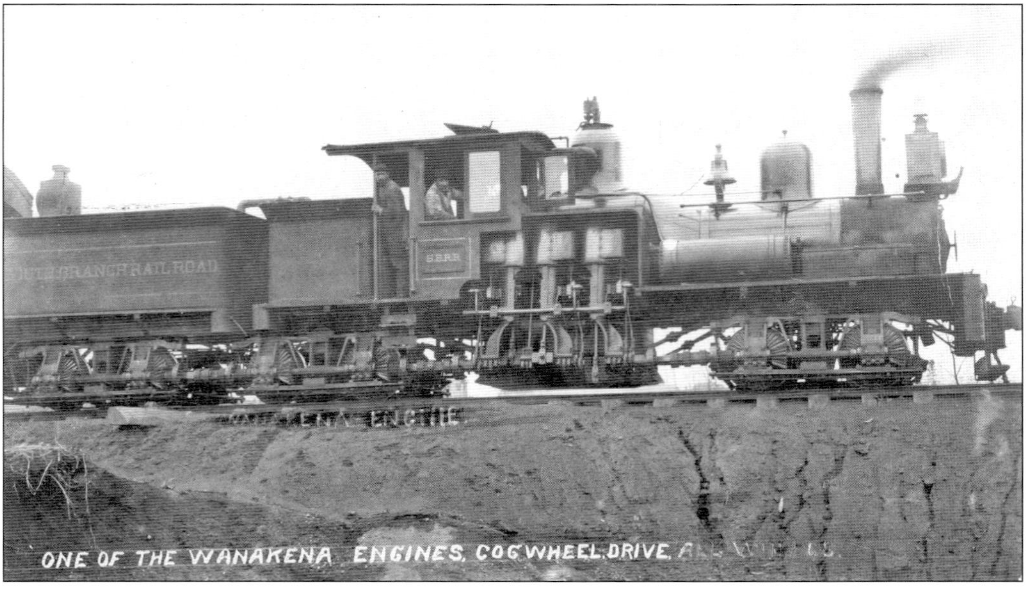

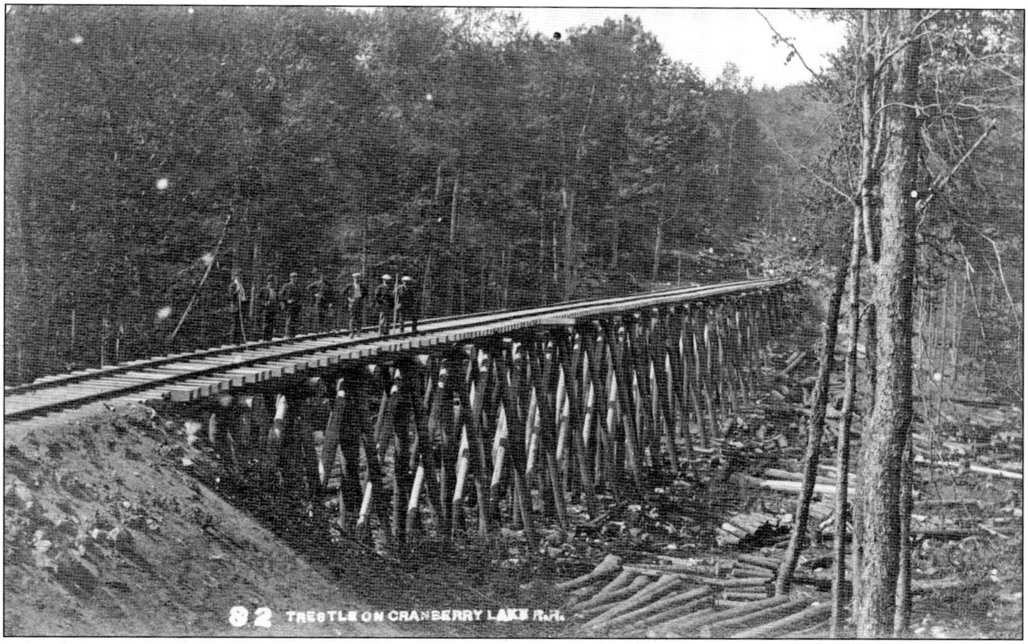

In 1902, Swedish and Italian crews laid track from Benson Mines using second-hand rails and hewing ties along the way. On April 15, 1903, the *Ogdensburg Journal* reported that "an excellent service of three trains daily is furnished and arrangements are being made with the NY Central for parlor car service." Parlor cars did not appear on the schedule until 1909. For a few thrilling years, passengers endured crossing a 400-foot timber trestle over Hayes Creek, seen in the card above. Herb Keith described it in *Man of the Woods*: "About 2 miles from Wanakena we crossed over a high wooden trestle which allowed the train to sway from side to side . . . it felt as if we were going to tip over." The trestle was filled in with tailings from Benson Mines and called the "Big Fill." In 1917, an auto road was created after the rails were sold for scrap. The card below shows a truck with a water tank spraying water to minimize dust. In 1926, Route 3 was rerouted to the north, and the Big Fill was abandoned.

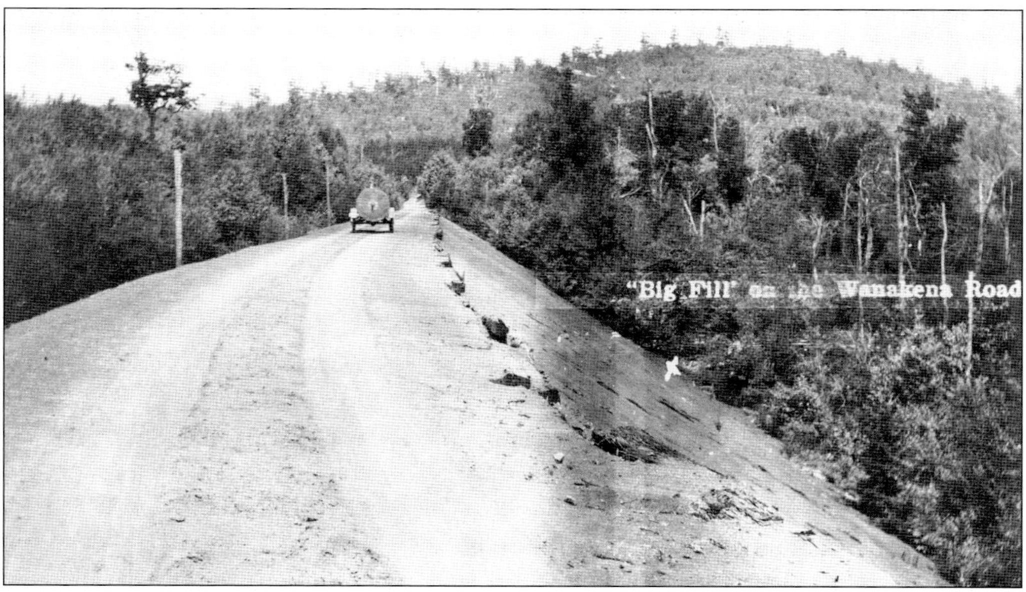

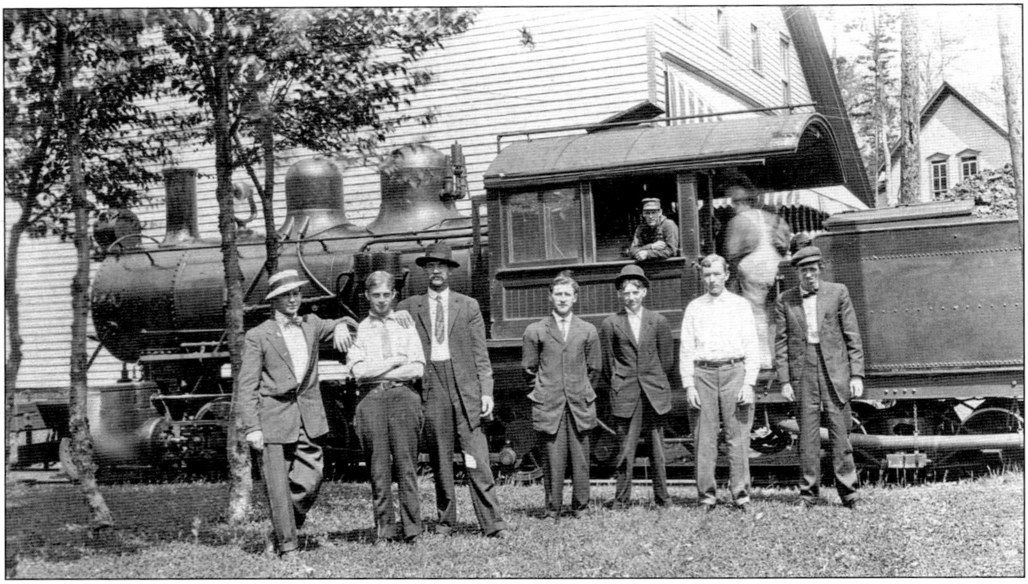

Above, the No. 5 Lima is parked on the main track in central Wanakena next to the general store. The card below of "The North Bound Limited Express" pokes fun at the six-mile short line. The locomotive made three daily round trips to the Benson Mines union station, leaving Wanakena at 6:10 a.m., 12:00 noon, and 5:30 p.m., and departing Benson Mines at 6:50 a.m., 1:05 p.m., and 6:35 p.m. Lumber and mill products were freighted to Benson Mines and beyond from Wanakena and other operations on Cranberry Lake; staples were hauled to Wanakena. On May 28, 1903, the *Lowville Journal & Republican* announced that a boat would run from Wanakena to all points on the lake, connecting with the 1:05 p.m. train from Benson Mines. This was Rich Lumber's passenger boat the *Wanakena*; it went into service in early August. Thousands of sportsmen and tourists came yearly to Wanakena, staying in the village or using it as a jumping-off point for the Cranberry Lake region. Rich Lumber's railroad provided an unexpected earnings bonus of $3,000 to $5,000 yearly.

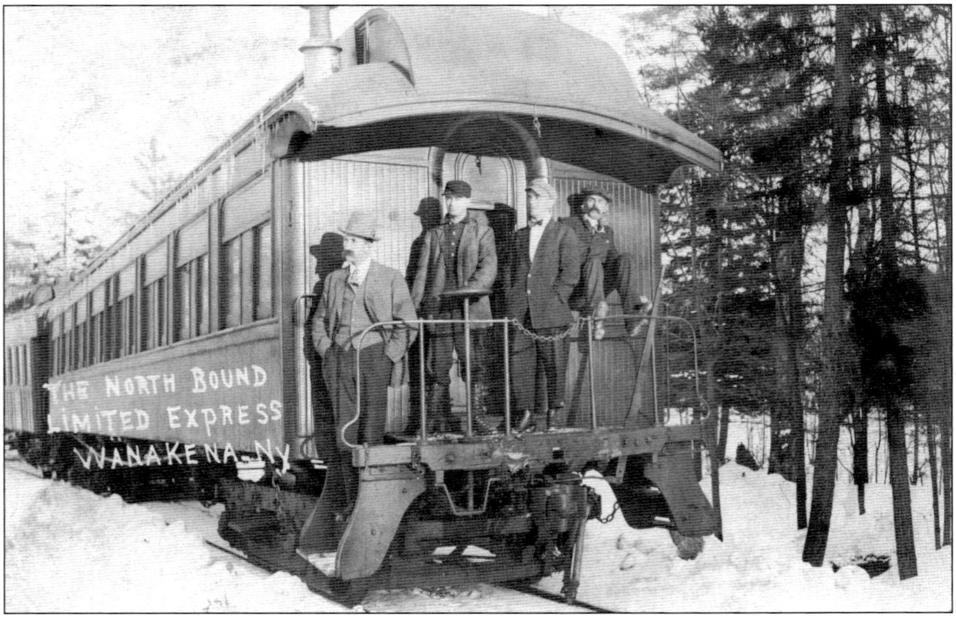

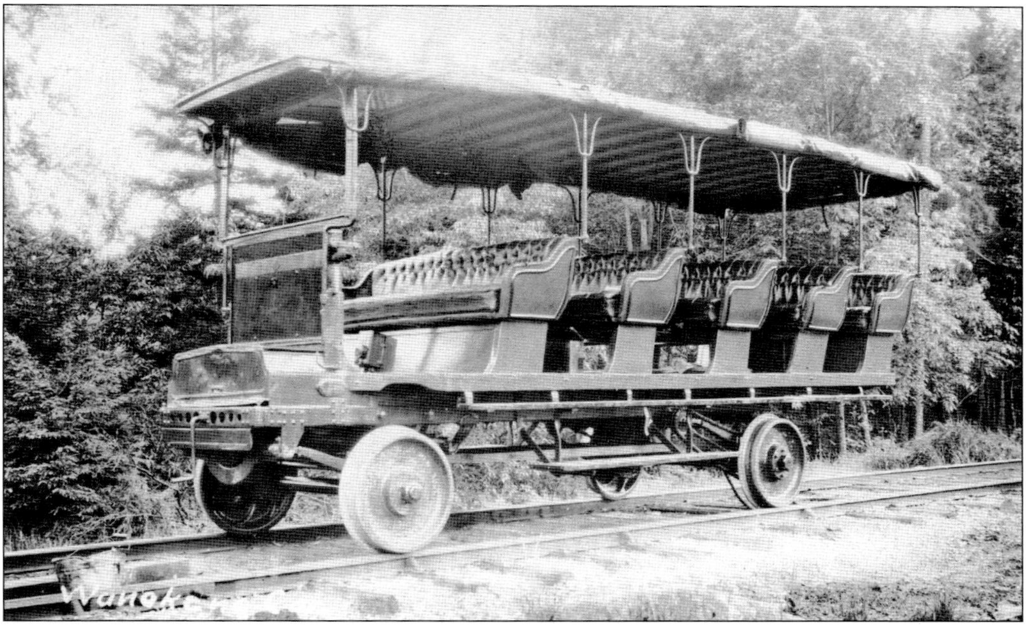

Rich Lumber ended operations in Wanakena and moved to Manchester, Vermont, in 1912–1913. The railway between Wanakena and Benson Mines remained until 1917, served by two gas-powered speeder cars. One was a former Buffalo, New York, sightseeing bus converted into an open rail coach with a canopy over the seats; capacity was 20 to 25 passengers. Rubber tires were replaced by flanged railroad wheels, as seen above. The photograph below from a family album shows the second speeder, a compact enclosed railcar, next to the Wanakena depot. The image can be dated by the large posters on the speeder advertising the Woods Moot taking place at Wanakena during the week of August 21, 1916. The moot, or meeting, was sponsored by the Adirondack Park League and ran for six days with lectures and programs on Adirondack preservation, forestry, camping and woods life, nature study, and outdoor sports, plus evening entertainment. J. Otto Hamele of Wanakena was secretary of the league and arranged for the moot to be held at the New York State Ranger School.

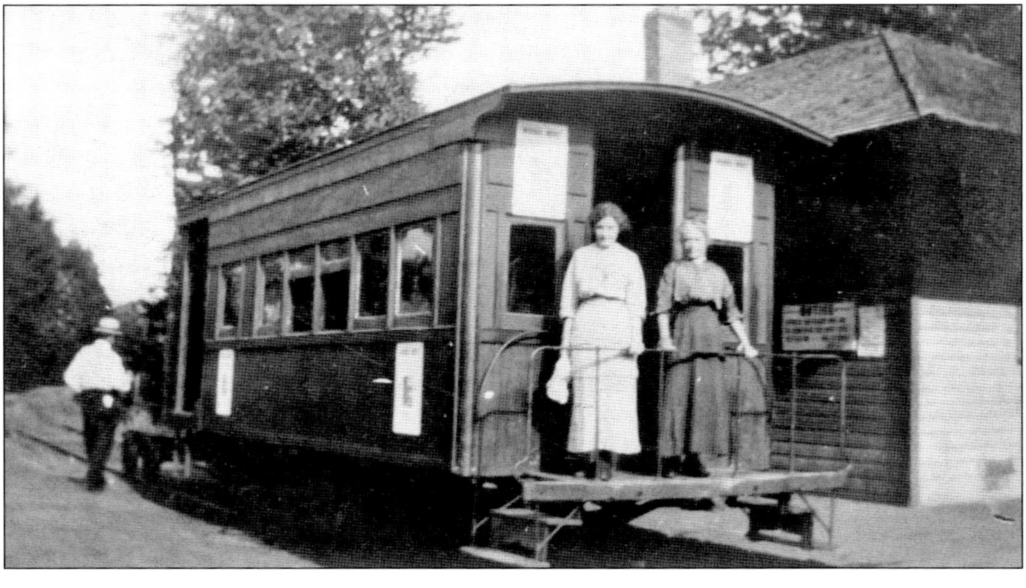

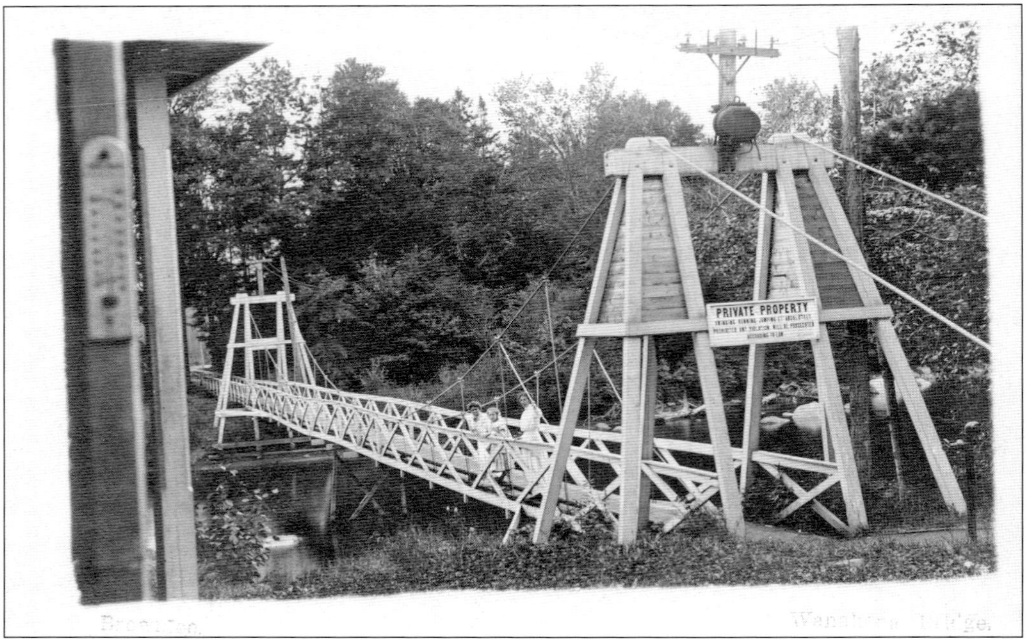

In 1902, Rich Lumber built a 170-foot suspension bridge between Wanakena village and the mills on the south shore. In this 1920s card, the bridge is supported by a cross frame mid-river; a sign warns against "swinging, running and jumping." Wood was replaced, but the original cables and anchors were retained until the bridge was crushed by an ice jam in January 2014. An intensive campaign funded a complete rebuild, finished on November 11, 2016. Grants, gifts, and the work of volunteers raised the $450,000 needed for the project.

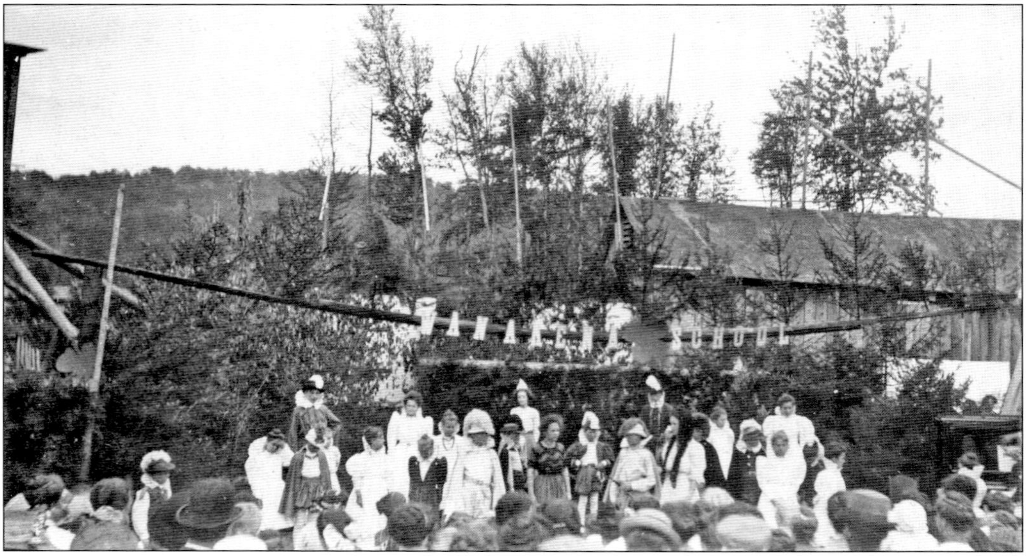

Wanakena's first school was built at the western edge of the village in 1902; it taught primary through junior high students, with over 100 pupils. This c. 1907 card shows a pageant day under a banner reading "Wanakena School." A play is being performed with piano accompaniment. About 25 students and several teachers are taking part in front of families and townspeople. Costumes seem to display an Elizabethan theme, with high ruffled collars, feathered caps, capes, pantaloons, and wigs. Rich Lumber's railroad machine shop is the long building in the background.

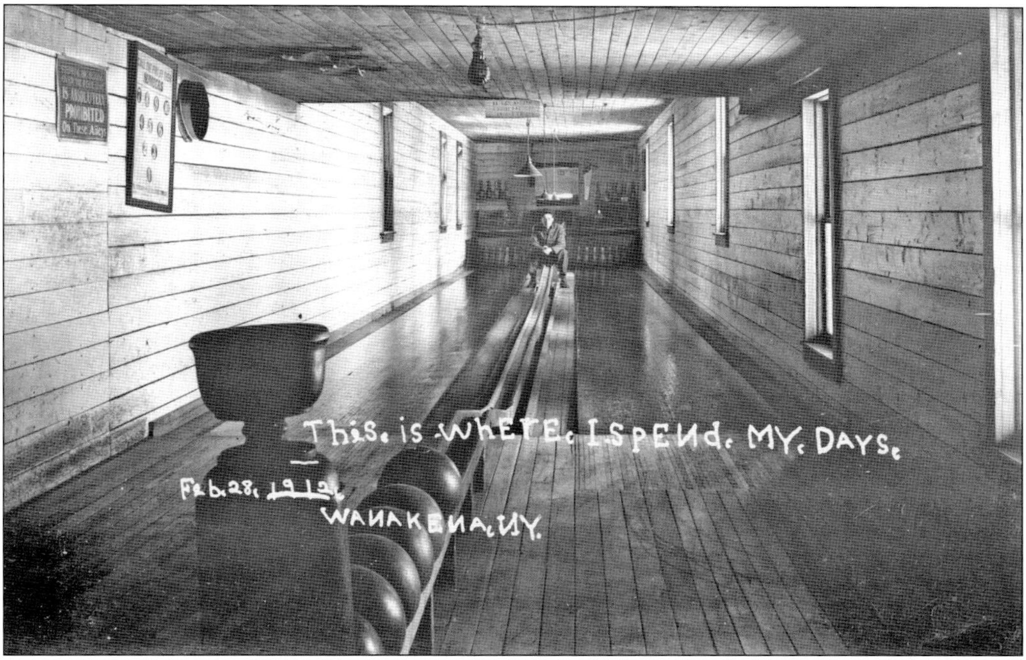

Rich Lumber encouraged wholesome activities by building a clubhouse and reading room. A two-lane bowling alley in the basement was completed in January 1907. The Reading Room Association held a yearly New Year's Reception that opened with bowling contests between the mill and town teams. Bowlers also competed in tournaments held in Carthage and Watertown. This card of the alley attendant reads, "This is where I spend my days, February 28, 1912." The alley was a cash operation; a sign warns "11 Men Asking Credit Lay Dead in Our Cellar."

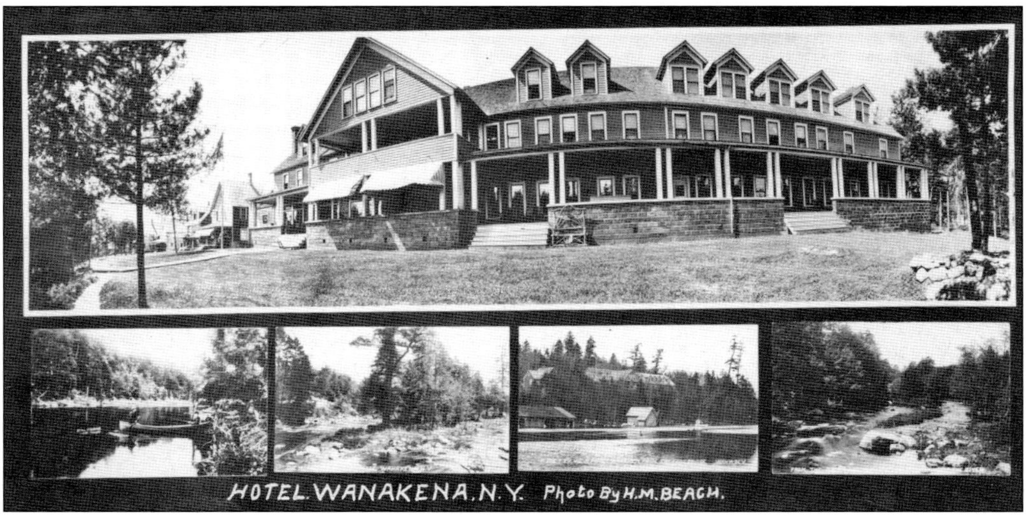

This "fisheye" card by Henry Beach features the Hotel Wanakena. William Bean managed the hotel until Rich Lumber left Wanakena. Bean grew up in East Aurora, New York, and attended school with Elbert Hubbard, founder of the Roycrofters arts and crafts community. In 1913, the Roycroft Press published a booklet, *Health and Recreation in the North Woods: A Little Journey to Billy Bean's Beanery . . . Being an Appreciation* by Elbert Hubbard. Written in florid prose and poetry, Hubbard extolled nature's rejuvenating value—especially when combined with a stay at a comfortable hotel.

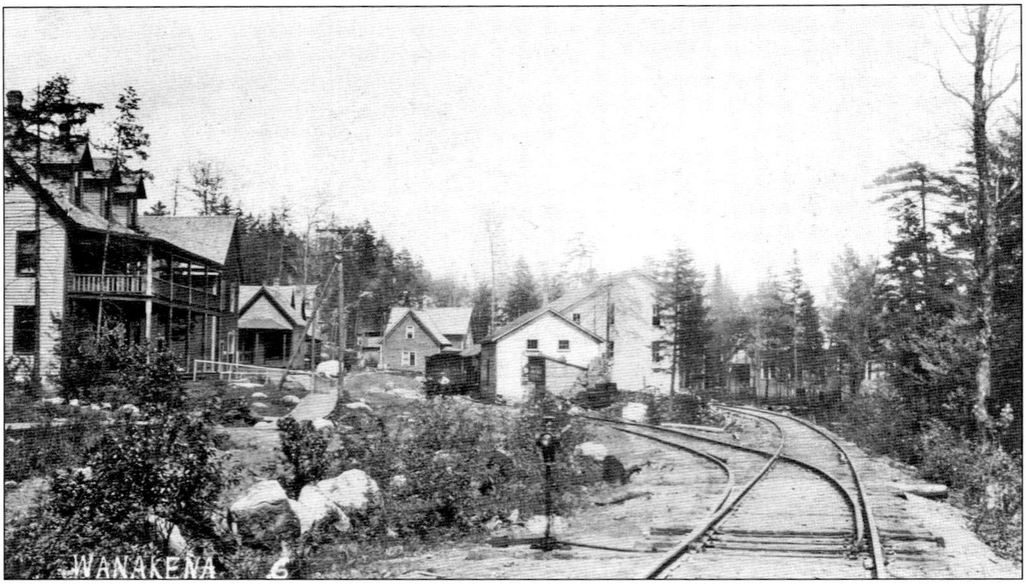

The Rich & Andrews general store was owned by Clayton Rich and Walter Andrews, operators of the Granere store. It held a large Marvin "burglar-proof" safe that thwarted safecrackers—with drills and nitroglycerine—in both Granere and Wanakena. A rail siding next to the store was used for deliveries and filling the adjacent icehouse. The store also packed flatcars with supplies for the logging camps. The card above is a c. 1908 view from the railway, approaching the center of town; the tracks at right lead to the depot and docks. The Conroy Hotel is at left; the weekend Pullman sleeper is on the siding next to the store. It left Grand Central Terminal for Wanakena every Friday night and returned home on Sunday afternoon. Sleepers were noisy and crowded; it was said that one could only get dressed in a Pullman if one knew how to dress under a sofa. The card below dates to after the rails were removed in 1917 and automobiles could drive to Wanakena on the bed of the former Cranberry Lake Railroad.

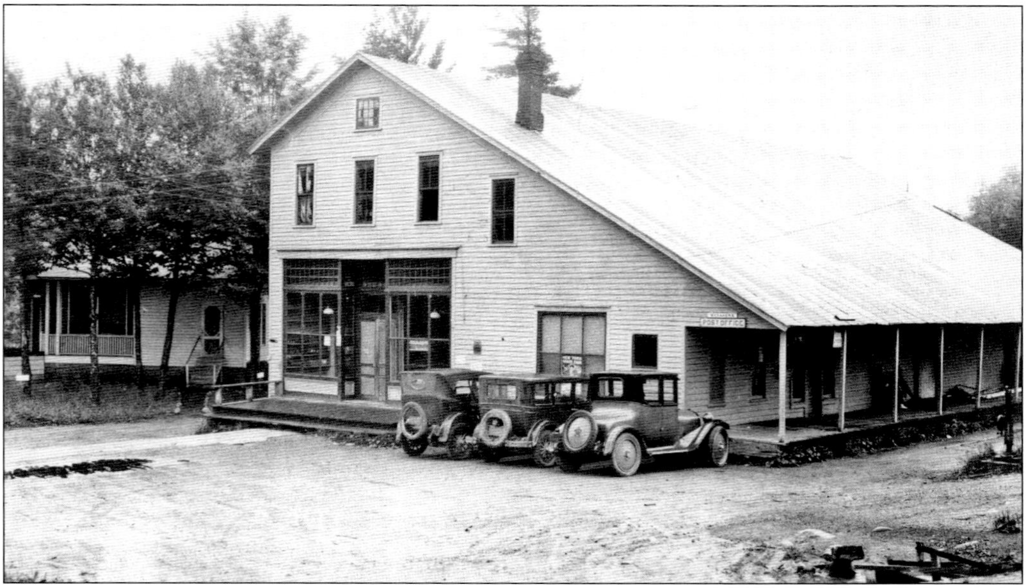

This c. 1915 card may picture Herb Keith at right; at left is Wilfred Morrison, foremost guide of the upper Oswegatchie. Wilfred has a stove roped to his back, possibly to pack into his own Camp Betsy. Keith's *Man of the Woods* recounts Morrison's exploits, often involving game wardens or flouting of Rich Lumber's dry laws. Raised in Quebec, Morrison was intended for the priesthood, but a visit to Benson Mines in the late 1880s interfered with his calling. He found work at Sternberg's Hotel and never returned home.

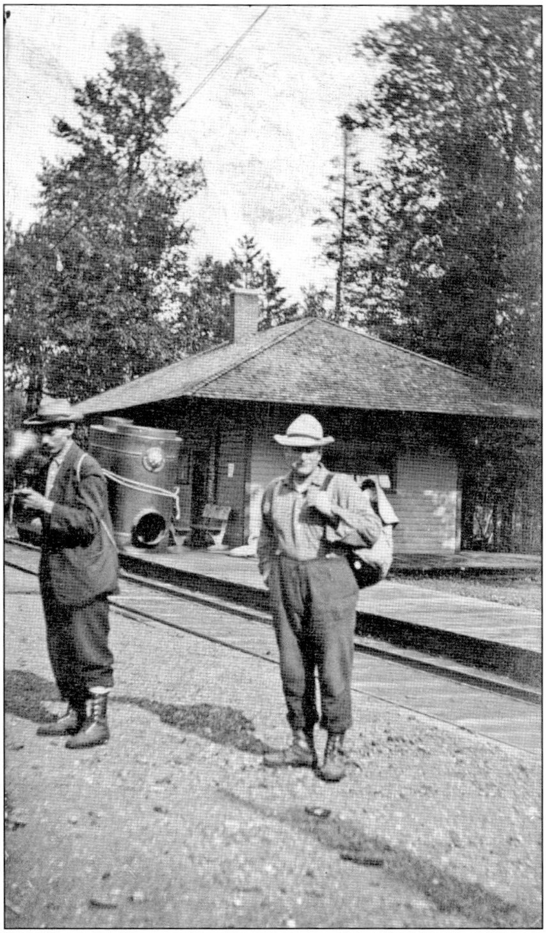

This early example of mechanical ingenuity, parked next to the depot, is not a true snowmobile. It does not use rear tracks and front skis, later developed by Joseph-Armand Bombardier of Quebec. Instead, it appears very similar to the Aerosled invented in 1909 by Russian Igor Sikorsky: a lightweight wood frame on runners, fitted with an airplane engine and open propeller. Russians working in Rich Lumber's logging camps may have introduced the incredibly hazardous design to Wanakena.

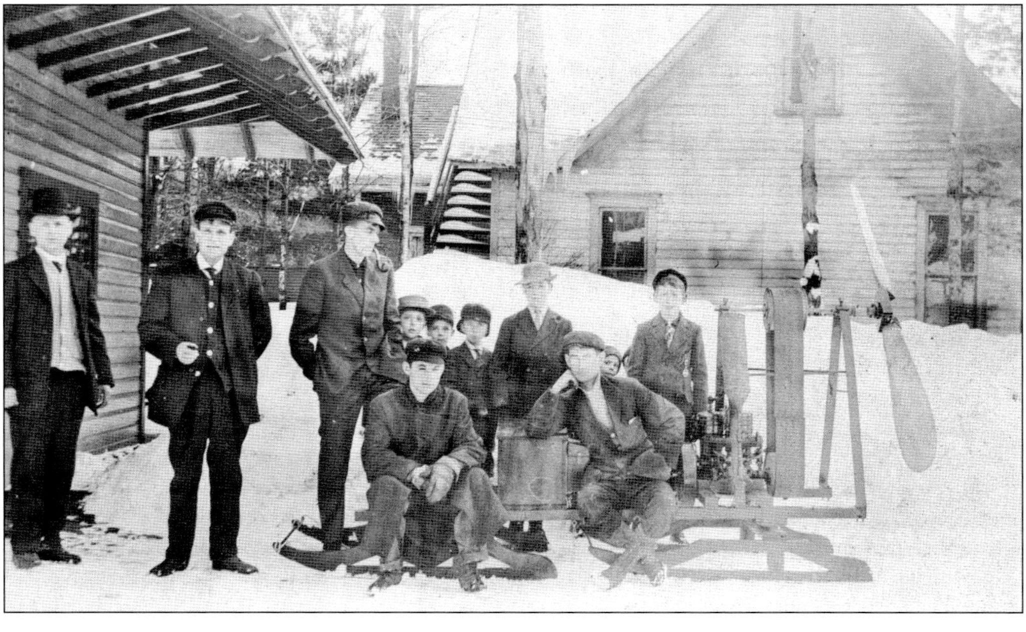

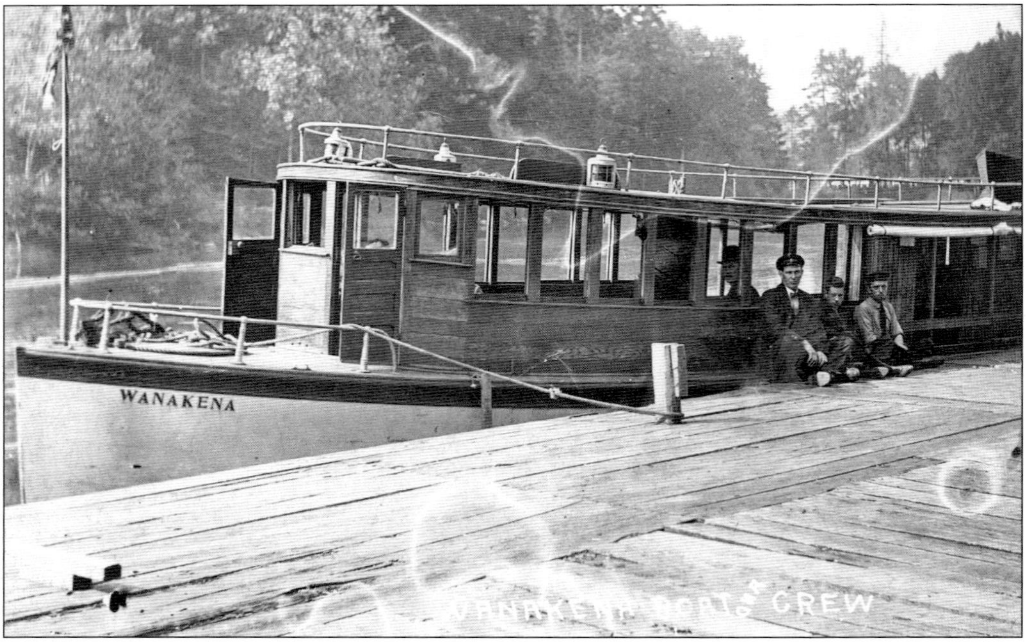

This card, "Wanakena Boat and Crew" was produced by Harris Locke. The man seated at right is probably the boat's engineer; at center is purser Stanley Locke, a 1908 Wanakena School graduate; at left is Captain George Schamp. His 1935 obituary in the *Ogdensburg Journal* stated he came from Buffalo in 1903 to pilot the first commercial gasoline boat on Cranberry Lake. The *Wanakena*'s fate was reported by the State Bureau of Navigation: "On July 14, 1917 the motorboat *Wanakena* burned at the Wanakena dock. Cause—engine backfire. Estimated loss $2,500."

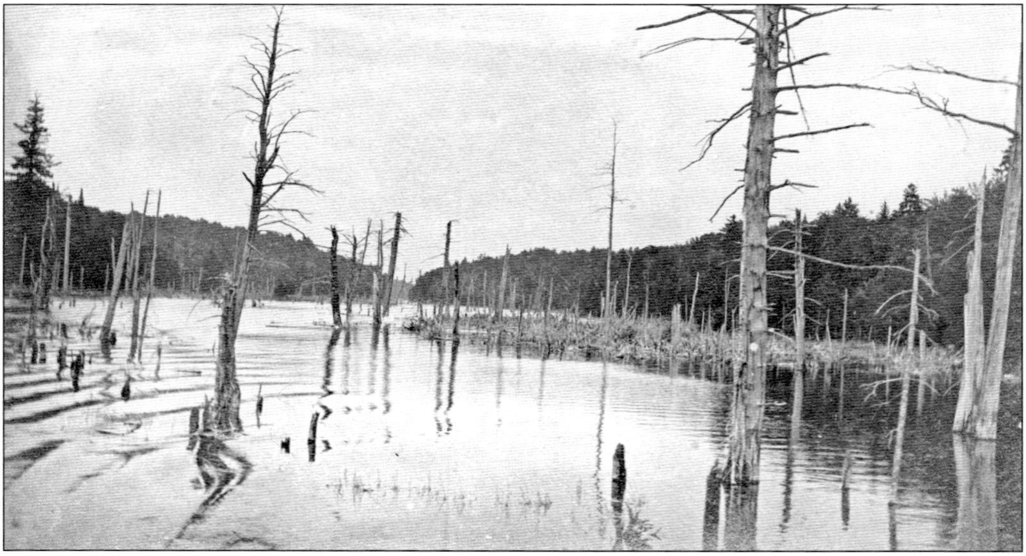

The same *Lowville Journal & Republican* article that announced the launch of the *Wanakena* also reassured readers about the state of the channel: "The state legislature has just appropriated $8,000 for clearing out the Cranberry Lake inlet, so that there will be no obstruction to navigation." Anyone familiar with Cranberry Lake in 1903 would have been skeptical. The land was not cleared before a dam was built at the foot of the lake in 1867; the actual state of the inlet, downriver from Wanakena, is shown in this 1905 card.

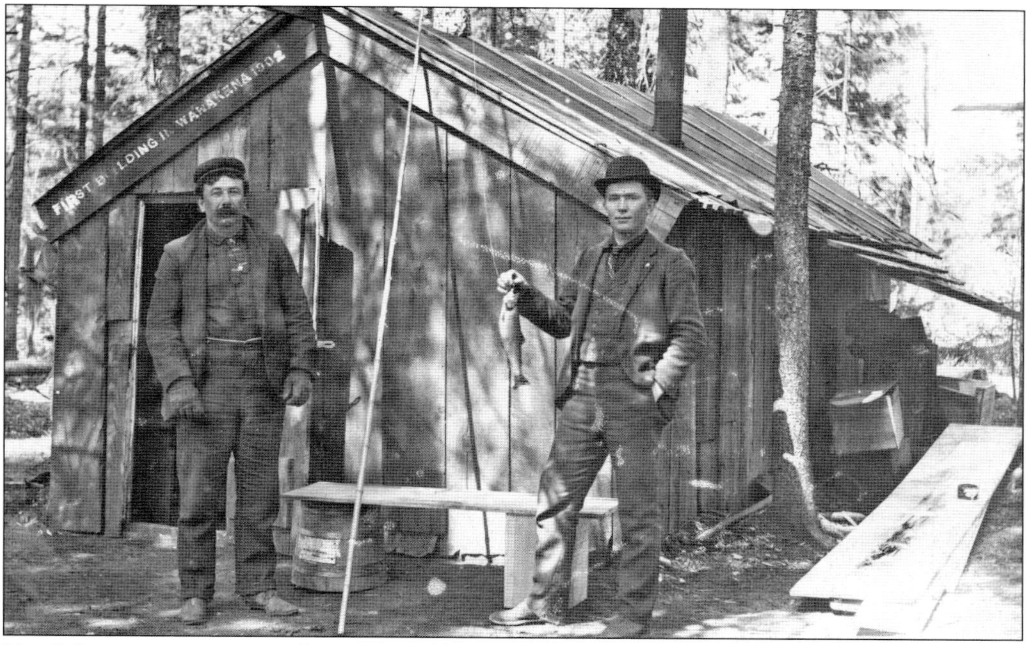

Two fishermen pose next to the "First Building in Wanakena 1902." Wanakena was first mentioned in the September 24, 1902, edition of the *Gouverneur Free Press*: "Rich Lumber proposes to erect a town for business and pleasure purposes. The village will be known as Wanakena." A July 1903 article in the *Lowville Journal & Republican* reported that "last October there was not one house, now there are 35 and 70 more are being built . . . it will take 12 years for the timber to be stripped, when the town will disappear."

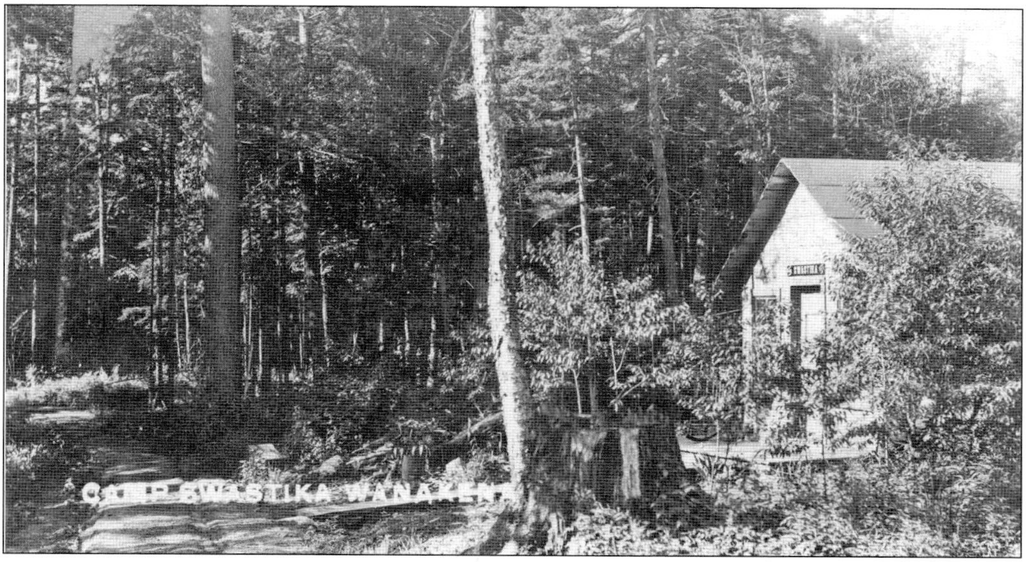

The swastika is an ancient symbol of well-being; it was used by the Swastika Gift Shop in Star Lake and Camp Swastika in Wanakena. This card's message reads, "Another view of my camp showing the old road it is situated on and how near I am to the dense forest where there has never been a stick of timber cut." This could have been the 1812 Albany Road or one of its branches near Inlet. Wherever Camp Swastika was located, it is unlikely the surrounding virgin timber remained for long.

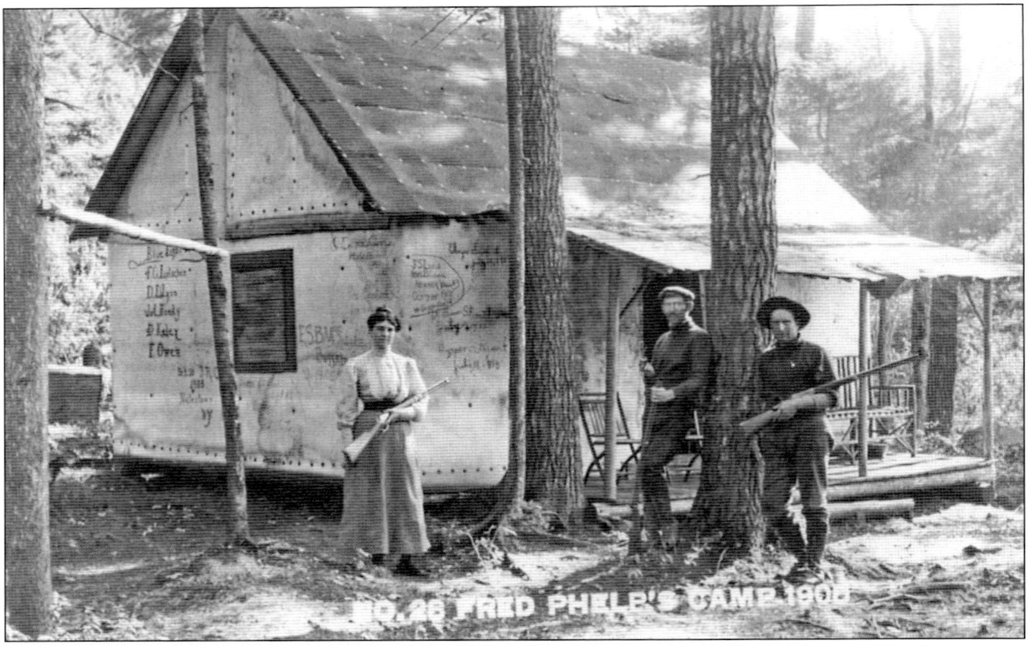

Guide Fred Phelps, at far right, owned this Wanakena camp; the walls were signed by his guests and fellow guide Walter Gates between 1903 and 1905. In May 1905, Phelps purchased Sternberg's Hotel at Inlet. In August 1912, he was quoted by the *Norwood News* in an article celebrating the "amazing return of the beaver to the Adirondacks" and the upper Oswegatchie. Phelps reported sighting a 30-pound beaver. Readers were assured that "everything is being done by the Inlet residents to guard the animals from being killed or molested."

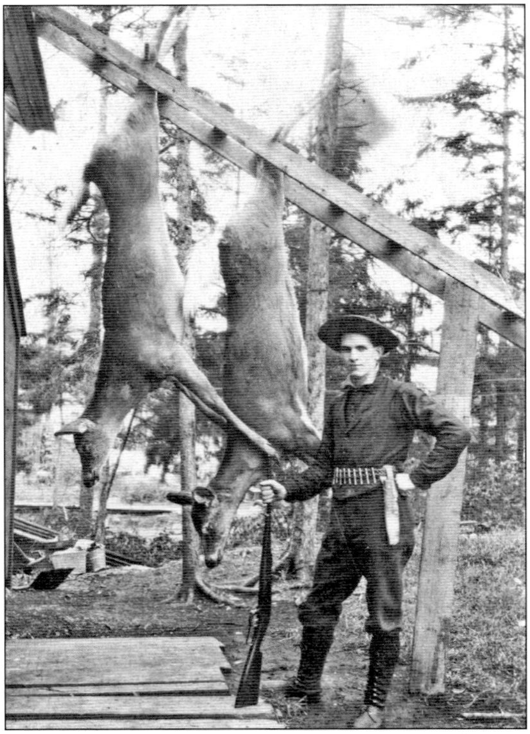

The successful hunter in this card is probably not a local. He may have been a fan of movie star Tom Mix, who appeared in his first silent Western in 1909, *The Cowboy Millionaire*. Mix was a one-man Wild West show, and his outlandish costumes were much imitated. The hunter's fancy cartridge belt, large hunting knife, and all-black outfit tend to mark him as a "sport," a term used by guides to describe their citified clients. Some eventually became skilled woodsmen, earning the respect of the guides.

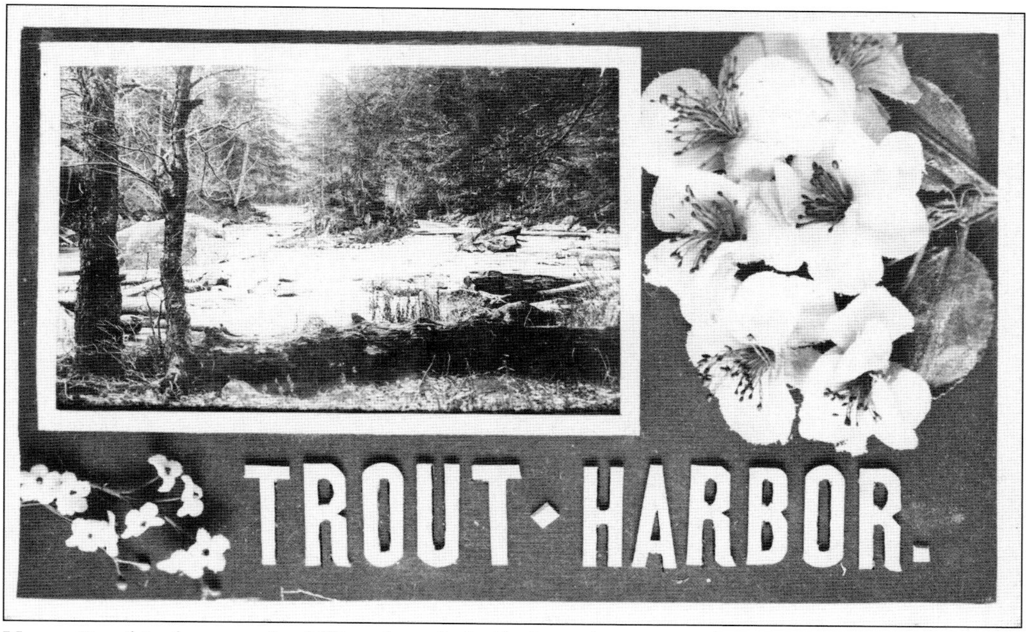

Henry Beach's photograph of "Rapids on Inlet," taken above Wanakena, is featured in one of his composite postcards. These added graphic designs, such as pictures of flowers, and large block lettering. "Trout Harbor" was an accurate description of the upper Oswegatchie. Bert Dobson, in a 1907 brochure advertising his Inlet River Camps, stated that "After May 30th springhole fishing begins on the Inlet and other brooks, where we get nothing but brook trout weighing up to six pounds. June, July, and August are the best months for splendid fly fishing."

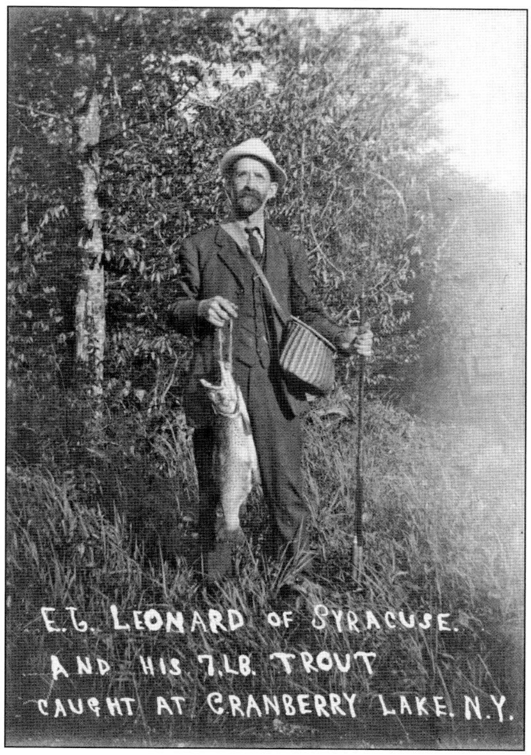

This card of "E.G. Leonard of Syracuse and his 7 lb. Trout Caught at Cranberry Lake N.Y." is dated July 26, 1912, at Wanakena. Brown trout, a European species, were introduced between 1884 and 1890 in the Upper Oswegatchie and throughout the United States. In January 1886, the *Ogdensburg Journal* reported the receipt of 50,000 brown trout fry from Germany by the Cold Springs hatchery. In April 1890, the *Journal* reported that the Adirondack Fish Station would be distributing 250,000 brown trout into the waters of northern New York.

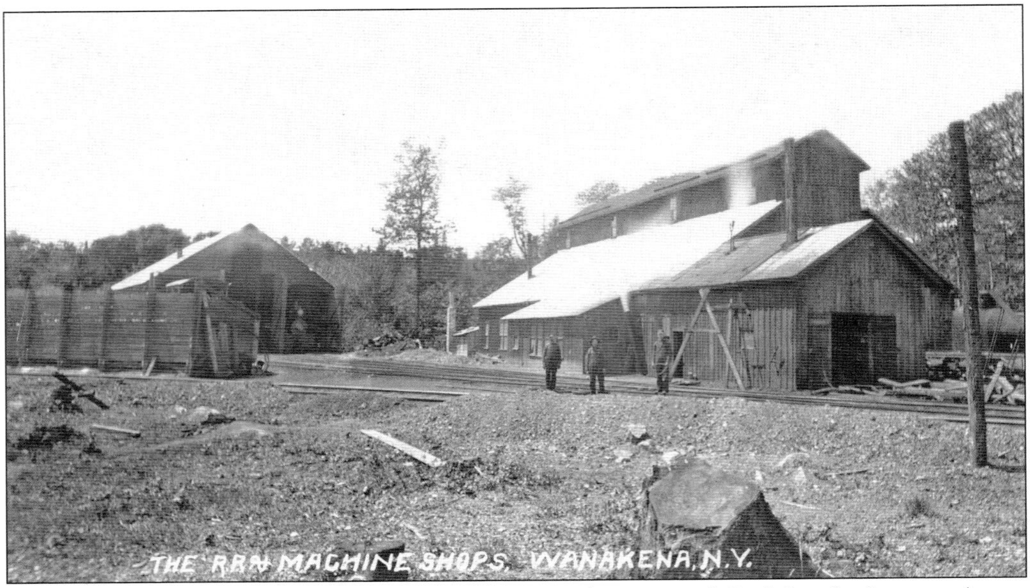

"The RR & Machine Shops, Wanakena N.Y." is a Beach series card. Rich Lumber's engine house and machine shop were located at the western edge of the village. The No. 4 Shay has backed into the smaller shed; a steam boiler is on a railcar in front of the main engine house. Locomotives saw daily maintenance here—oiling, greasing, and cleaning—and more extensive repairs. Water tank cars and fire hose were also kept on sidings at the machine shop; forest fires were a constant danger with coal-fired locomotives.

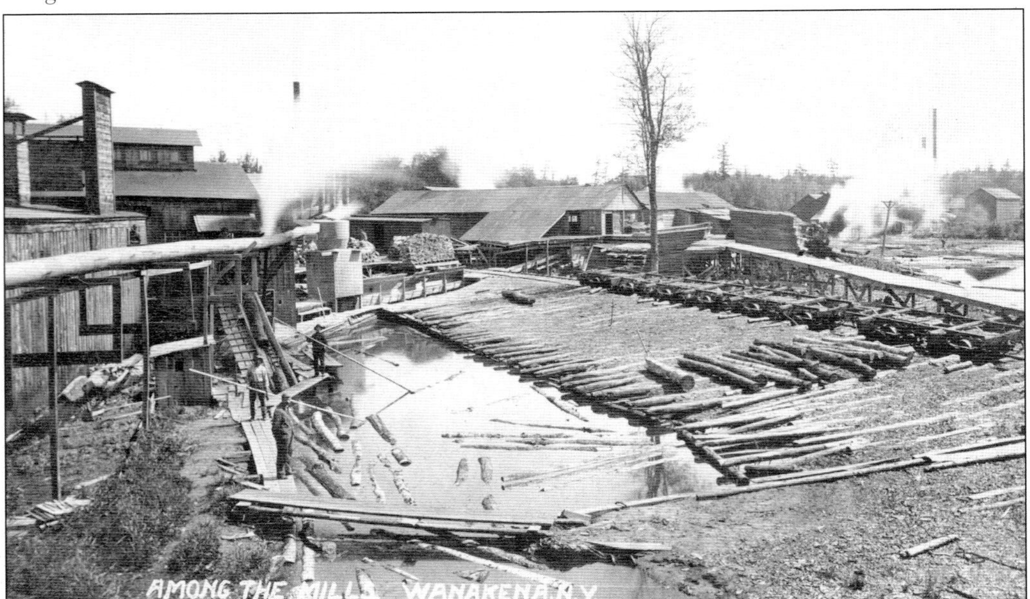

"Among the Mills, Wanakena N.Y." is a view of the mill complex. On September 24, 1902, the *Gouverneur Free Press* reported that Rich Lumber was building the whip butt mill at left. It produced 1,000 buggy whipstocks daily, plus rake and fork handles, all turned from beech. The mill's unloading ramp has a string of empty log cars next to it. Logs in the water are pulled by workers with pike poles onto a conveyor. The mill closed in 1910, possibly because automobiles could not be motivated by whipping.

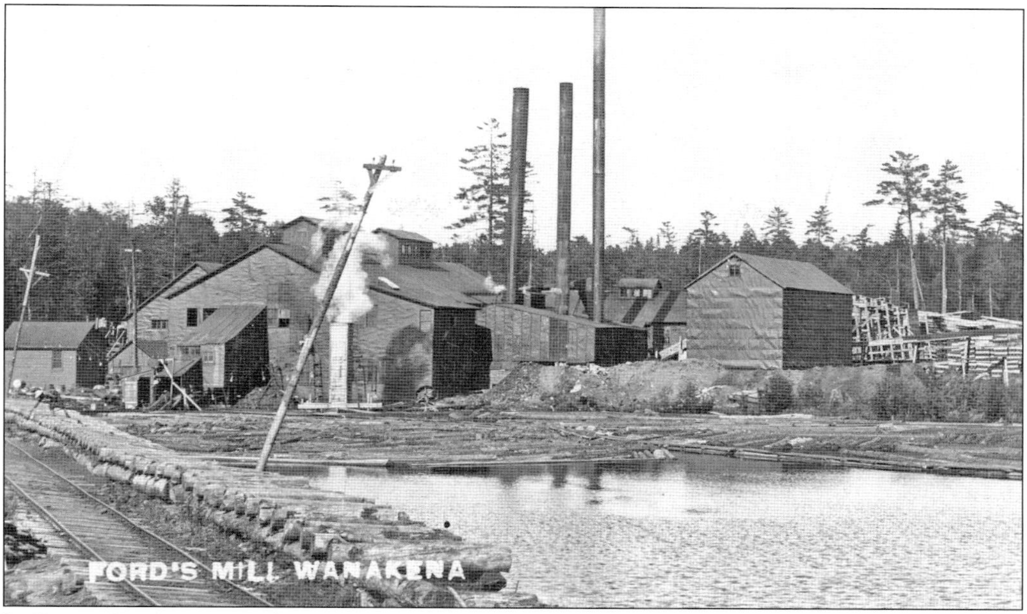

In December 1902, Potsdam's *Commercial Advertiser* reported that Rich Lumber's sawmill was nearly complete. It was of steel construction, would cut up to 60,000 feet of lumber daily, and employ 50 to 60 men. After air drying, boards were sent to the adjacent planing shed. All of Rich Lumber's mills were operated by other firms. The Ford brothers sawed logs on contract for Rich at its first venture in Gardeau, Pennsylvania; they later set up sawmills at other company locations. Rich Lumber maintained similar partnerships during the company's 34-year lifetime.

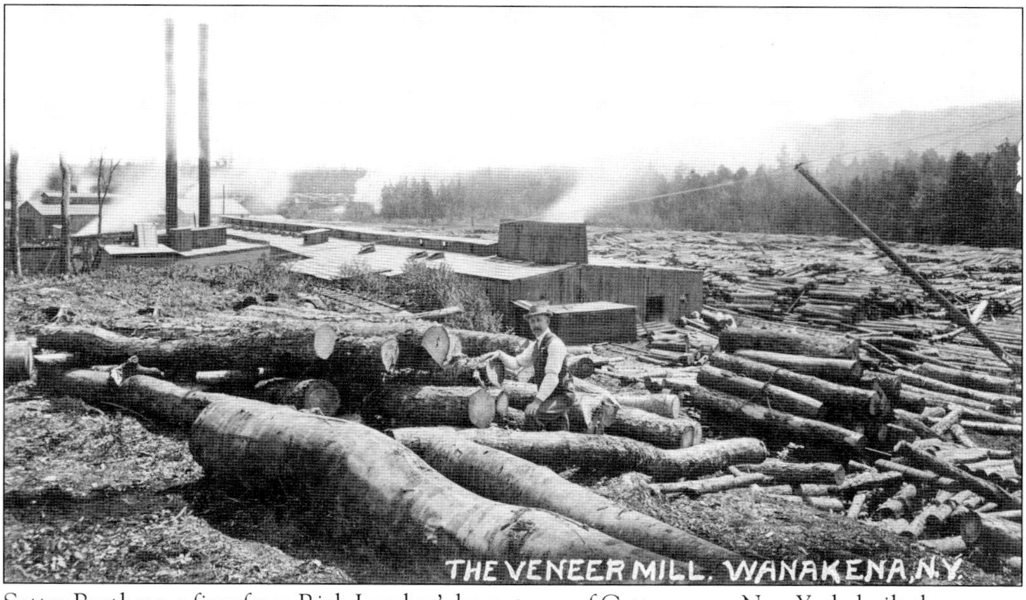

Setter Brothers, a firm from Rich Lumber's hometown of Cattaraugus, New York, built the veneer mill. Joseph Setter oversaw its operation—intermittent, according to local papers. In February 1909, the *Northern Tribune* noted that "the mill has closed down until they get a fresh supply of logs." Fine yellow birch, the only wood used, was getting scarce. The last report came in the September 9, 1909, edition of the *Ogdensburg Journal*: "We are very sorry to hear that the Wanakena veneer mill must close for an indefinite period."

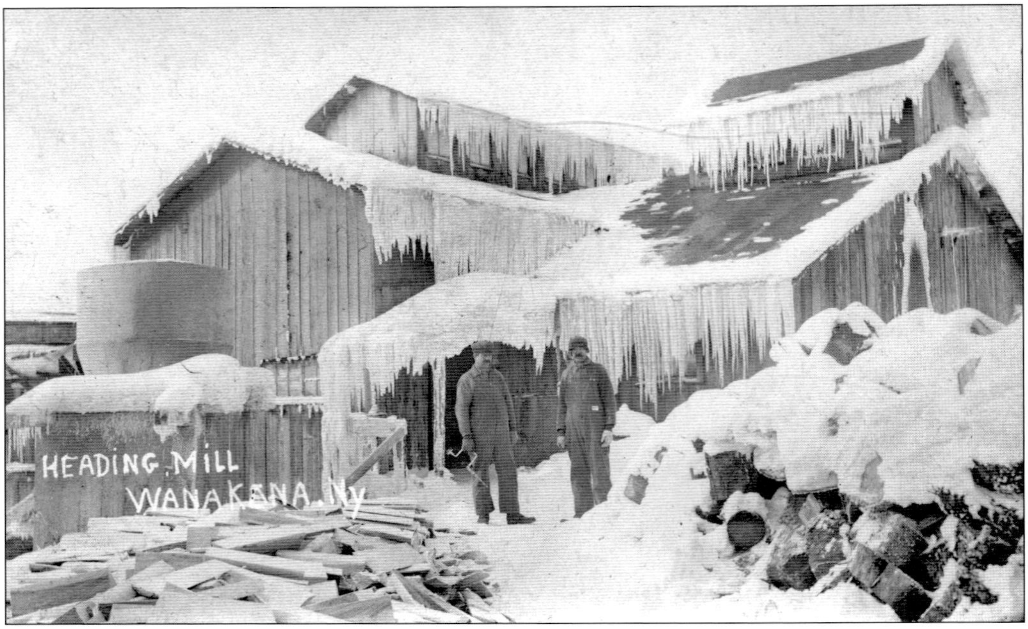

The Heading Mill pictured here burned in December 1906, but was rebuilt; on February 5, 1907, the *Ogdensburg Journal* reported that "the new heading mill is all enclosed and machinery is being put in." Equipment included a rosser to debark logs and a circular bolter saw that cut short logs, slabs, and edgings into pieces for making barrel heads. On September 29, 1908, the *Journal* noted that "the heading mill is closed as men are fighting the forest fires." The terrible Adirondack fires of 1908 shortened Rich Lumber's stay in Wanakena.

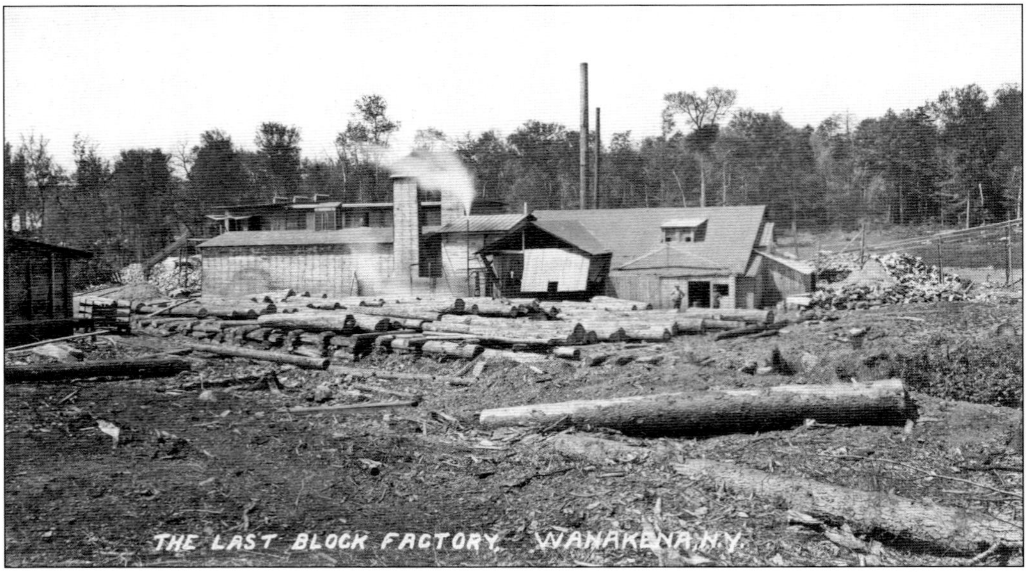

In November 1903, the Wanakena Last Company was chartered to make last blocks and finished lasts, wooden cobbler's models of a foot. The capital stock was $10,000; directors included Rich family members. This view shows maple logs ready to be rolled into the mill. The mill burned in February 1912; owner Charles Bates needed to sell stock in the dry kiln and complained that the Cranberry Lake Railroad was not providing regular service. The New York Central declined to buy the railroad; it dissolved in August 1914.

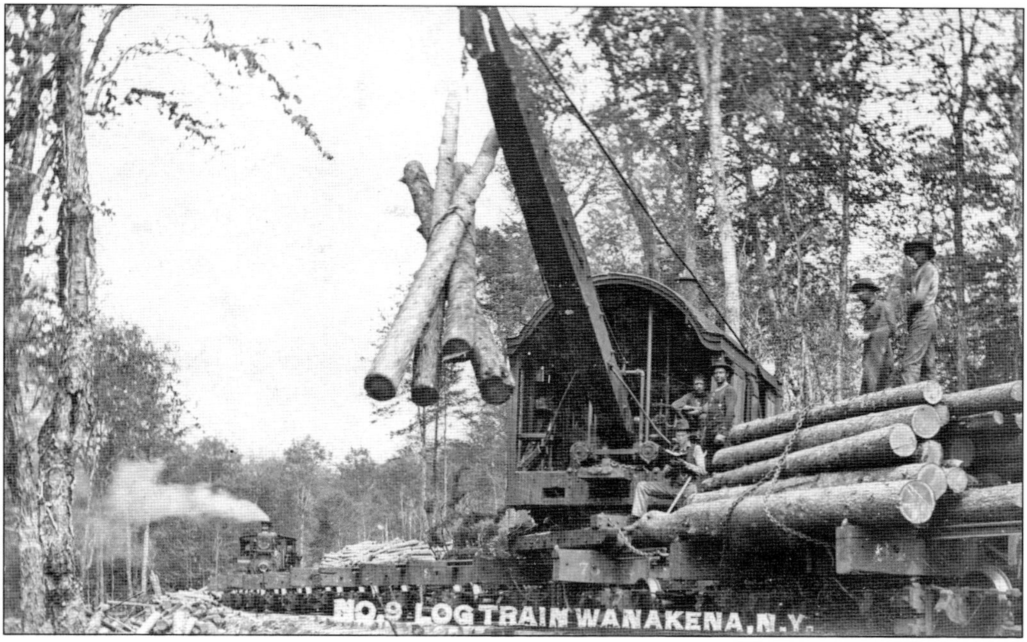

The card above shows the beginning of a log loading operation. The No. 2 Shay has pushed empty cars and a Barnhart steam loader to a railside skidway, where horse teams have drawn logs. Barnharts were small swing cranes, developed by Marion Steam Shovel co-founder and engineer Henry Barnhart. The first model in 1886 was an instant success. Barnharts moved on rails under their own power from car to car; "shoo-fly" rails were placed on the gaps between cars. It was not usual to chain four logs together or for the crew to stand under the boom reading a book. Once loaded, the logs would be chained to the cars. The card below, dated August 16, 1904, shows log cars fully loaded and ready for a Shay to pull them to the Ford Brothers sawmill. Barnhart loaders replaced the back-breaking work of manually loading logs but did not eliminate the danger entirely. On August 22, 1905, the *Ogdensburg Journal* reported the death of Rich Lumber's log train foreman as he was caught under logs falling from a railcar.

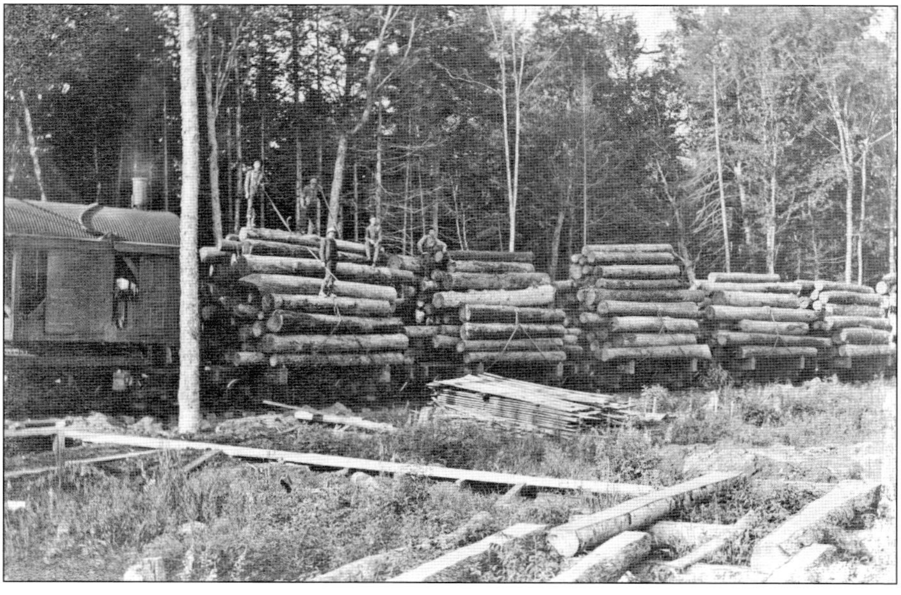

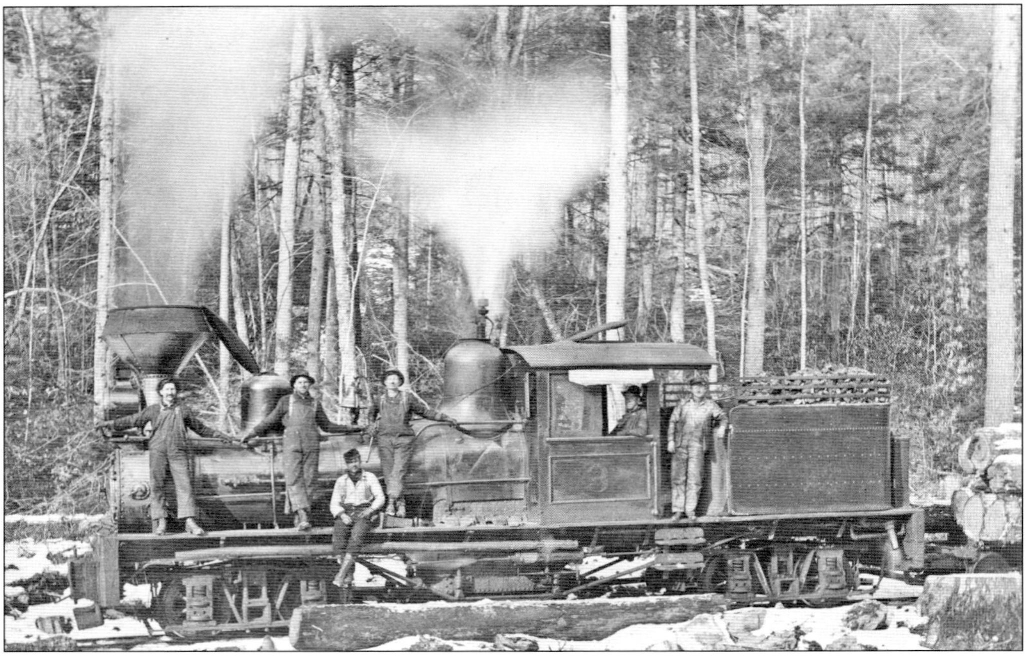

This undated card of a Shay at Wanakena is a puzzle. It is No. 3, with two trucks under the engine, matching the description of one of Rich Lumber's Pennsylvania Shays, but not recorded as being brought to Wanakena. The card, sent to Himrod in Central New York, reads, "This is a picture of the engine Eugene is running. He is standing in the engine. He says tell Uncle to come help him railroad." This could refer to either Eugene Mattison or Eugene Blodgett, both engineers on Rich Lumber's Shays.

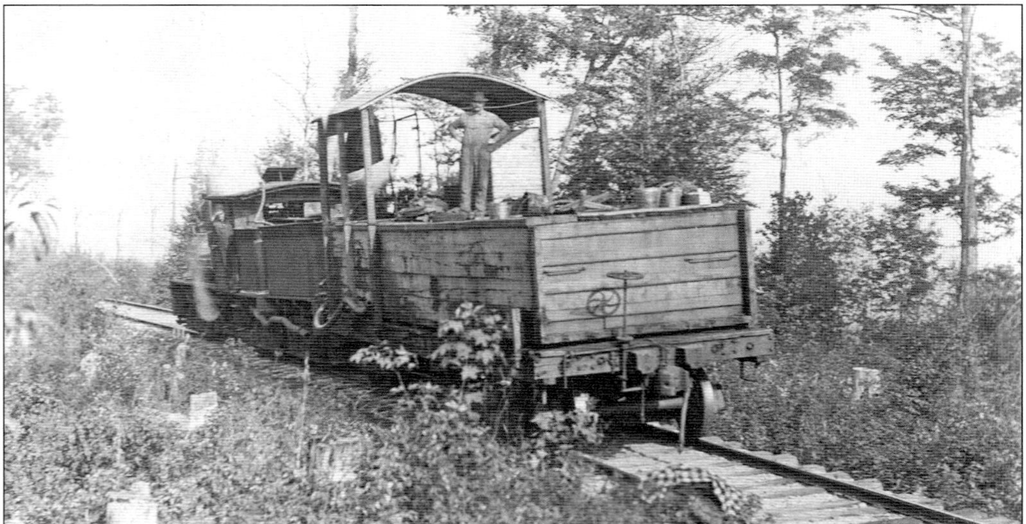

Harris Locke, with studios in Harrisville and Wanakena, produced this card of Rich Lumber's utility railcar. The car was kept on a siding at the machine shop. It is filled with rails, hammers, shovels, bars, chains, and pails. Apart from track and switch inspection and maintenance, the car might have carried parts to repair Shays in the woods, along with supplies like oil and lubricants. Automatic couplers and air brakes often had mechanical issues; Shays derailed and needed to be coaxed back onto the tracks. The utility car served many purposes.

Five

Newton Falls

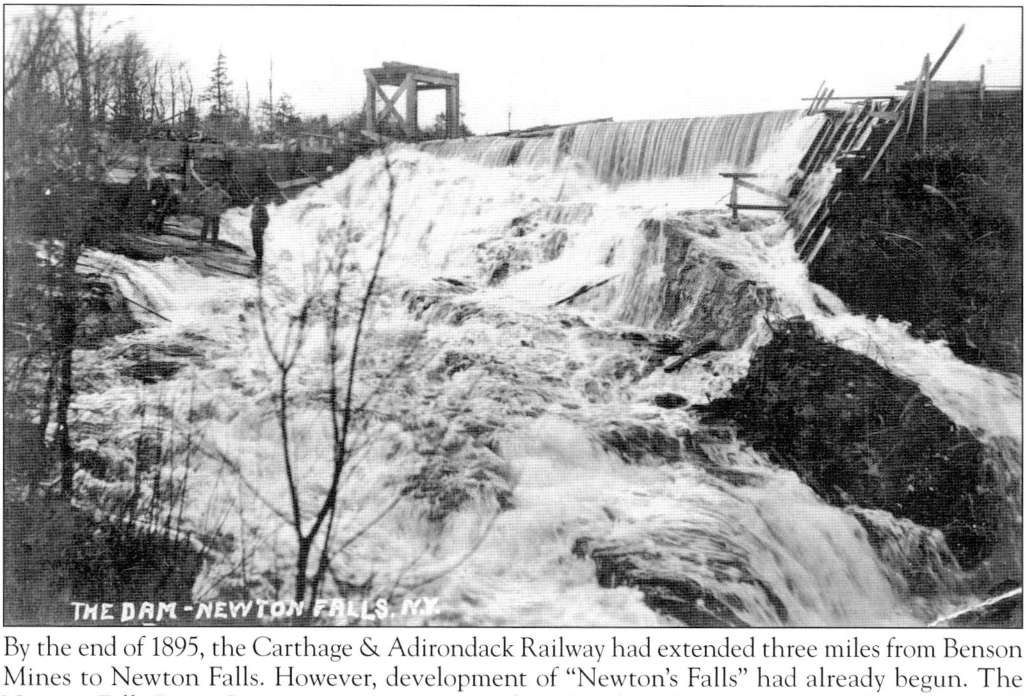

By the end of 1895, the Carthage & Adirondack Railway had extended three miles from Benson Mines to Newton Falls. However, development of "Newton's Falls" had already begun. The Newton Falls Paper Company was incorporated on October 17, 1894, "to manufacture and sell paper, mechanical and chemical wood fiber." Among the directors were James L. Newton, owner of 15,000 acres, and James A. Outterson, a paper business veteran. The capital stock was $200,000. The Oswegatchie River and adjacent timberlands would furnish power and raw materials for pulp and paper mills, reducing transportation and manufacturing costs. In 1894, a wagon road was dug to the site of the new village, and a dam and sawmill were constructed. According to the January 25, 1895, *St. Lawrence Herald*, the sawmill had a daily capacity of 30,000 board feet. In May, the lumber was used to construct the paper mill and company houses. The original dam is seen in this Beach series card.

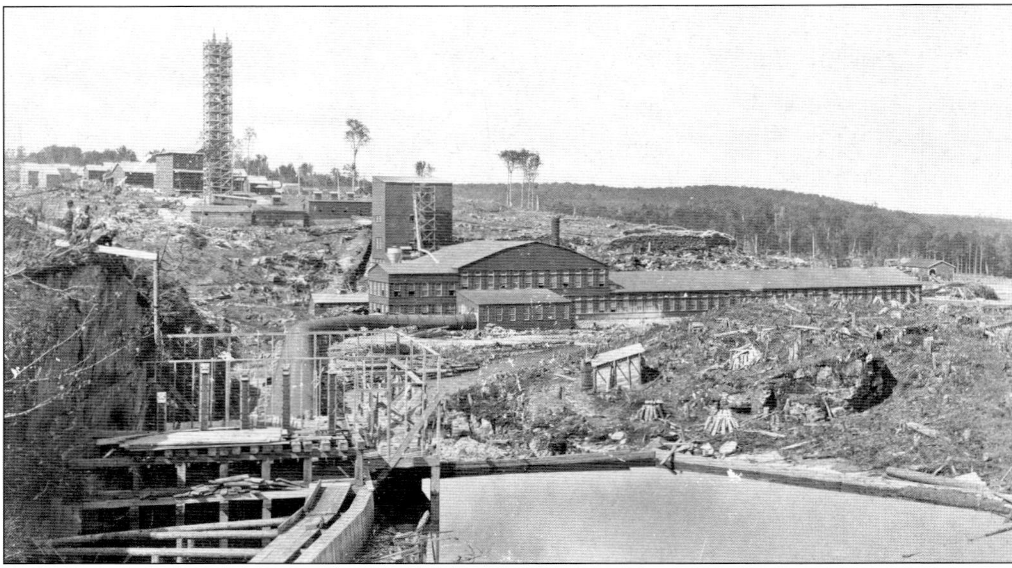

The *Ogdensburg Advance* of January 9, 1896, reported on the start of papermaking in Newton Falls, with two machines. One was a rotating 90-inch cylinder partly immersed in a vat of pulp, creating sheets of paper; the other a 112-inch Fourdrinier using a screen conveyor belt to drain the pulp slurry and making continuous paper that could be wound on large rolls. In the above c. 1898 cabinet card, the machine room is the long building at center right. The sulfite plant is the taller building at center. In front are the ground wood plant and the pulp room, where pulp from the sulfite plant and wood fibers from the grinding plant were combined. The slurry from the pulp room was fed to the paper machines, which could produce 25 tons of paper daily. The first papers made were bag, wrapping, manila, and light cardboard. Company houses are at upper left; the Newton Falls Hotel is behind the boiler stacks. The card below is postmarked October 12, 1905; original buildings have expanded, and the conveyor in the foreground added.

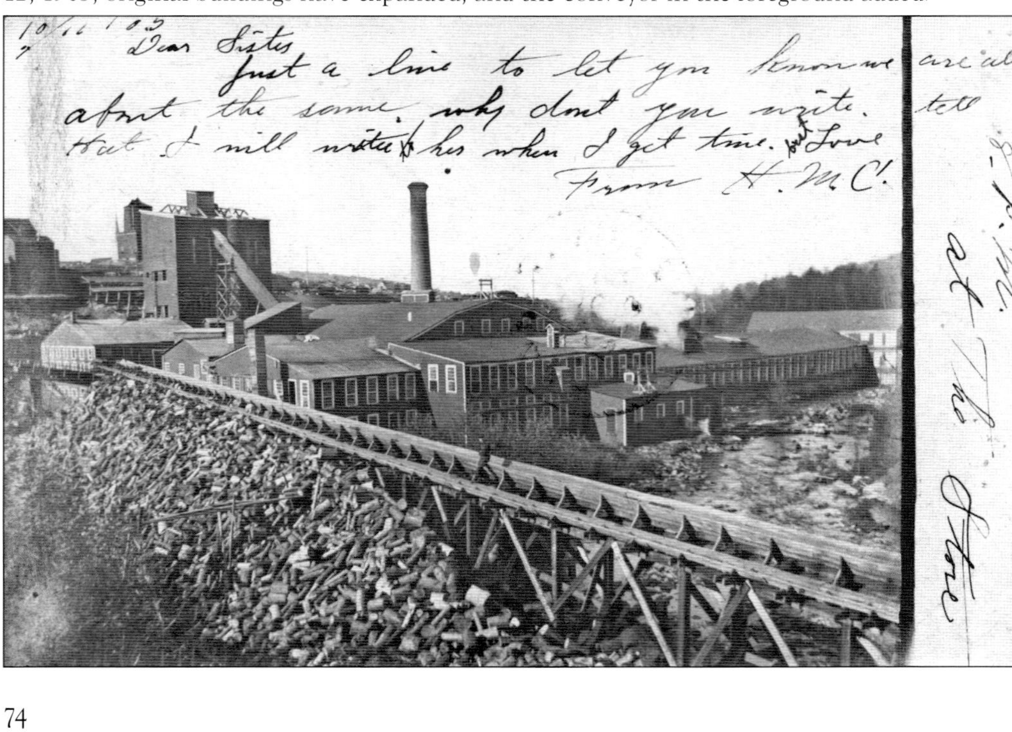

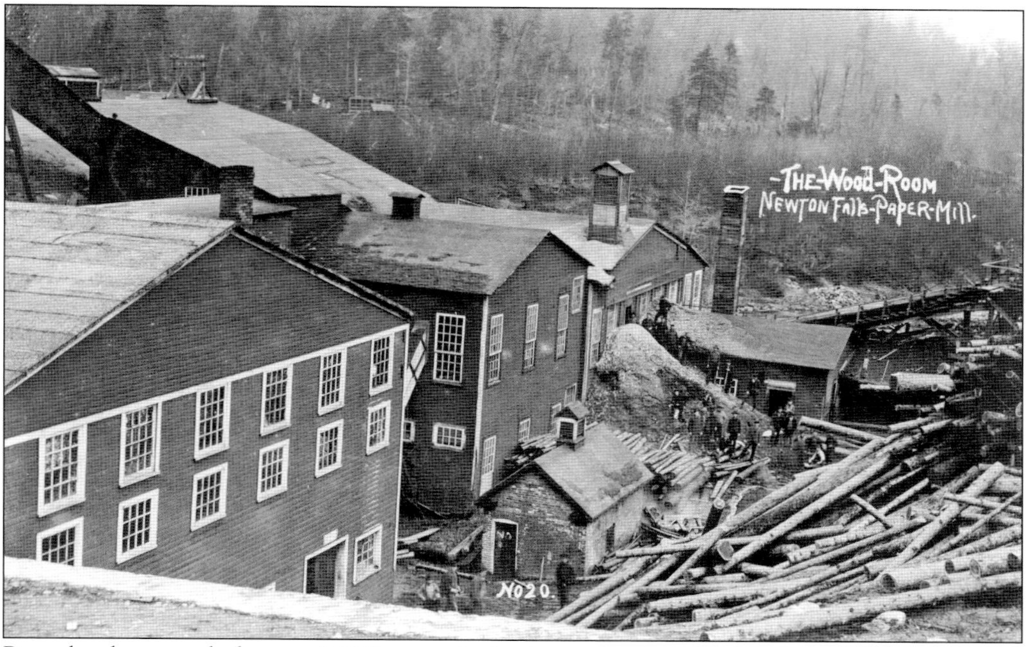

Paper has been made for over 2,000 years; the basic process drains a suspension of fibers in water through a screen to produce a mat of interwoven fibers. Water is removed by pressing, and a flat, uniform sheet of paper forms. Even after automation, paper continued to be made from rags—like US currency—making it expensive. In the 1860s, mechanical grinders were developed that allowed cheap wood pulp to be used, leading to a boom in papermaking. The card above, postmarked September 21, 1910, shows the Newton Falls wood room. Logs were moved by conveyor to the wood room, debarked, cut into blocks 20 inches in length, and then sent via chute to the ground wood plant. Its two mechanical grinders could reduce pulpwood to coarse fibers or provide chips for the sulfite plant. The card below is a view of one of the mill's pulpwood conveyors. Blocks of pulpwood were stored in huge piles to supply the grinders during winter when the Oswegatchie River was frozen and logs could not be floated to the mill.

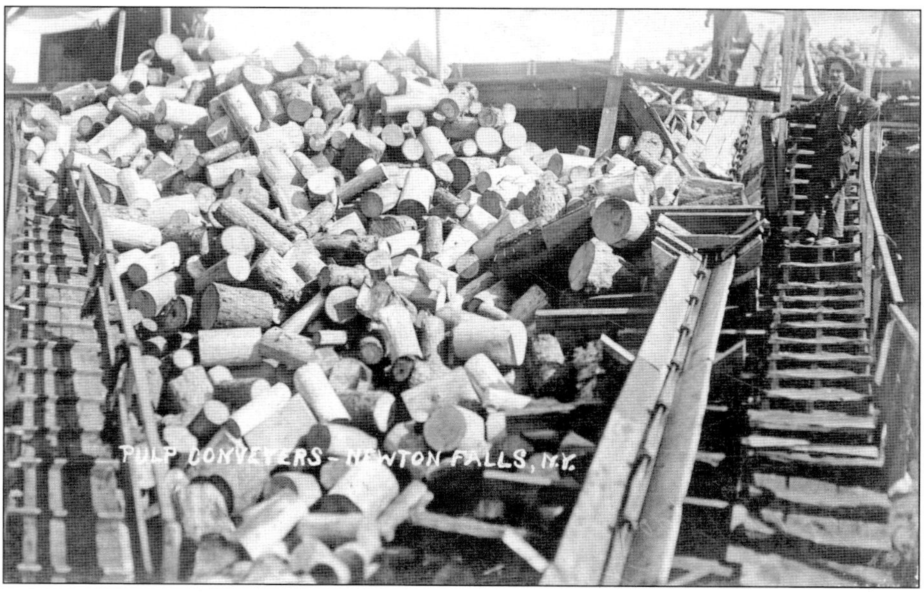

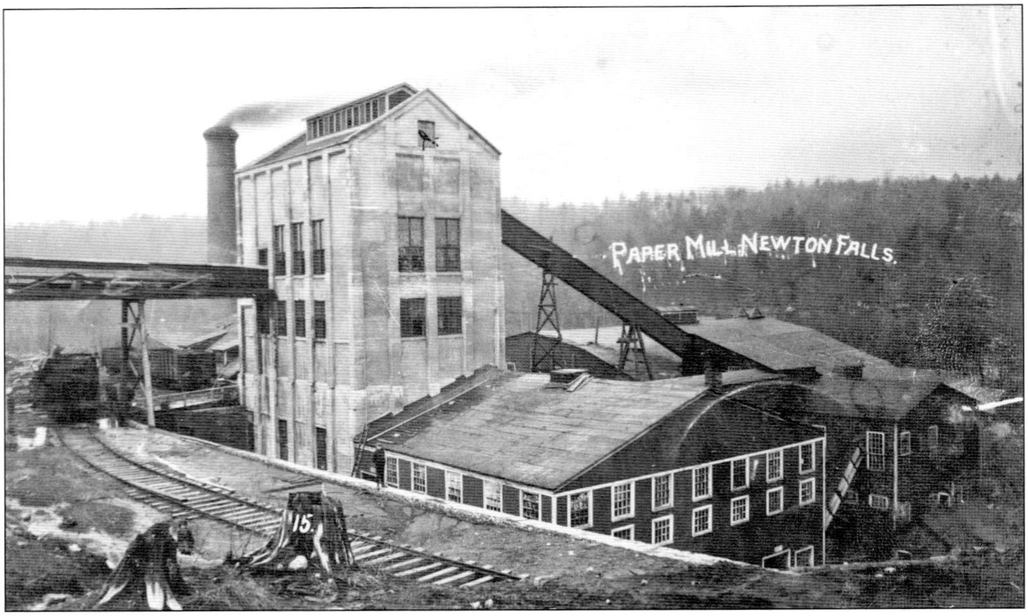

By January 1908, the date of the card above, the sulfite plant had been rebuilt using steel and concrete. The wood room still retains its wooden construction, but eventually, all buildings would be of steel and brick or concrete. The card below shows two Buffalo & Susquehanna railcars unloading coal at the plant; the reservoir in the background holds booms of sorted logs. The sulfite chemical process used at Newton Falls was developed around 1880. Wood chips were treated with salts of sulfurous acid to extract lignin—the "glue" holding wood together—in large pressure vessels called digesters. The end result after "cooking" was a wood pulp that was almost pure cellulose fibers, ideal for making paper. The sulfite process of pulping created toxic wastes that were discharged into rivers, killing vegetation and animal life. This was not of great concern in the 19th and early 20th centuries. In 1901, the village of Fine complained of pollution flowing from the Newton Falls paper mill 15 miles upriver, to no avail.

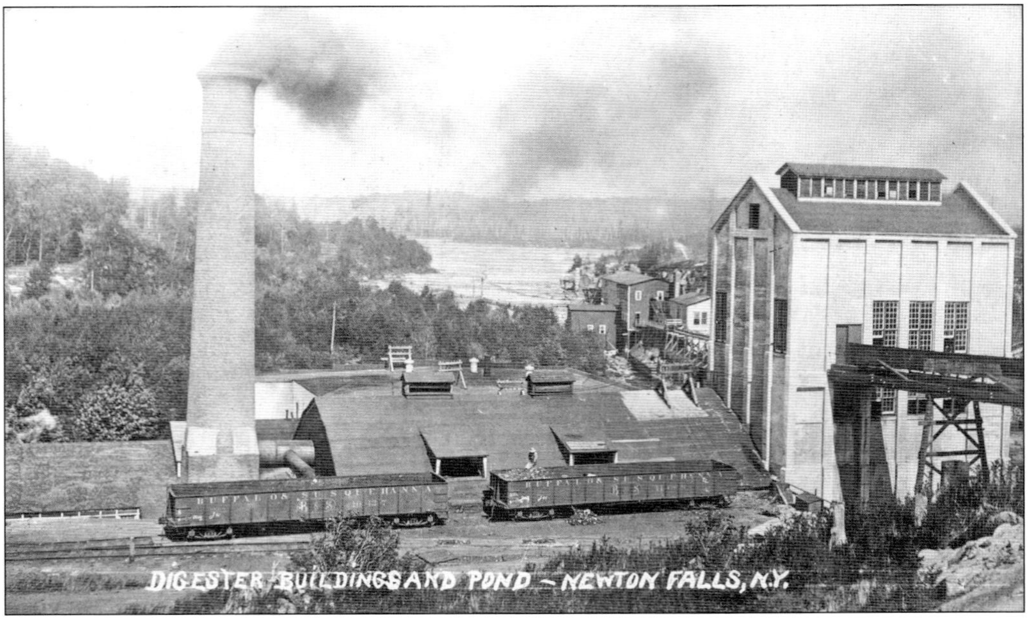

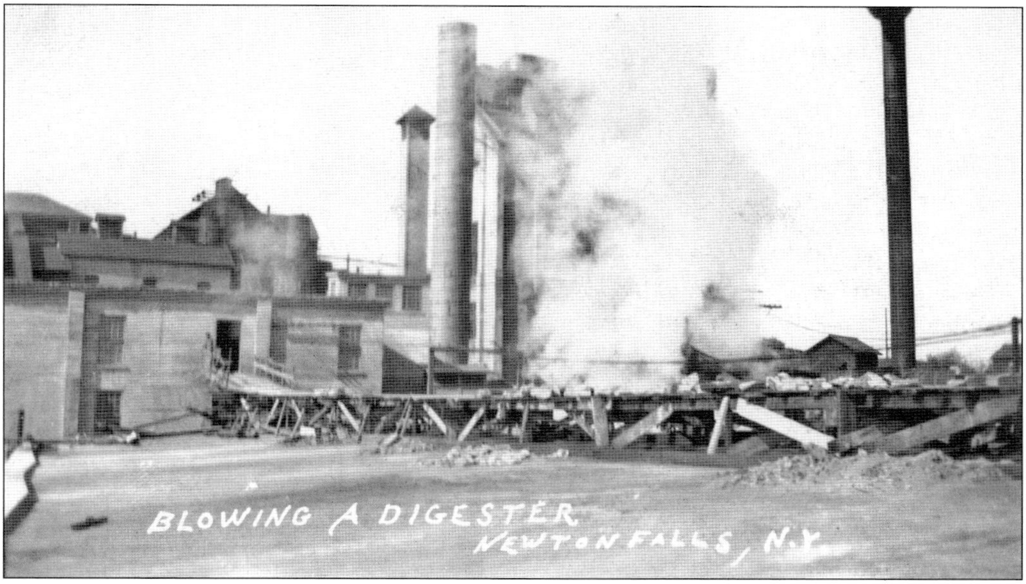

The Newton Falls sulfite plant contained two large digesters. After cooking at high temperature and pressure was complete, the digester was discharged via a large pipe into a blow pit, as seen here. The bottom of the pit was lined with perforated tiles, retaining wood fibers and allowing the cooking liquor to drain. The open pit allowed steam and gas to escape. The fiber was washed by flooding and draining the pit, then passed through screens and sent to a bleaching system.

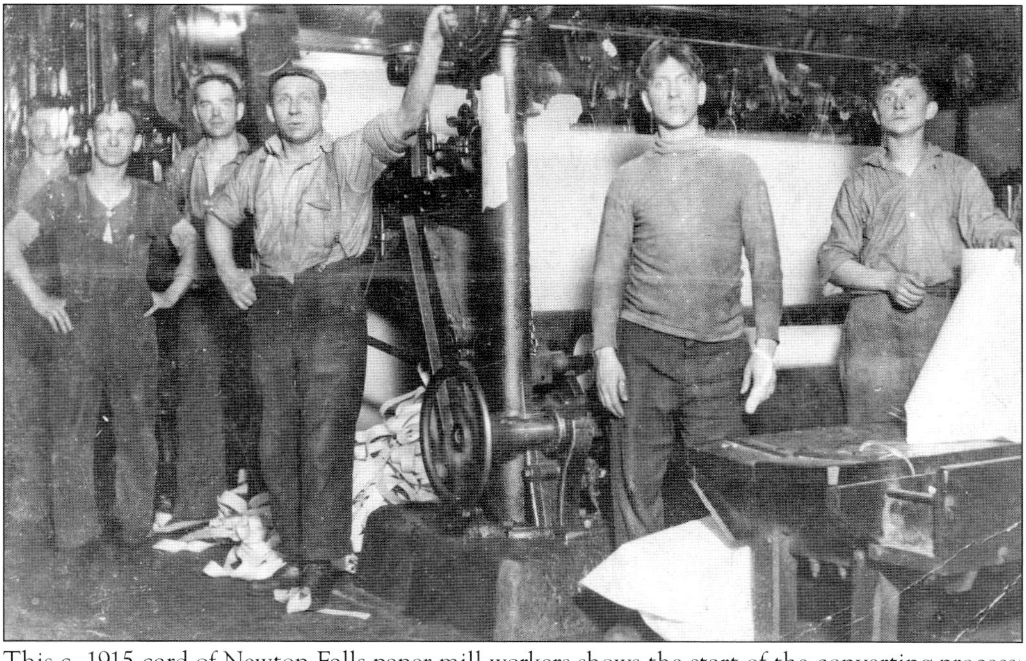

This c. 1915 card of Newton Falls paper mill workers shows the start of the converting process: making useful paper products from the large rolls coming off the paper machines. Finished dry paper was collected on large parent reels in jumbo rolls, which were usually scaled down. Slitters were used to cut the large rolls into narrower widths and trim off the rough deckle edges. A winder rewound the paper on cores, ready to be shipped to customers or cut into smaller sheets.

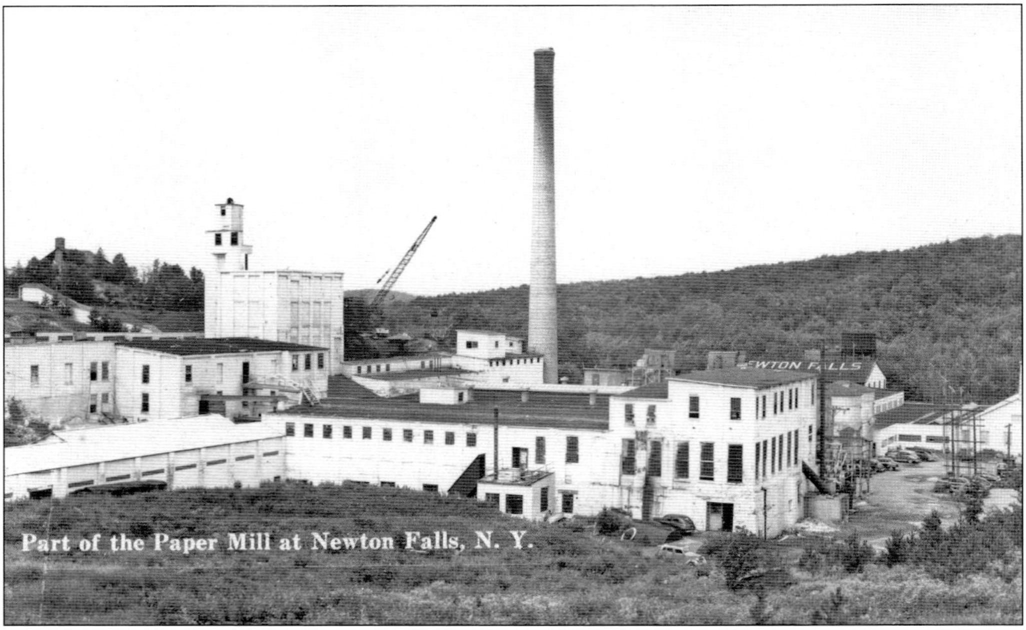

On March 6, 1920, the *Ogdensburg Republican Journal* reported on the "New Mill to Be Erected at Newton Falls." The 1895 paper machine building was the last to be converted to modern construction. A new concrete and steel structure would be built around the old wood one, and then the old one would be removed, with no interruption in operations. Charles Eaton, an Ogdensburg engineer, had already used this method to rebuild the mill's wood, beater, and boiler rooms, and the digester plant. Ongoing construction is evident in this 1920s card.

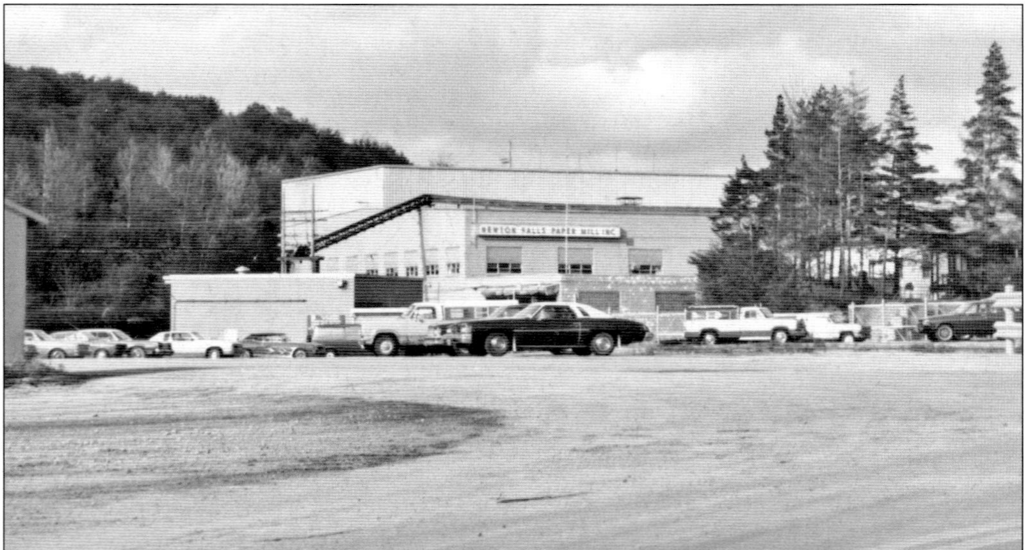

In 1920, McGraw Hill and United Publishers Corporation purchased the Newton Falls Paper Mill. It was modernized and converted to print book paper. In 1984, Sweden's Stora Kopparsbergs bought the mill to make coated paper, investing over $100 million in the plant. A total of 425 tons of paper was produced daily; 550 people were employed. In 1995, the mill was sold to Appleton Papers; it closed in 2000. After several changes of ownership, the mill operated from 2007 to 2010. In 2013, the machinery was sold. This card shows the mill on May 31, 1983.

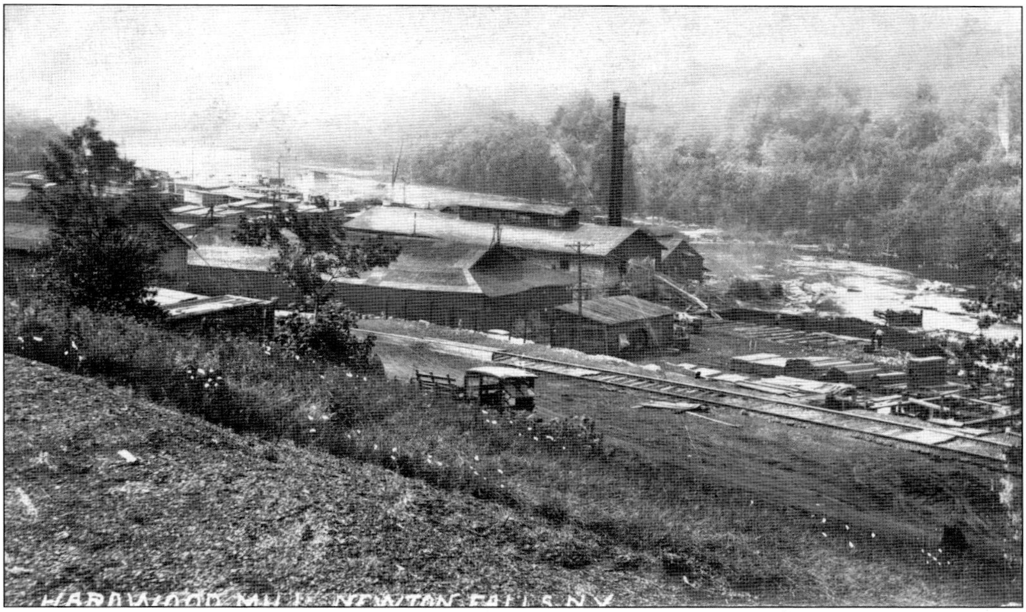

The Robert W. Higbie Company built the Newton Falls & Northern Railroad from Newton Falls to its lumber village, New Bridge. A hardwood sawmill in Newton Falls was also part of Higbie's plans. According to the September 1, 1907, edition of *Lumber World*, "Robert W. Higbie has returned from a business trip to the northern part of the state. He visited his new hardwood operation at Newton Falls, where the new plant is turning out some choice hardwood stocks for the eastern markets." Higbie's hardwood mill burned in 1920.

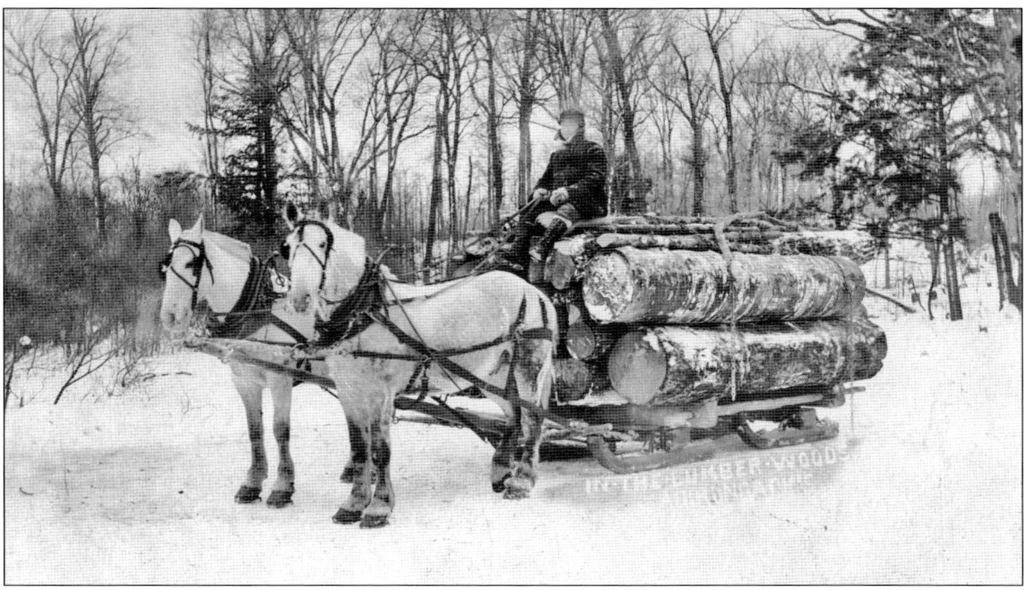

This card was postmarked at Newton Falls on March 9, 1908, and shows a load of hardwood piled on a logging two-sled—perhaps headed for Higbie's hardwood mill. Traditionally, only conifers like fir, spruce, and hemlock were used for pulping; softwoods have longer fibers than hardwoods and give paper more strength. Advancements in papermaking eventually allowed hardwoods to be used; the shorter fibers help make paper smooth and uniform. In 1923, the Newton Falls paper mill was one of the first to make paper out of hardwoods.

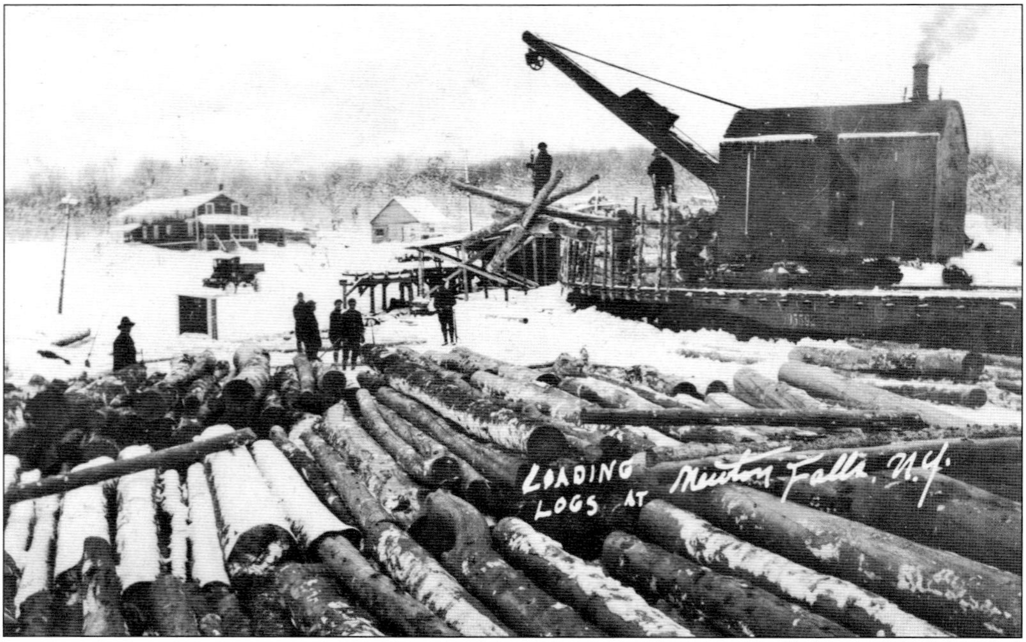

This card, labeled "Loading Logs at Newton Falls NY," was postmarked on March 31, 1922, and shows a Barnhart loader transferring logs from a skidway onto railcars. A worker is grandstanding on the load of six chained logs. The Newton Falls Paper Company initially practiced vertical integration—logging its own land for pulpwood that it processed from tree to finished paper. Between 1929 and 1931, the company closed its ground wood and sulfite plants; all pulp fiber was then purchased and brought in on the Carthage & Adirondack Railway.

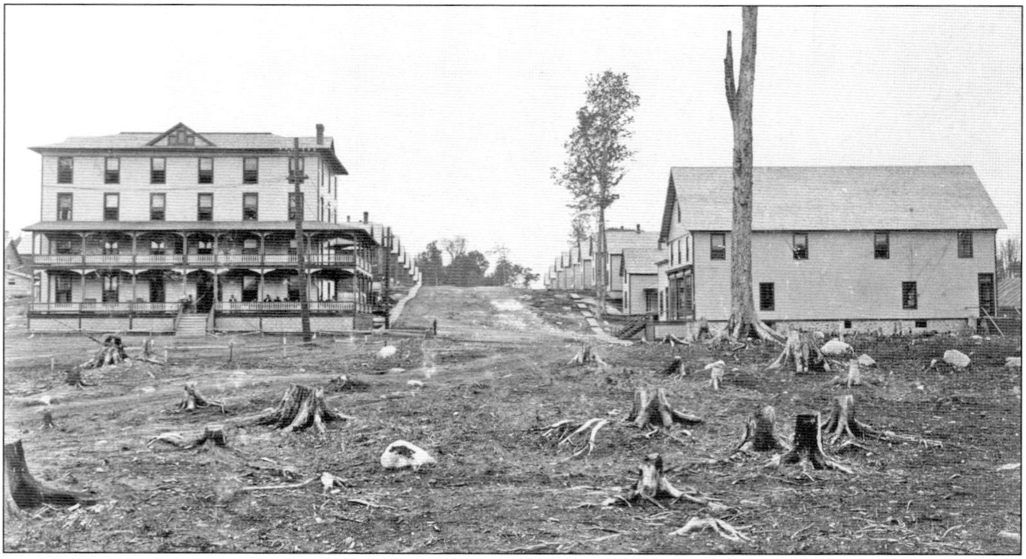

An *Ogdensburg Advance* headline on January 9, 1896, proclaimed "Newton Falls Hustling." This 1896 cabinet card shows village construction was well underway, with the hotel at left, the company store at right, and houses lining the street behind them. By March 1914, the *Gouverneur Free Press* reported that the paper company owned 59 houses, a hotel, a store, and two large boarding homes, and employed 225 men. In 1915, the mill built Sears pre-cut homes for its workers; construction continued until 1955, when the mill sold all houses to employees.

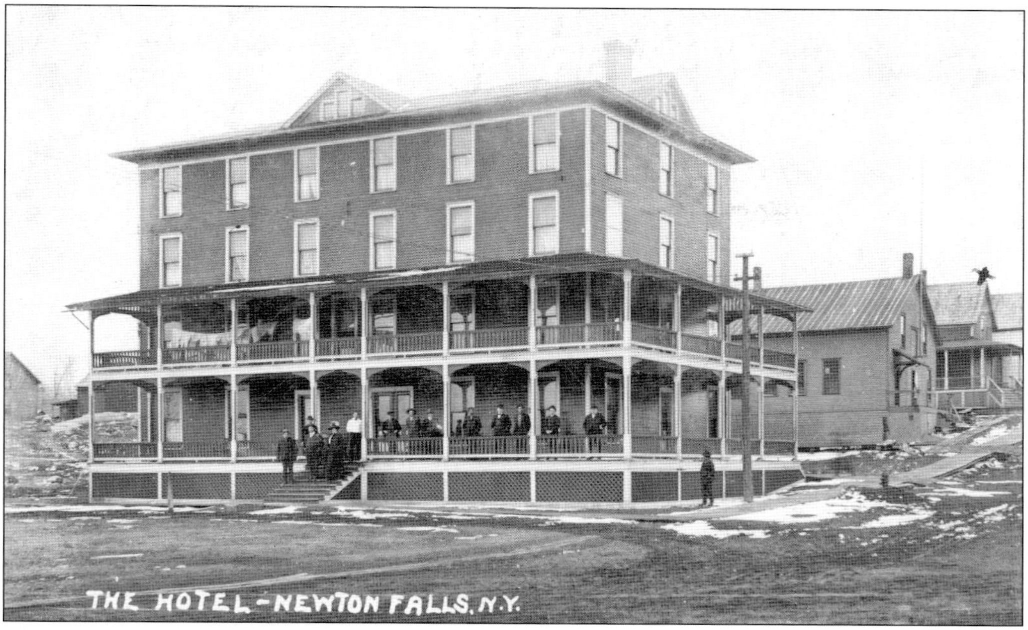

The Newton Falls Hotel was one of the first buildings constructed by the paper company, which hired many managers over the years. In the 1950s, the company renovated the hotel and then sold it; it still stands, but is no longer in operation. The early hotel was a community center and served many purposes besides food and lodging—polling place, courthouse, doctor's office and surgery, and other public functions. In October 1918, during the Spanish flu pandemic, the *Republican-Journal* reported that the hotel housed 60 patients "with one or more ill in nearly every house." This influenza was fatal primarily to healthy, young adults—the main age group of mill workers. The card below was postmarked January 27, 1909, at Newton Falls, and features the hotel's bar. A sign on the wall reads, "Wadsworth Whiskey—the Real Stuff. Beech Hill Distilling Co." The bar is equipped with an ornate brass National cash register weighing over 200 pounds, meant to discourage patrons who might have consumed too much Wadsworth from making off with it.

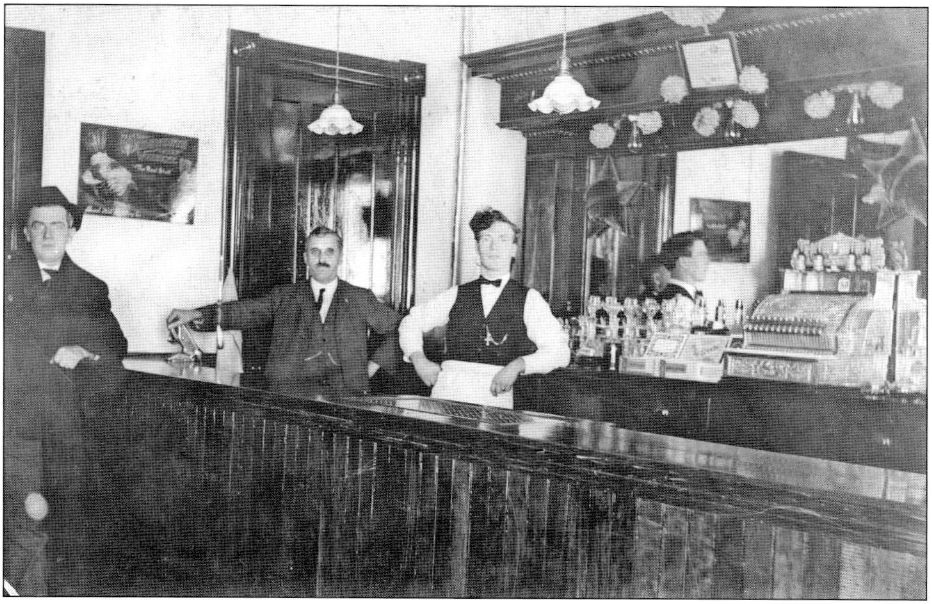

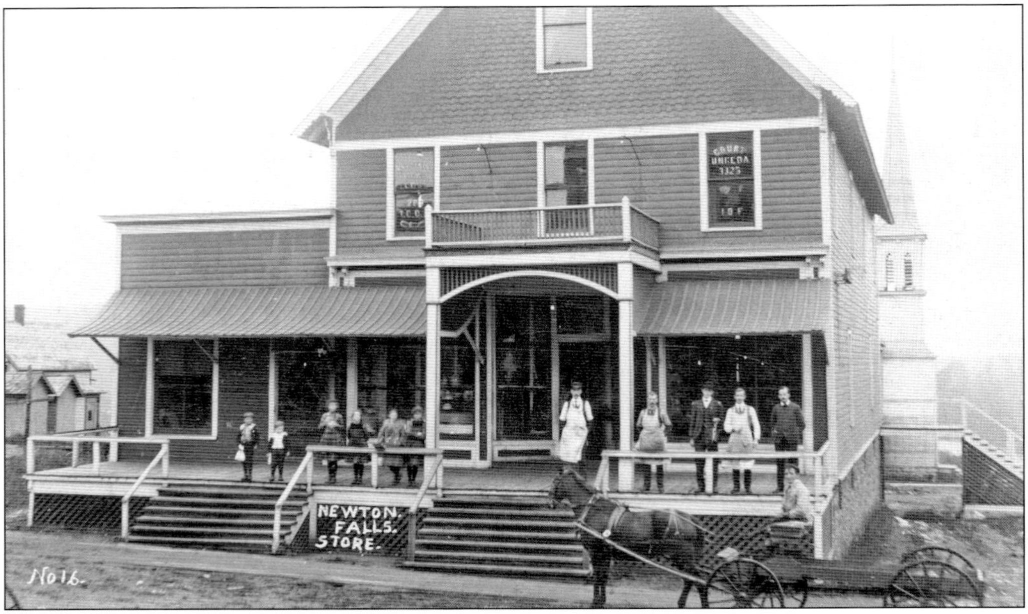

The Newton Falls company store, like the hotel, was built in 1896. It held the first post office; the upstairs was rented to local chapters of the Independent Order of Foresters and the Independent Order of Odd Fellows, two fraternal groups that were among the first to make insurance available to the average working family. In 1919, the store became Clifton Supply, owned by James Leonard, office manager of Benson Mines Company for 18 years and later supervisor of the Town of Clifton. The original store, pictured in 1908 above, burned on December 24, 1927. It was rebuilt in cinder block in 1928 and continued as Clifton Supply until 1957; after the retirement of James Leonard that year, it became a Great Atlantic & Pacific Tea Company (A&P) store. A&P may have had an earlier presence in Newton Falls, as the 1925 census lists one salesman. The card below shows Clifton Supply at left; note the Texaco Fire Chief gas pump. The apartment building at right was built in the 1920s; it was eventually demolished.

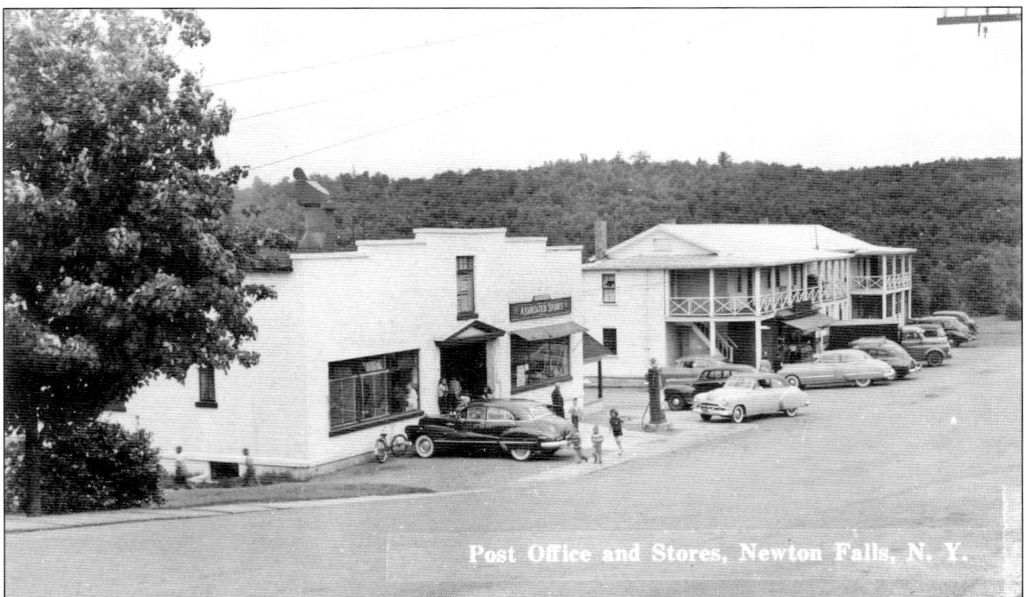

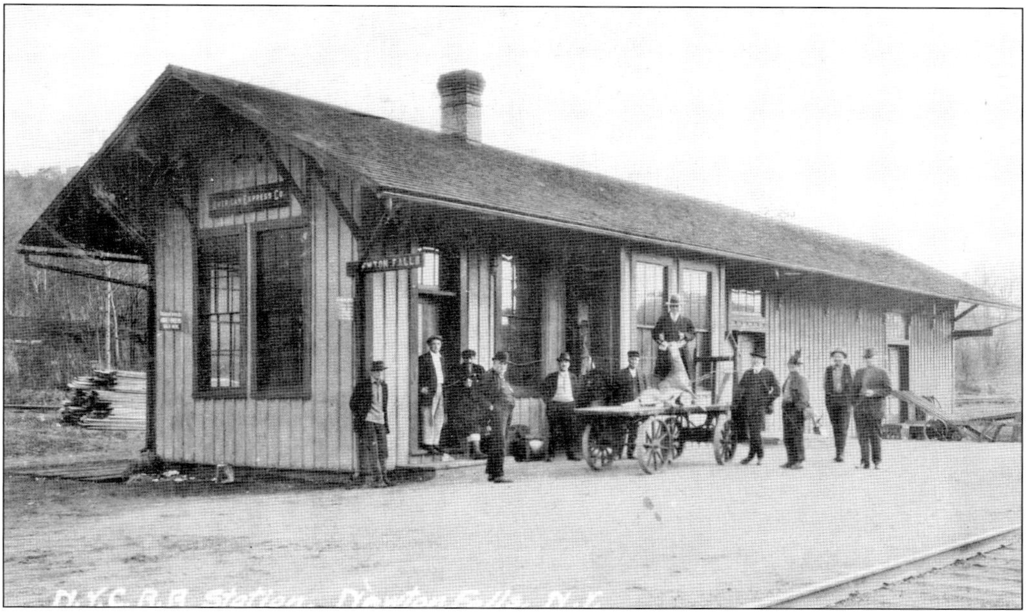

The November 6, 1895, Potsdam *Courier and Freeman* described an early rail trip to Newton Falls when the depot was not yet built: "The railroad deposits everything used in the manufacture of the company's product right on the ground." In 1931, the New York Central received permission from the Public Service Commission to reduce daily train runs to Newton Falls; passenger service was discontinued by 1944. In late 1958, the Central closed the station, but was required to continue handling carload freight on sidings, and to provide pick-up and delivery services for less-than-carload freight. The agent at Benson Mines was given jurisdiction over shipments to and from Newton Falls. The card above of the depot is postmarked July 29, 1920; a hunter displays a deer on the luggage wagon. The card below was postmarked in 1922, with a message written by a former paper mill worker from Rumford, Maine: "So like Rumford and yet so far superior. The hotel is in back of the Catholic Church; the mill is up to the left. Main Street is on top of the hill."

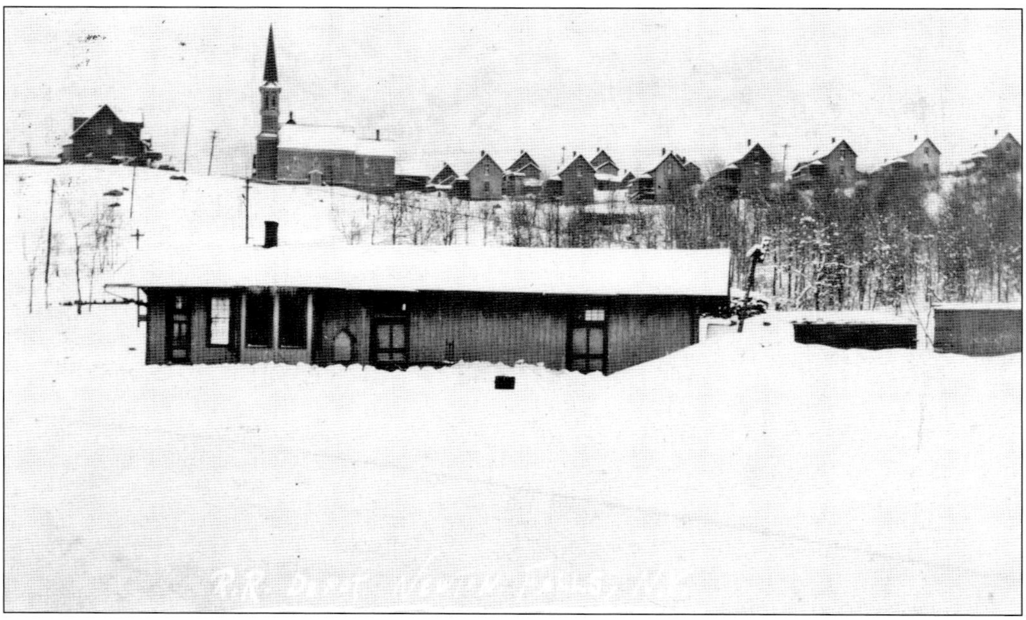

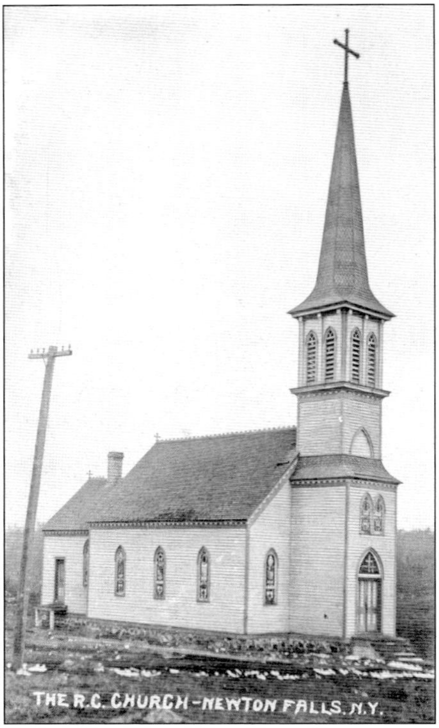

Before St. Anthony's Church was built in Newton Falls in 1904, pastors from Harrisville or Benson Mines said Mass in the community hall over the company store. In 1962, a campaign was started to build a new St. Anthony's, chaired by trustee Ronald Hynes. Hynes started at the paper mill in 1920 at age 18, rising from coal handler to become chairman of the board and chief executive officer. The new St. Anthony's was dedicated on November 24, 1963; it was affiliated with St. Hubert's Church in Star Lake before finally closing.

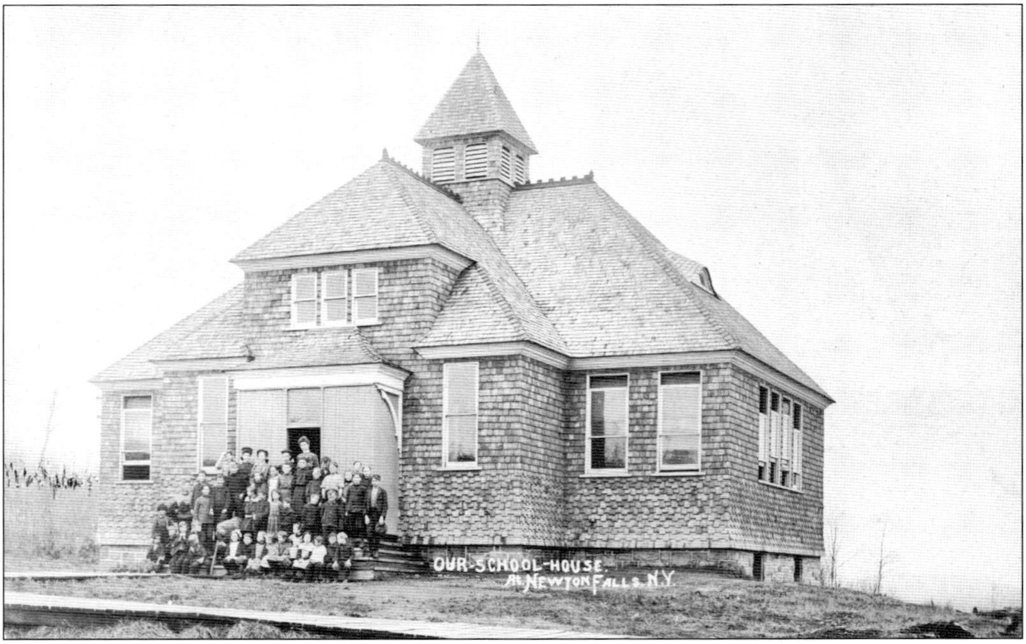

A teacher and 40 pupils are pictured in this card of the first Newton Falls School. Built around 1898, it held primary and middle grades; a separate high school was eventually built. In April 1913, the *St. Lawrence Republican* reported that the school was closed due to a smallpox outbreak; in January 1921, another outbreak closed the school for weeks. In May 1951, voters in the district, which by then included Benson Mines, voted to close their school and send pupils to the new Clifton-Fine Central School.

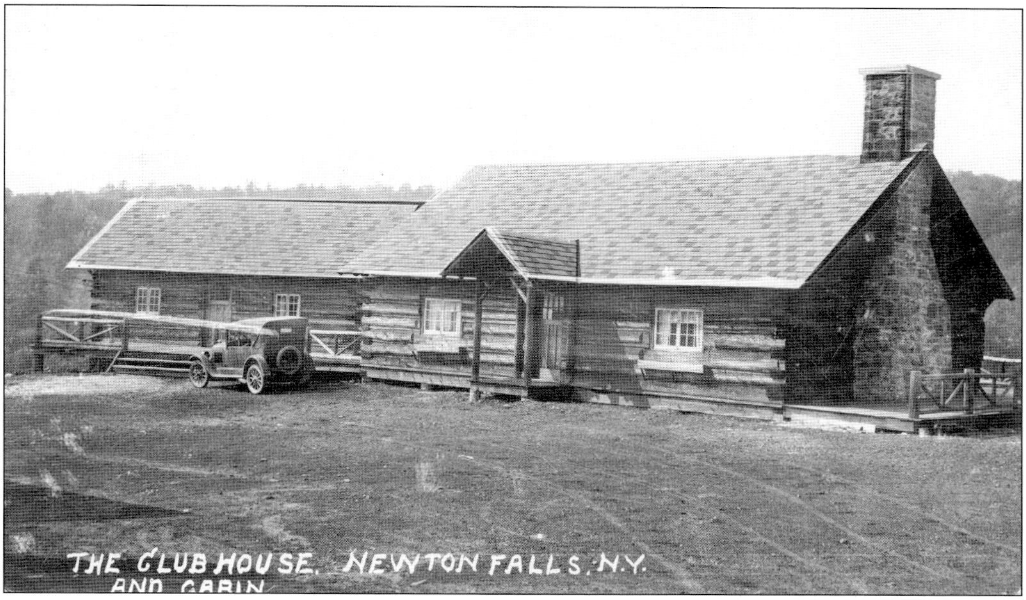

Built around 1920, the Club House hosted community and social events. A 1952 McGraw Hill booklet offered the adjacent guest cabin to prospective customers who could tour the mill and then (hopefully) place an order for paper. The building is now the Adirondack Community Church. This card was postmarked on October 27, 1929; the message reads, "Well Dad get your teeth set for venison. . . . Don't forget to get the Whippet going OK, and come up on Sunday." The Willys-Overland Whippet was one of the most popular cars of its day.

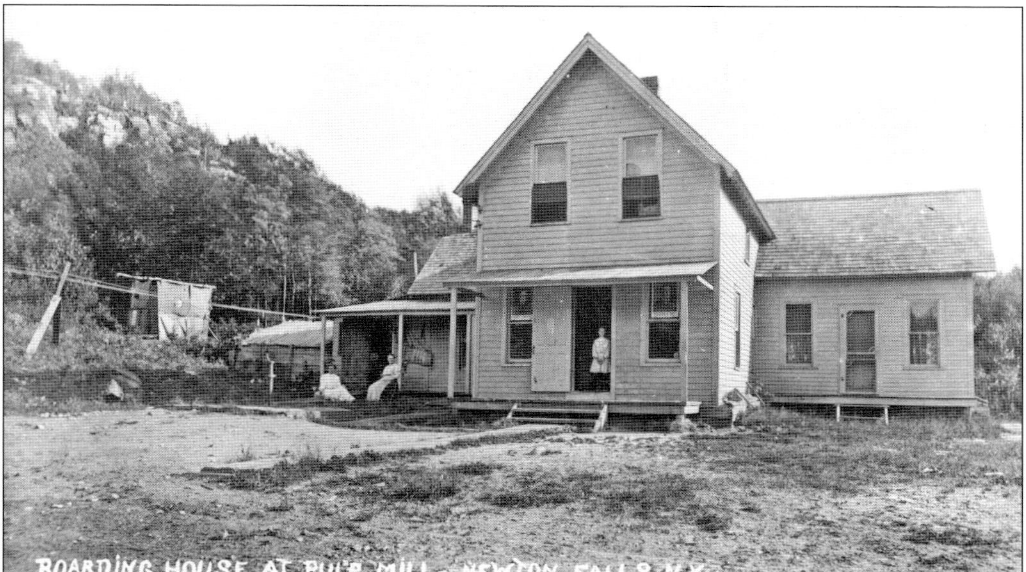

This Beach card of a "Boarding House at Pulp Mill, Newton Falls, N.Y." can be dated by the posters of William H. Taft. Taft was president from 1909 to 1913. By 1900, the paper company had built two large boardinghouses in the village. The 1900 census listed 121 residents of Newton Falls as "boarders"—a third of the population, mostly young single men. They lived in the hotel or boardinghouses or roomed in private homes. Company houses were assigned to workers with families, as at Benson Mines.

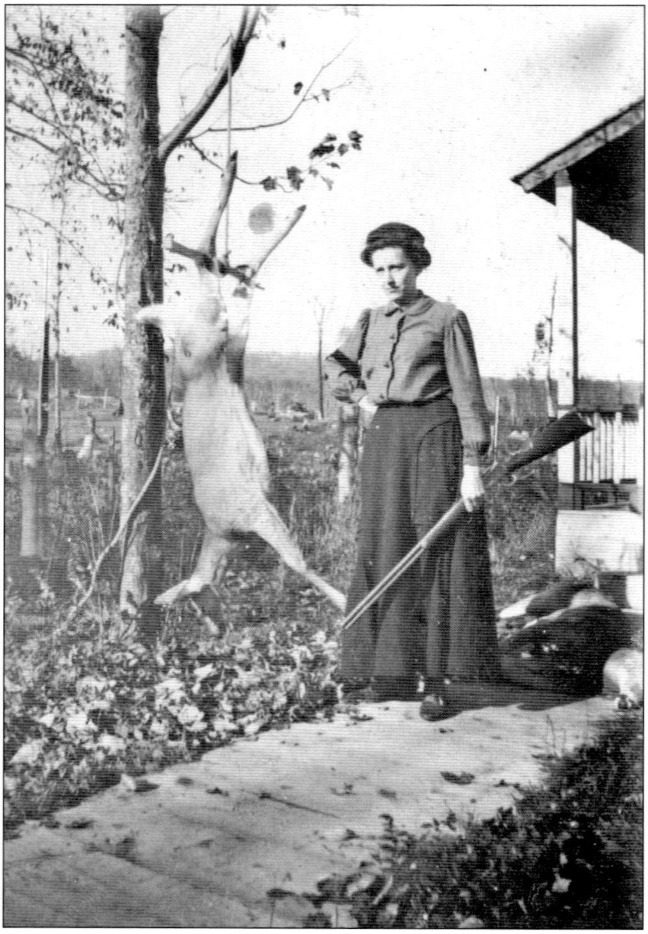

Both these cards were postmarked at Newton Falls in October 1908 and are examples of the revolution in photography then taking place. In 1900, Kodak introduced the $1 Brownie camera, with 15¢ film and 40¢ developing. Amateur picture taking took off, and Kodak achieved its objective—to sell large quantities of roll film. From 1906 to 1910, Kodak also offered a service processing and printing real-photo postcards from a customer's roll of film. The message on the card at left reads, "Here is a picture of—guess who—and the deer she shot & killed Oct. 12th 1908. This card is some of my own work." The card below, sent by a school teacher, has a message reading, "This is the family where I am boarding now. The little girl goes to school with me. She makes me think of you and I call her Florence." Unique, personal cards like these give the best look into the lives of ordinary people of the time.

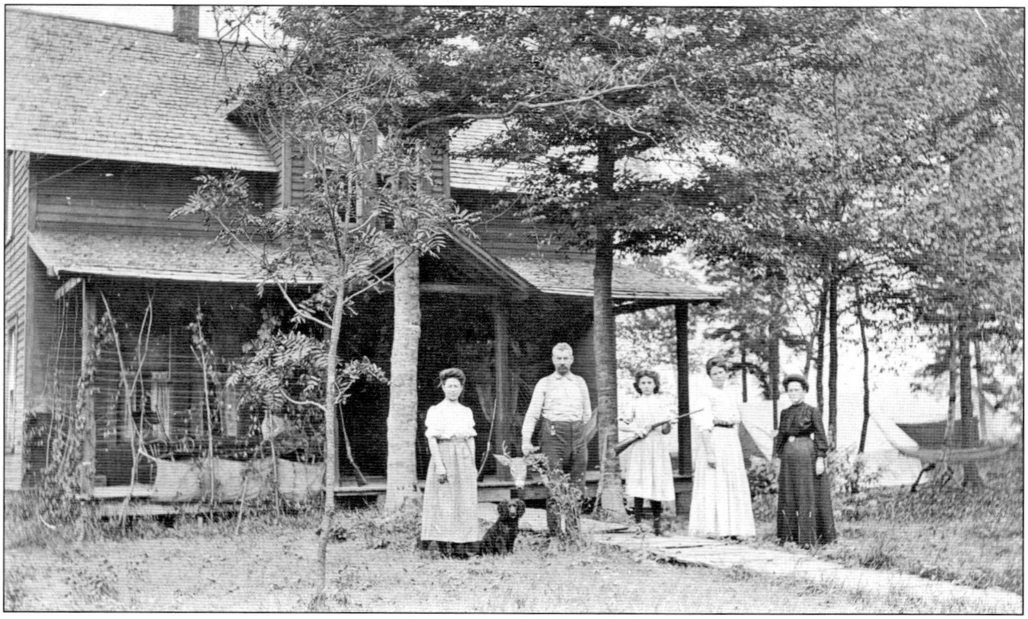

Six

New Bridge and Clifton Mines

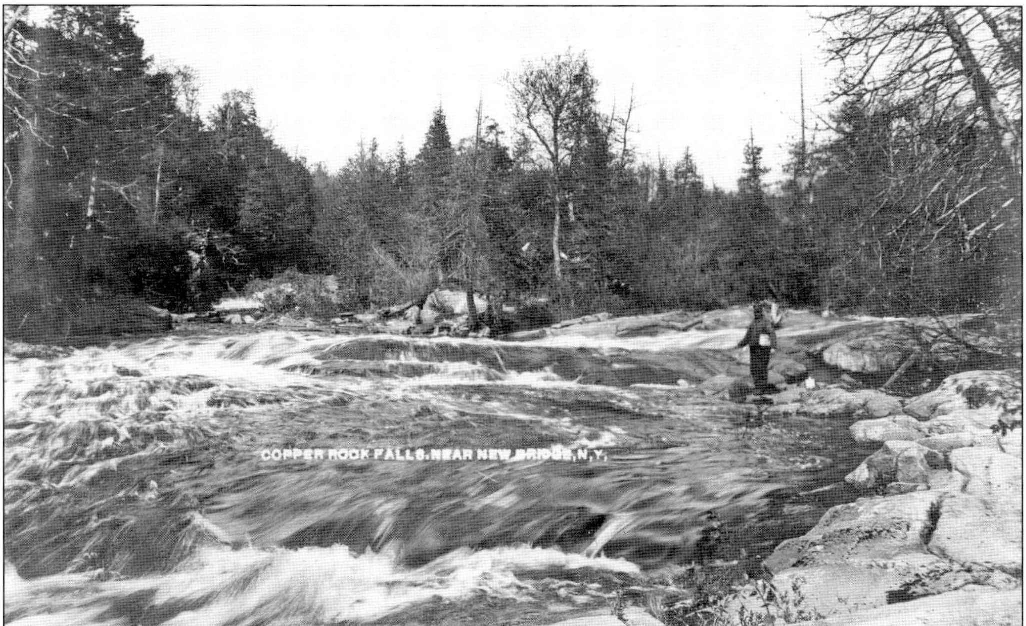

An *Ogdensburg Journal* headline on November 27, 1905, read "A Boom for Clifton—Immense Lumbering Operation to be Carried On." Robert Higbie had purchased a large tract in the towns of Clifton and Clare, and a railroad had been surveyed from Newton Falls to Copper Rock Falls, near the location of the proposed company mill town of New Bridge. The seven-mile Newton Falls & Northern Railroad, from Newton Falls to New Bridge, was built in 1906. Copper Rock Falls is a series of small waterfalls and rapids on the south branch of the Grasse River, about eight miles from Cranberry Lake along the Tooley Pond Road. Along with nearby waterfalls, Copper Rock Falls has been a popular scenic and fishing site since the 1860s and is pictured during high water in this card by A.W. Santway of Star Lake.

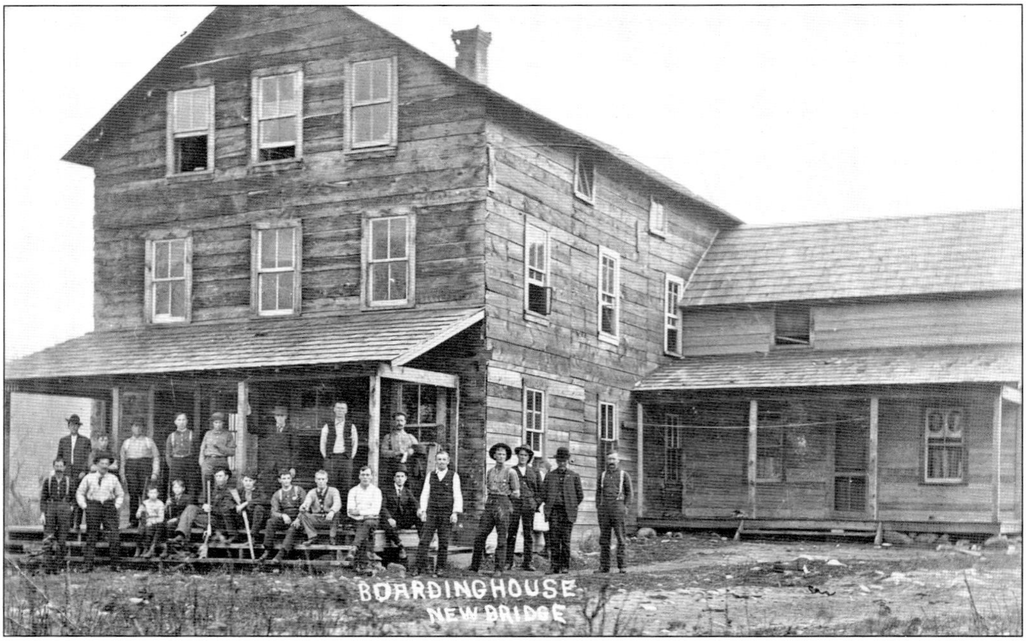

The periodical *Wood Craft* reported in April 1906 that "the Robert W. Higbie Company of Newton Falls N.Y. has been incorporated with a capital stock of $500,000 to manufacture lumber. The company will begin operations in spring, when it will put in a small band mill." First, a temporary village at New Bridge was needed to house mill workers and families and supply goods and services to residents and outlying logging camps. In 1906, a small sawmill was set up at the village site to produce lumber to build the settlement. Within two years, there were 50 homes, a boardinghouse/hotel with a general store and post office, a school, and a resident doctor. The boardinghouse was built first—as usual—and is pictured in the card above postmarked at New Bridge on April 20, 1909. The card below is dated September 13, 1911, and shows the hotel at right with added porches, and some of the company houses. The message reads "The 1st building is the store. I bought postcards at same."

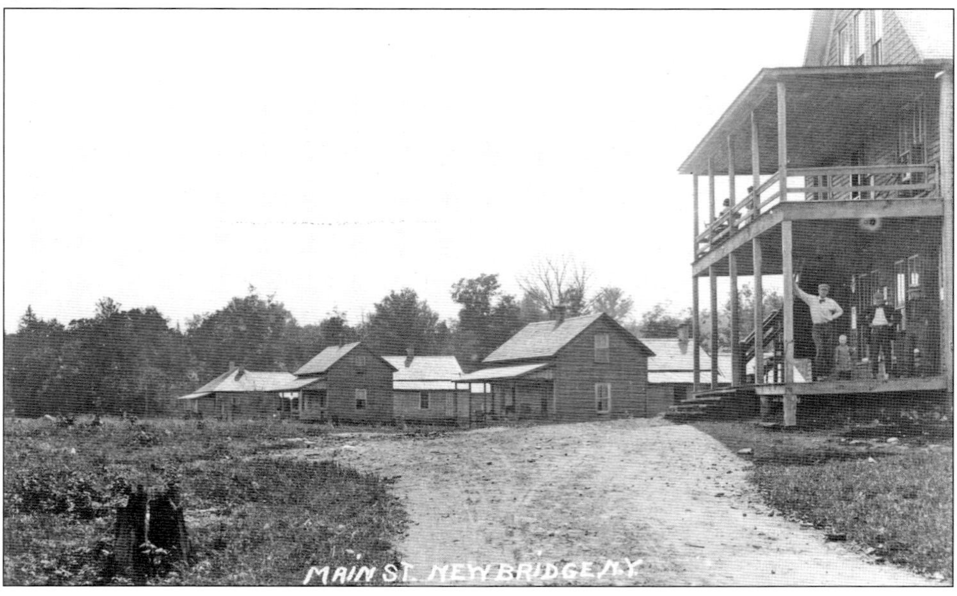

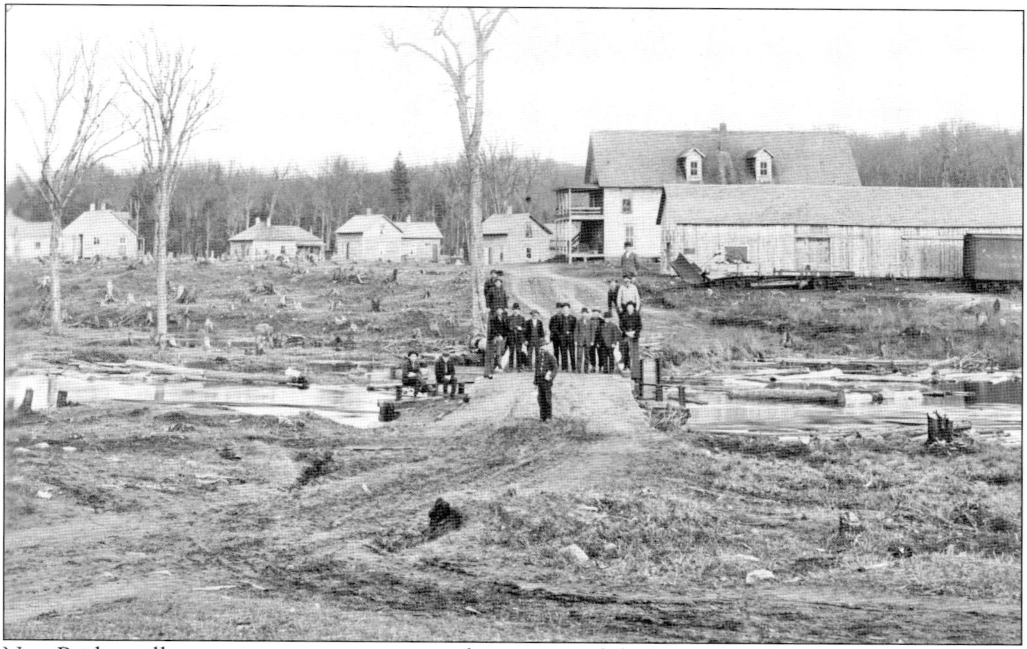

New Bridge still retains a raw appearance in these two cards by Henry Beach. The card above shows workers on a wagon bridge over the Grasse River, with the hotel and homes in the background. The long building next to the hotel may be the railroad machine shop; a flatcar lettered for the Newton Falls & Northern Railroad is on the siding. Below, there is a Shay engine parked next to a shed on the opposite side of the Grasse River. Since Higbie only used Climax locomotives, ownership of the Shay is uncertain. Once the timber was cleared, New Bridge quickly vanished. On August 21, 1919, the *Ogdensburg Advance* reported that homes were being sold for $75 to $100, with purchasers required to move them; many became summer cottages elsewhere. On March 24, 1921, a headline read, "State Orders Houses Burned in New Bridge." After the sale of Higbie Company lands to the state, new fire ranger Moses Lafountain of Cranberry Lake was assigned to clear what remained of the abandoned village.

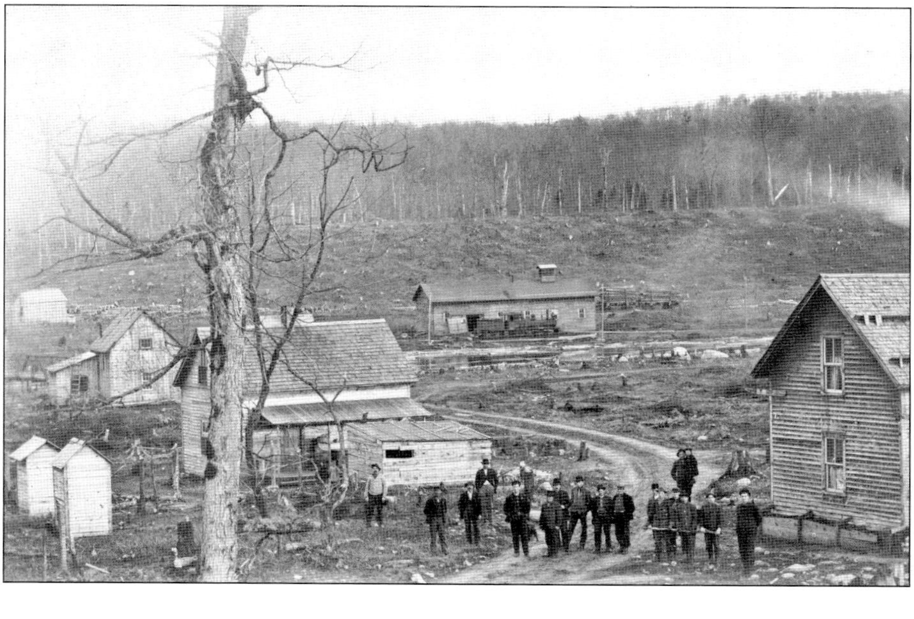

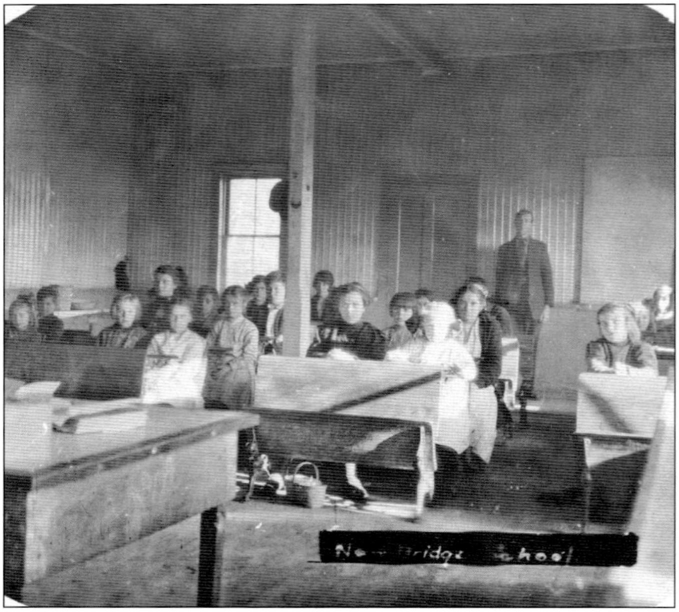

The one-room schoolhouse at New Bridge is shown in this card; a male teacher is pictured. Female teachers were preferred, since they could be paid less. In December 1915, a Potsdam *Commercial Advertiser* article described how older students had organized the New Bridge Student Union. Its motto was "Our School is Our Kingdom." Officers were elected and a school song composed. On Halloween, the union turned the school into a haunted house complete with ghosts, fortune telling, and refreshments. Admission was 10¢.

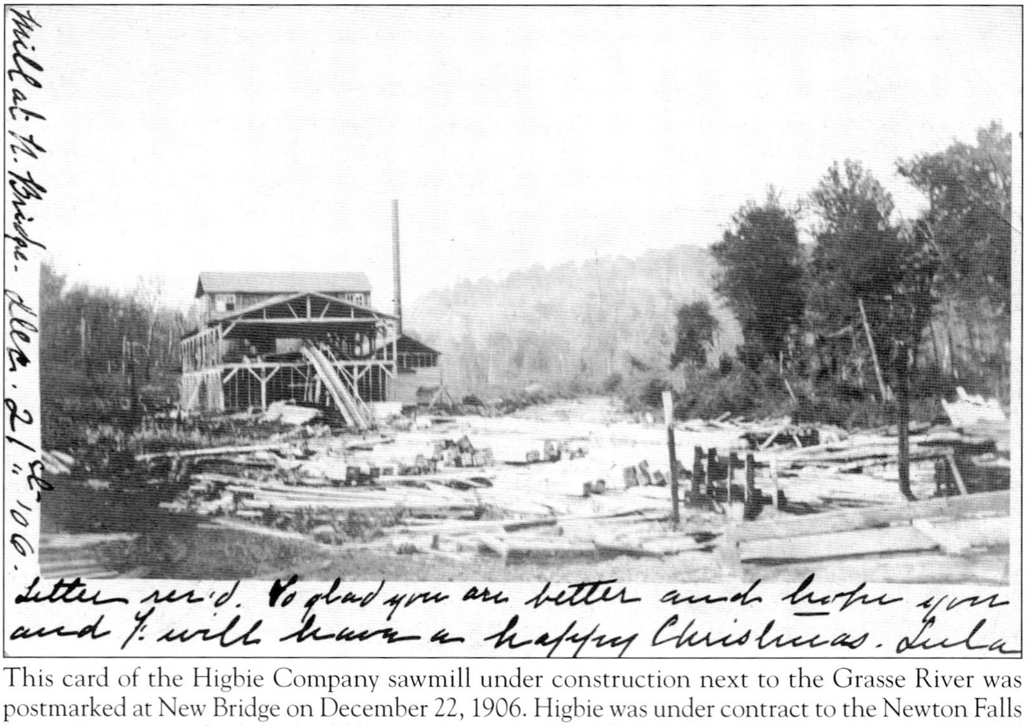

This card of the Higbie Company sawmill under construction next to the Grasse River was postmarked at New Bridge on December 22, 1906. Higbie was under contract to the Newton Falls Paper Company, which had sold him 21,500 acres of timberland in 1905. In return, Higbie had to deliver all softwood, pulpwood, and pine and cedar sawlogs by railroad to the paper company, dumping them into the pond above the dam at Newton Falls. Higbie cut and manufactured the hardwoods at his mills in New Bridge and Newton Falls.

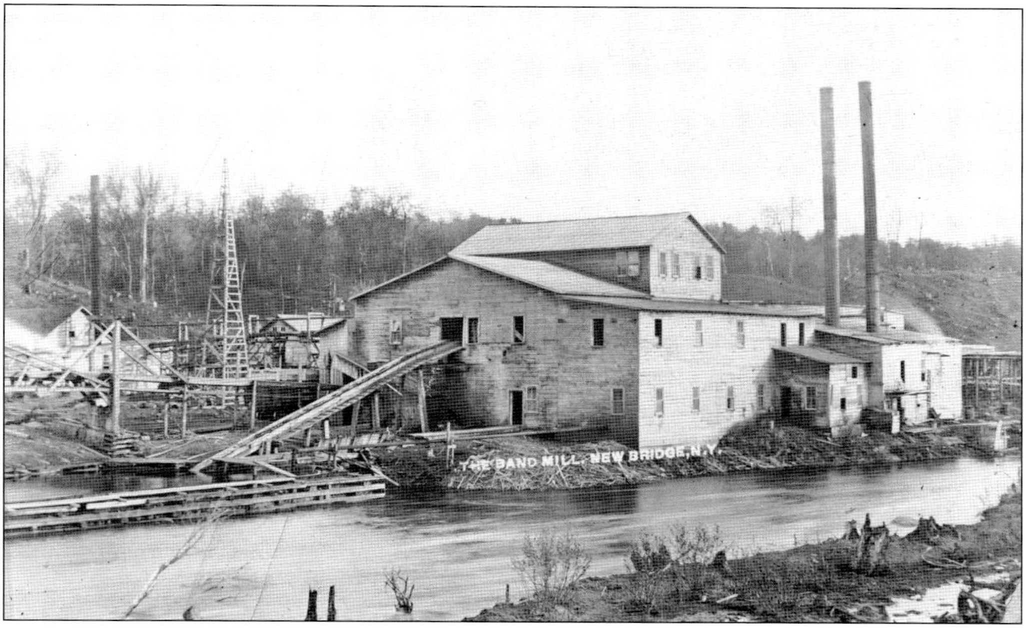

The large steam double-band sawmill is shown completed in the card above, postmarked at New Bridge in 1909. Its boiler was fed with scrap wood and sawdust. The mill also used small saws to make lath. At far left is a broom handle factory. The front of the card below reads, "The Mills at New Bridge N.Y., from the Boarding House." The reverse message reads, "Saw Mill in front. Broom Handle Mill in background. Saw about 40,000 feet of hardwood in 10 hour day." The *Gouverneur Free Press*, on March 11, 1914, reported that Higbie Company expected to have enough timber to keep its mills in operation for at least three more years. This was an accurate prediction; Higbie's main logging jobber, Leslie Spicer, finished his last New Bridge lumber job in February 1918 and returned home to Russell. Spicer began working for Higbie in 1910; local personal columns followed his progress as he and his wife lived at logging camps "in the lumber woods above New Bridge" for the next eight years.

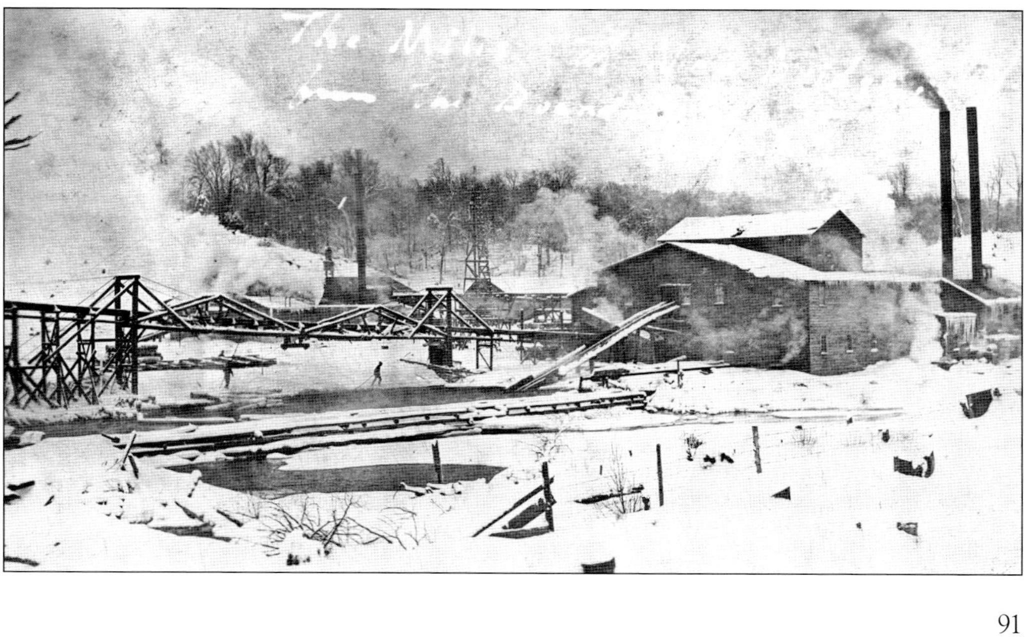

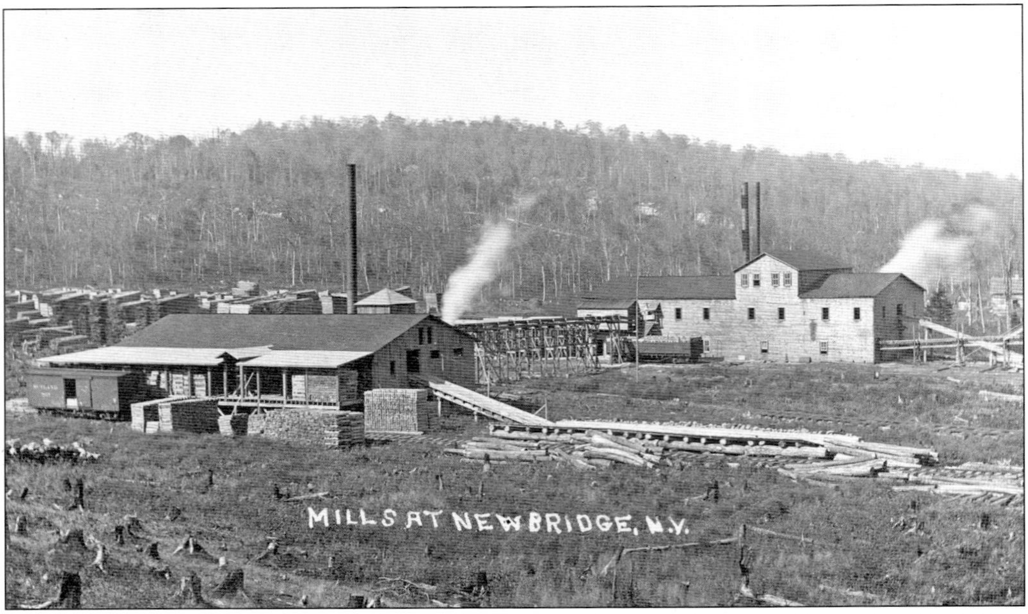

The broom handle mill is at left in this card, postmarked at New Bridge on November 11, 1908; it used hardwood logs unsuitable for lumber. The sawmill at right was rebuilt after a fire in July 1908; a steam loader was also destroyed along with 100,000 feet of logs. Next to the sawmill are its docks, where lumber was sorted and stacked to air dry. Carloads of lumber were transported to Newton Falls on the company rail line and then taken to markets via the New York Central system.

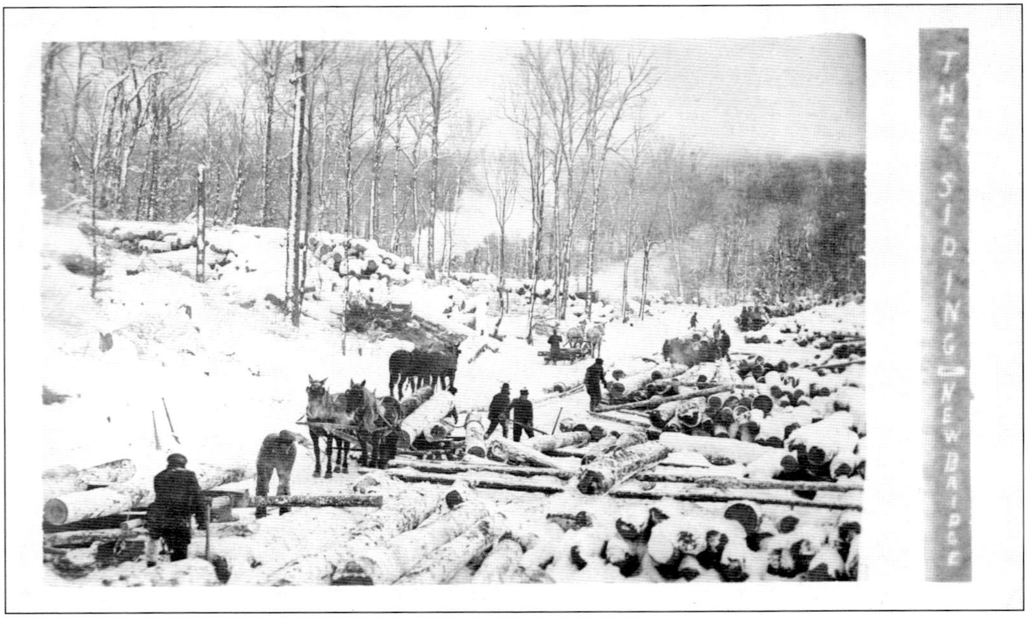

This undated card is titled "The Siding—New Bridge." Teamsters and their horses were in great demand for the winter work of hauling logs to railway sidings. A January 10, 1912, article in the Potsdam *Courier Freeman* noted that "George Brown and Fred Short went to New Bridge on Thursday with their teams to draw logs." The men returned home in late April. On March 4, 1913, the *Ogdensburg Journal* reported that Cranberry Lake jobber Warren Guinup had gone with his teams to work for Higbie Company at New Bridge.

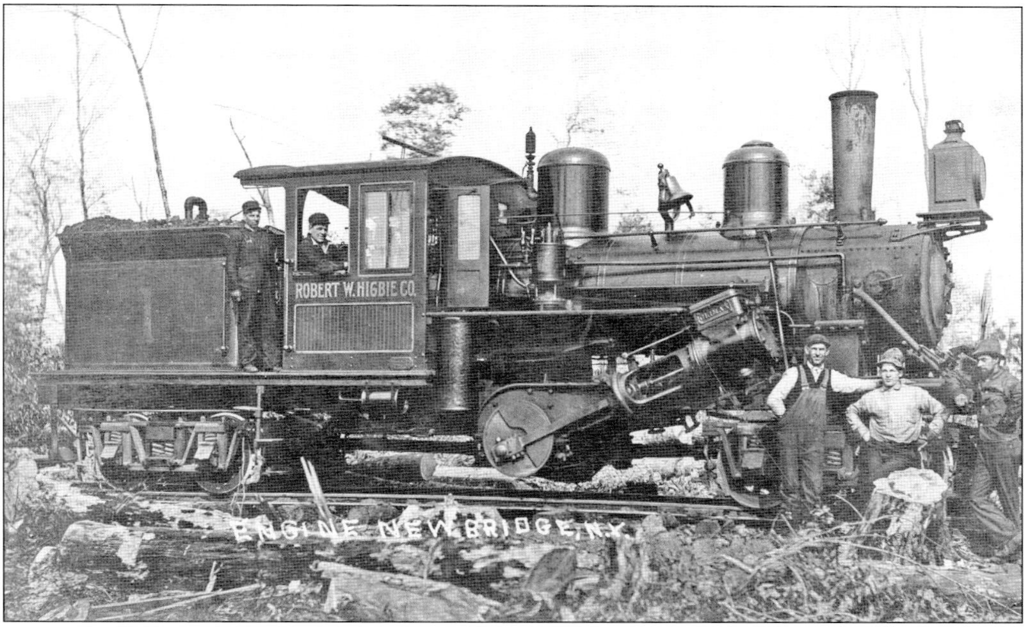

Higbie Company used two Climax locomotives on its Newton Falls & Northern Railroad. No. 1 is pictured in the card above, postmarked on September 3, 1909, at Clarksboro. It was purchased new in 1907 and weighed 45 tons. The Climax was a geared engine, powered by two angled cylinders mounted on opposite sides and connected to a central drive shaft. They held track well but were rough riding for the crew. The photograph below shows No. 1 on a bridge over the Grasse River at Newton Falls, pulling three boxcars. The *Ogdensburg Journal* reported on November 10, 1908, that the Newton Falls & Northern Railroad had applied to the Public Service Commission for "a certificate of convenience and necessity . . . and to issue $70,000 in common stock." The railroad was also given common carrier status. On June 7, 1919, the *Gouverneur Free Press* reported that stockholders of the Robert Higbie Company had voted to dissolve the corporation; on November 14, 1919, the paper stated that the Newton Falls & Northern Railroad was granted dissolution in state supreme court. The rails were then pulled up.

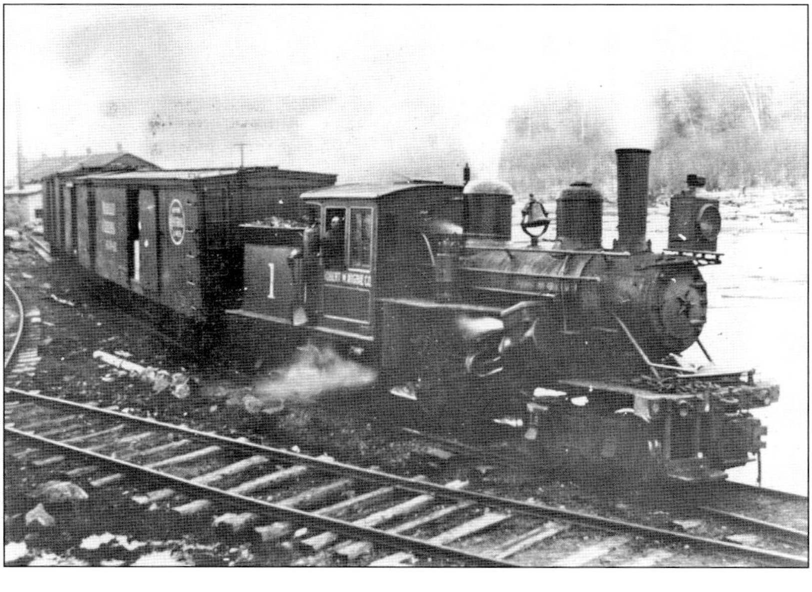

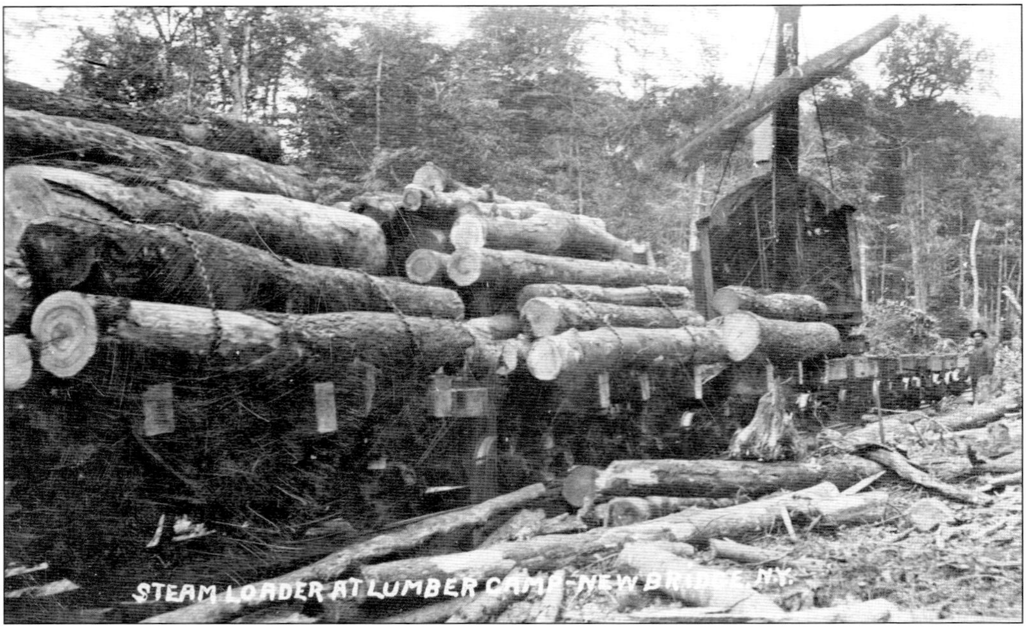

These two 1909 cards show Higbie Company's Barnhart loader at work. Cars loaded with beech and other hardwoods are pictured above, headed for Higbie's mills. The card below shows crew standing on a softwood sawlog over piles of pulpwood intended for the Newton Falls Paper mill, although Higbie also milled softwood lumber after a few years. Rail spurs at New Bridge were also built and were moved every summer to reach new stands of trees. One spur led to Flat Rock Falls, about three miles northwest of New Bridge, where a large skidway was located. Softwoods could also be banked next to the Grasse River and driven in spring to New Bridge, where a boom caught the logs. Hardwoods float poorly and had to be transported to the mill by rail. New Bridge was an isolated town that offered little but hard labor; lacking a church and social amenities, worker turnover was high. One postcard sender lamented, "This is a rather lonesome place and I am going to leave it soon."

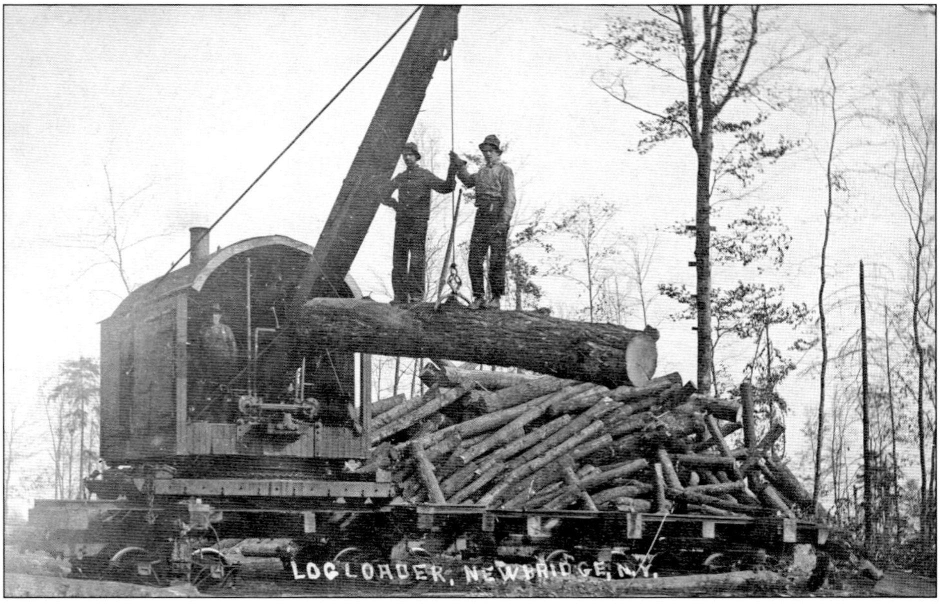

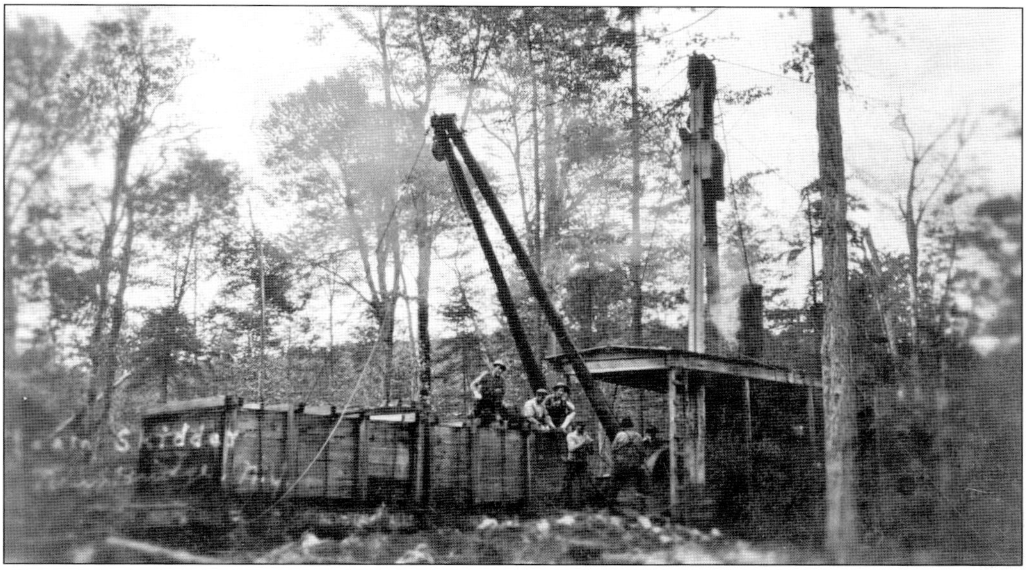

This card, postmarked on December 6, 1913, at New Bridge, shows a rail-mounted, overhead cable steam skidder that was uncommon in the Adirondacks. It was basically a large winch with long cables that were wrapped around logs; two to four logs could be pulled to the railhead at high speed through the air for hundreds of feet. The skidder also had a boom for loading the logs onto railcars. This system was highly destructive to young trees; what happened to any worker caught in the way can be imagined.

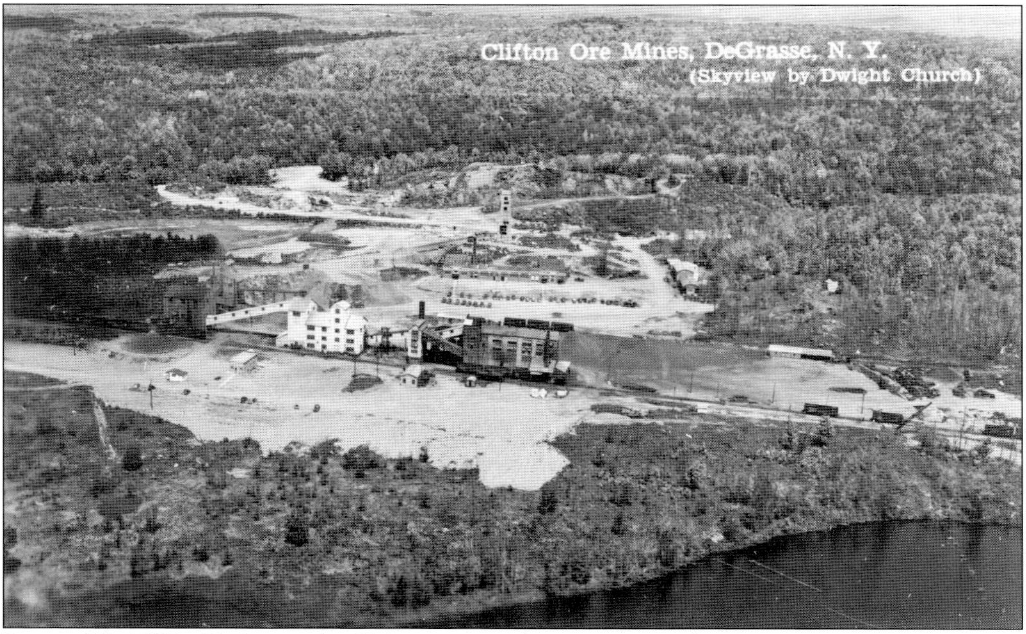

During World War II, the nearby Clifton iron mines were reopened. In 1941, Hanna Ore Company re-laid track on the Newton Falls & Northern grade to New Bridge, then probably followed the spur to Flat Rock Falls; less than two miles of new grade were needed. The mine operated from 1942 to 1952 on power from Browns Falls; this card shows the crushing, concentrating, and sintering plants at center. Nearly two million tons of ore were shipped from underground and open pit mining. The 10-mile rail line was abandoned in 1955.

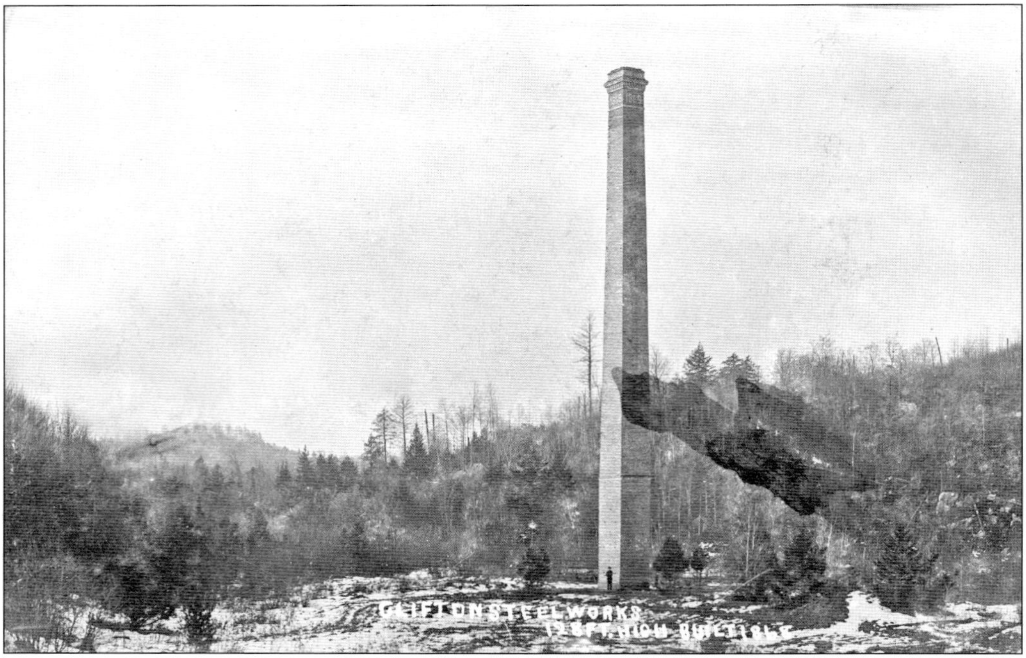

The Clifton Mines were first reached in January 1868 by a railroad built from the opposite direction. The Clifton Iron Company's wood railroad ran 21 miles southeast from the Rome, Watertown & Ogdensburg station at East DeKalb. Mining had begun in 1866, with ore and pig iron hauled out by wagon road. The company village of Clarksboro was located across the Grasse River; a rail spur connected the village to the main line. Clarksboro was the site of a Myers Furnace Company blast furnace for smelting the ore into pig iron. A fire on September 4, 1869, destroyed the steel works; the splintered wood railroad was also a contributing factor to the mines' shutdown. The chimney shown in the card above, with a man standing at its base, was built in 1868 and stood 160 feet tall; its master mason reportedly stood on the last brick laid, drank a pint of squirrel whiskey, and then scaled the ladder to the ground. Hanna demolished the chimney in 1942. The card below shows the ruins of a charcoal fuel pit.

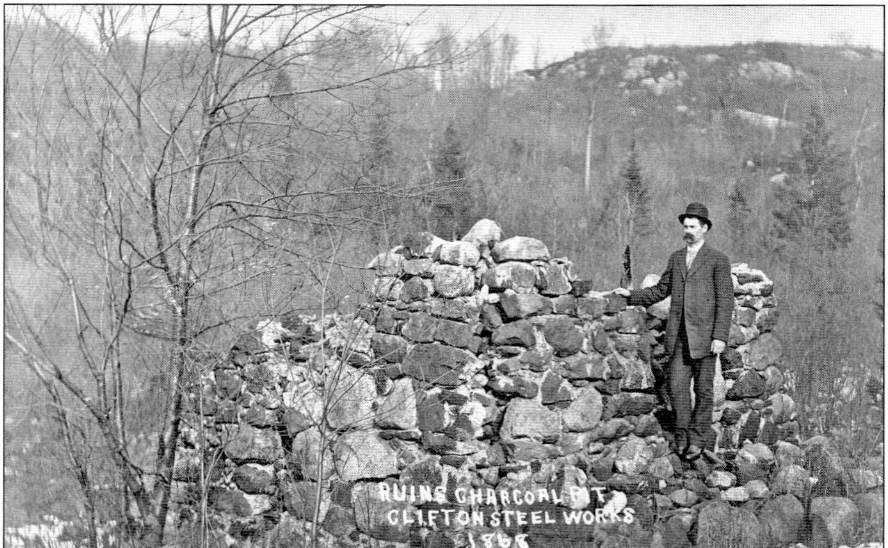

In 1866, Clarksboro boasted several stores, two hotels, a school, and about 50 houses, all company owned. After the mines closed, the hotels continued as overnight stagecoach stops on the Tooley Pond Road leading to Cranberry Lake. Hugh Gordon began renting the three-story Log Hotel around 1870 at $60 a year; he and his wife soon became famed for their board and hospitality. Gordon purchased the hotel in 1886 and operated it until a few years before his death in 1911. Subsequent owners turned the Log Hotel into a lumberjack roadhouse notorious for brawls, blasphemy, and bed bugs. The card to the right shows the abandoned Log Hotel in the 1920s. The card below of the Clifton Hotel was postmarked at Clarksboro on July 8, 1912. While not as well-known as the Log Hotel, the Clifton Hotel had a longer history. In 1920, it was renovated and regained appeal as a sporting and tourist resort. The Clifton Hotel was open into the late 1930s and may have housed Hanna Ore Company geologists when they arrived in 1939 to evaluate the old mines.

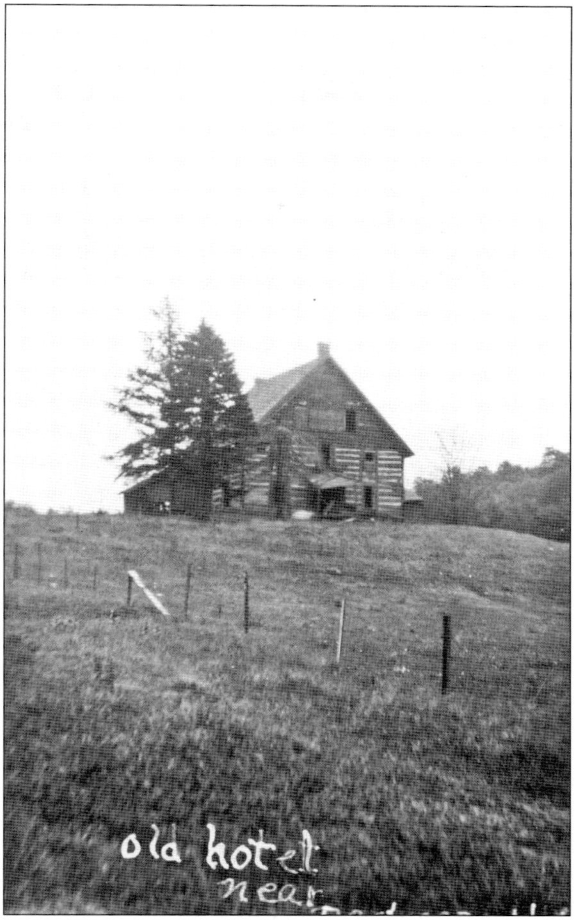

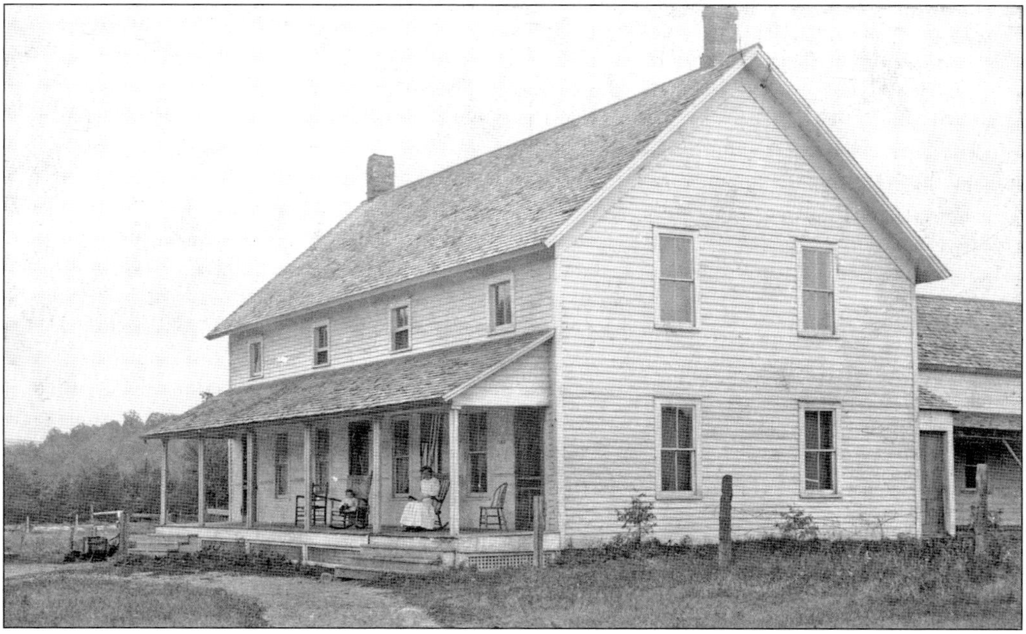

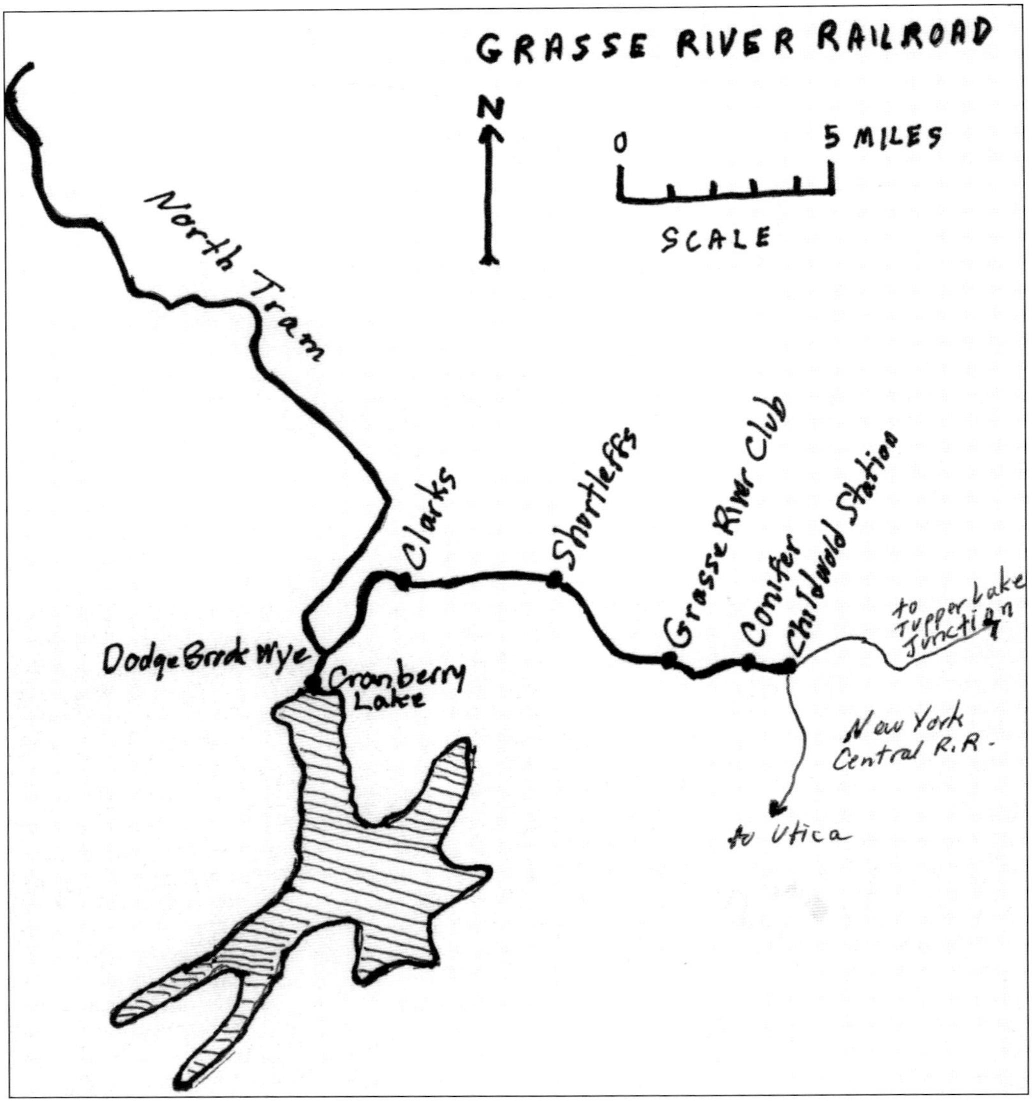

The Grasse River Railroad main line between Childwold Station, Conifer, and Cranberry Lake, and the North Tram from around 1925 are shown in a simplified map drawn by the author. The numerous logging spurs off the main line and the North Tram are not indicated.

Seven

CONIFER AND THE GRASSE RIVER RAILROAD

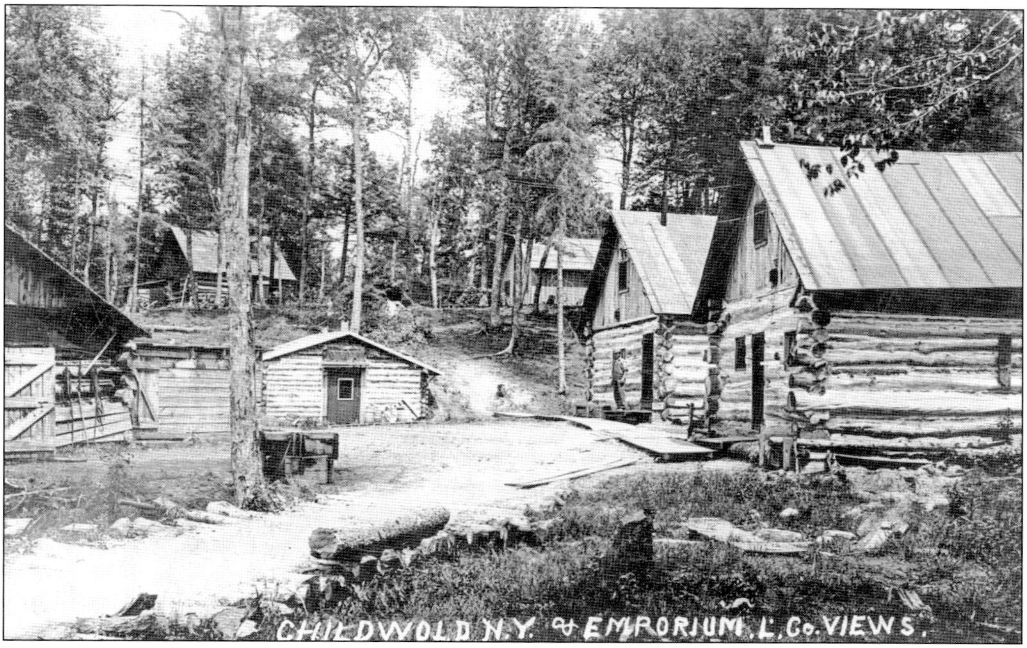

Emporium Lumber Company purchased large tracts of Adirondack land from 1905 to 1909. A *Norwood News* article on October 26, 1909, "Lumbering on a Grand Scale," reported that "one of the biggest lumber enterprises on this side of the Adirondacks is developing the country east and north of Cranberry Lake . . . new land purchases will give the company around 165,000 acres." After years of Pennsylvania logging, Emporium was also said to be "immensely rich." Emporium chose a location about 10 miles west of Tupper Lake village for its new sawmill town, Conifer. In 1910, the site was purchased from George A. McCoy and Son, which had already built log camps, set up a sawmill, and constructed a corduroy road to Childwold Station. McCoy's original village at Conifer is seen in this Beach series card. From left to right in the foreground are the horse barn, root cellar, dining room, and cook shack. In the background, the blacksmith shop is at left, and the bunkhouse at right.

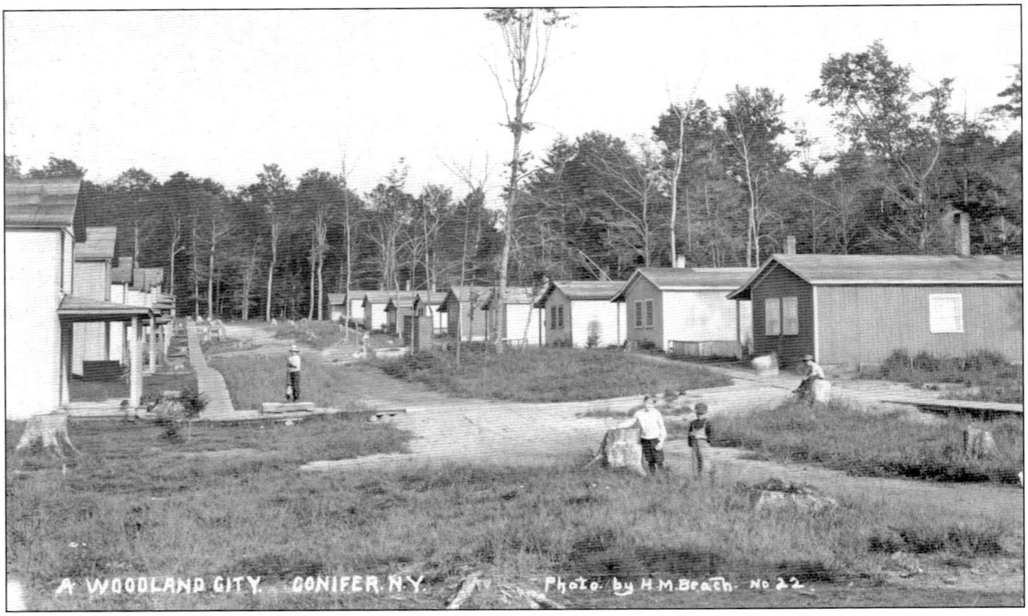

Emporium hired contractors to build homes for its Conifer employees. Worker housing is shown in the card above, "A Woodland City," postmarked at Conifer in March 1918. The card below shows a larger home at right, built for an owner or manager. At left is the school and community center; a footbridge over the rail line connects the school with the residential section. A March 25, 1914, article in the Potsdam *Courier and Freeman* described Conifer's progress: "For a two year old town it is doing very well. It has about 50 families, 300 residents, and a well-stocked store. The streets of painted frame houses are laid out around a central plaza. . . . The Conifer Inn, with 30 rooms, will open in May. Conifer has a school attended by 50 pupils; the school is also used as a church, and for rehearsals of the Conifer Brass Band." Conifer grew into one of the largest—and last—of the company lumber towns, with over a hundred homes, a boardinghouse, post office, doctor's office, and pool hall, plus the store and hotel.

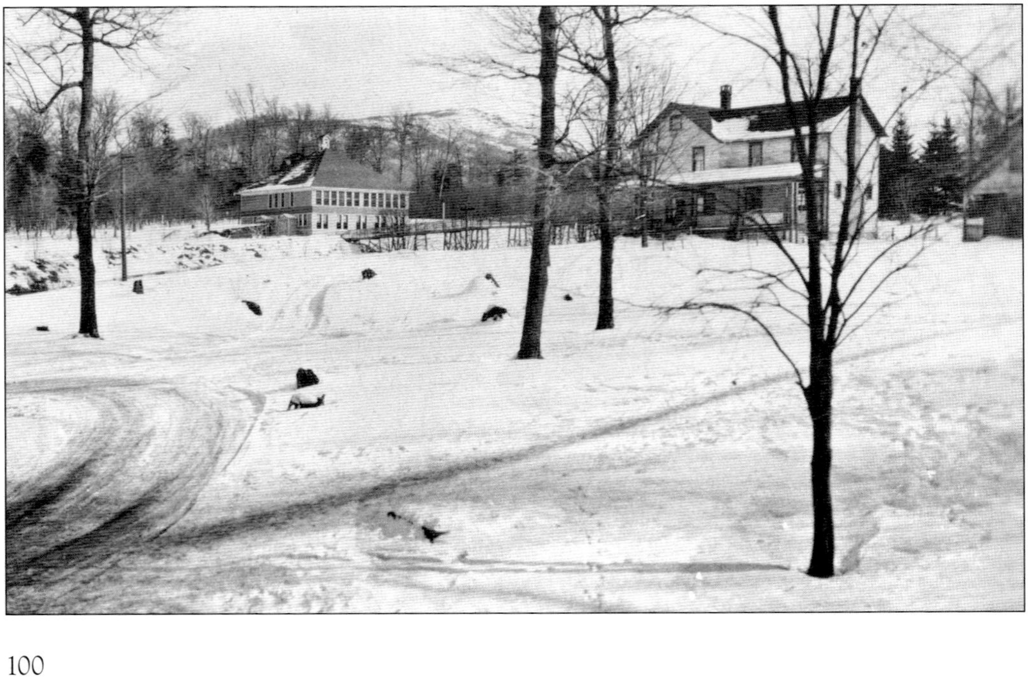

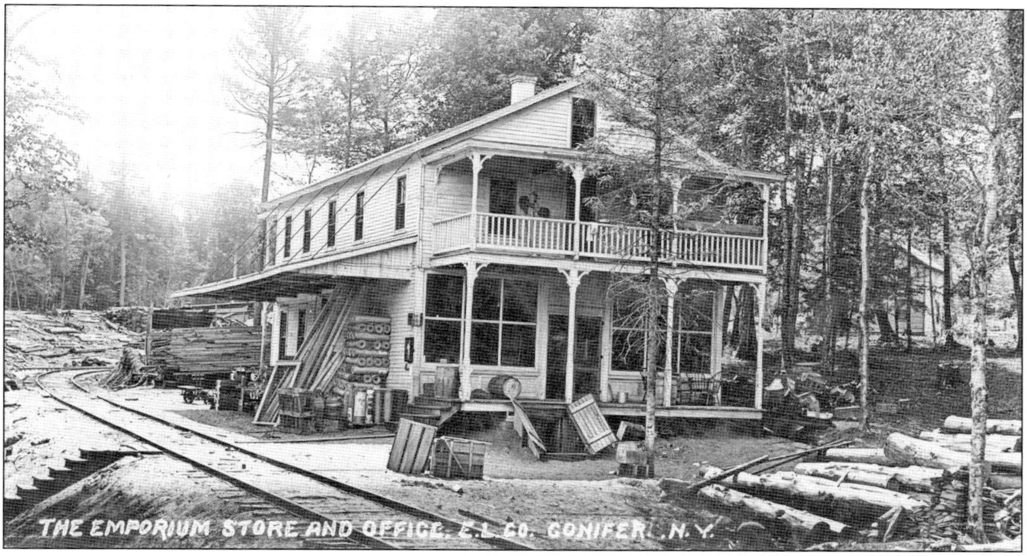

The Emporium company store and depot, with general offices on the second floor, was new when this card was mailed on November 14, 1912. This was also the year Emporium formed a New York corporation, Emporium Forestry Company. Signs advertise Hurd Shoes, Ox-Heart Chocolates, and the store's ice-cream soda fountain. An open hatch leads to underground storage. All sales at the store were strictly on a cash basis, as was the entire village; Emporium paid workers weekly in cash and collected house rents monthly in cash.

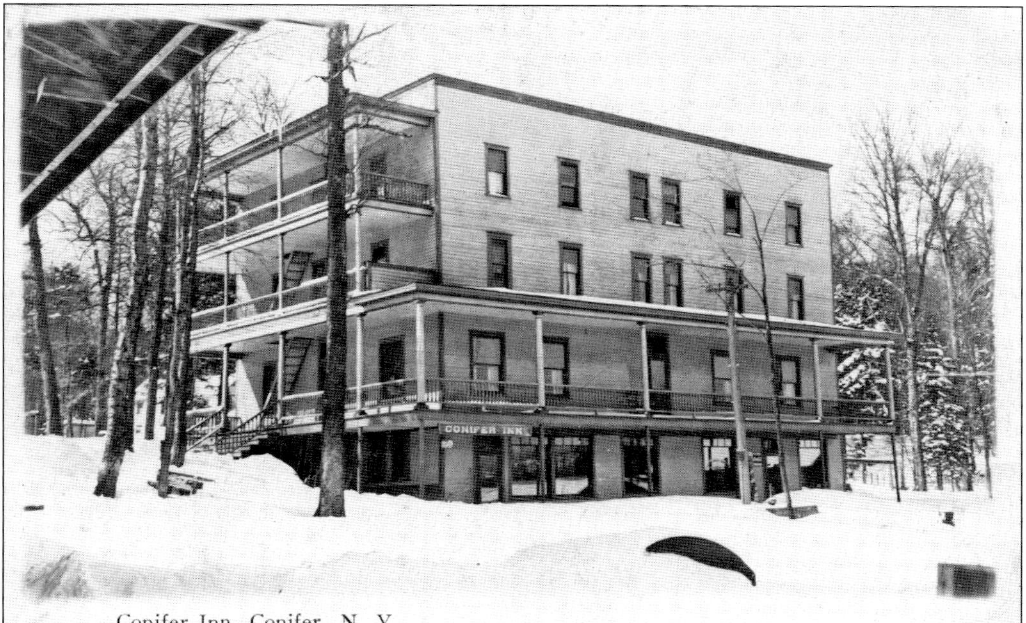

The Conifer Inn offered meals and lodging to passengers headed for Cranberry Lake on Emporium's Grasse River Railroad. The message on this card's back reads, "This is the company hotel at Conifer, New York. Will accommodate all travelers and boarders passing through the Adirondacks." Emporium advertised the hotel as being "modern in every respect, with steam heat, electric lights and shower baths." It had no bar during Emporium's ownership; all company properties were dry. The inn closed after being heavily damaged in a fire in May 1967.

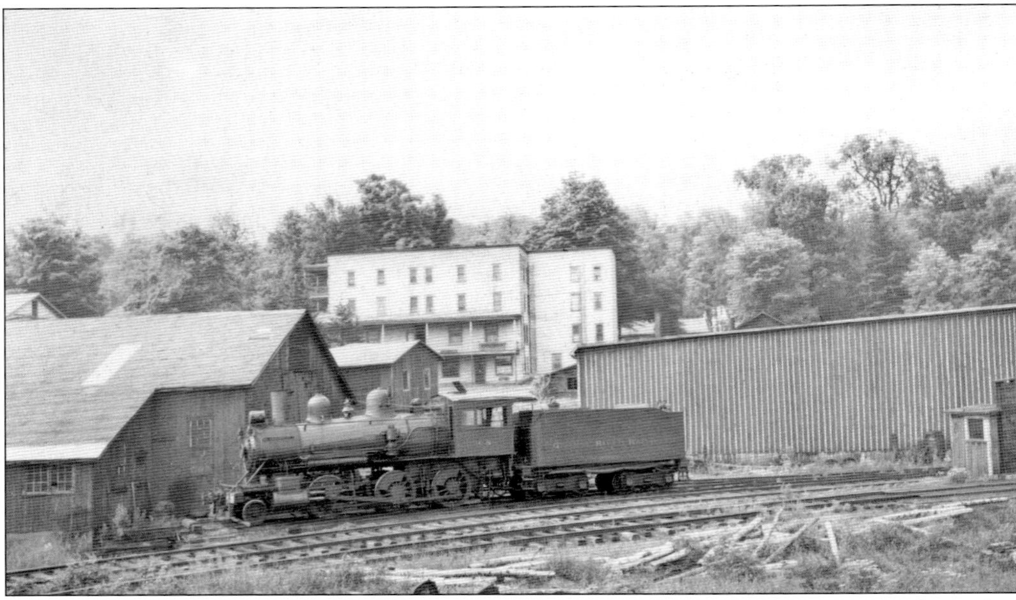

This photograph frames the north side of the Conifer Inn between Emporium's machine shop and engine house. It dates to 1923 or later; in that year, Emporium purchased the engine in the foreground from Pennsylvania Wood & Iron Company. Engine No. 68 was built by Schenectady Locomotive Works in 1892. The 60-ton Mogul locomotive was used on both the Grasse River Railroad main line and its logging branches. In 1949, it was sold to Emporium's successor, Heywood-Wakefield Company; it was scrapped in 1951 at Conifer.

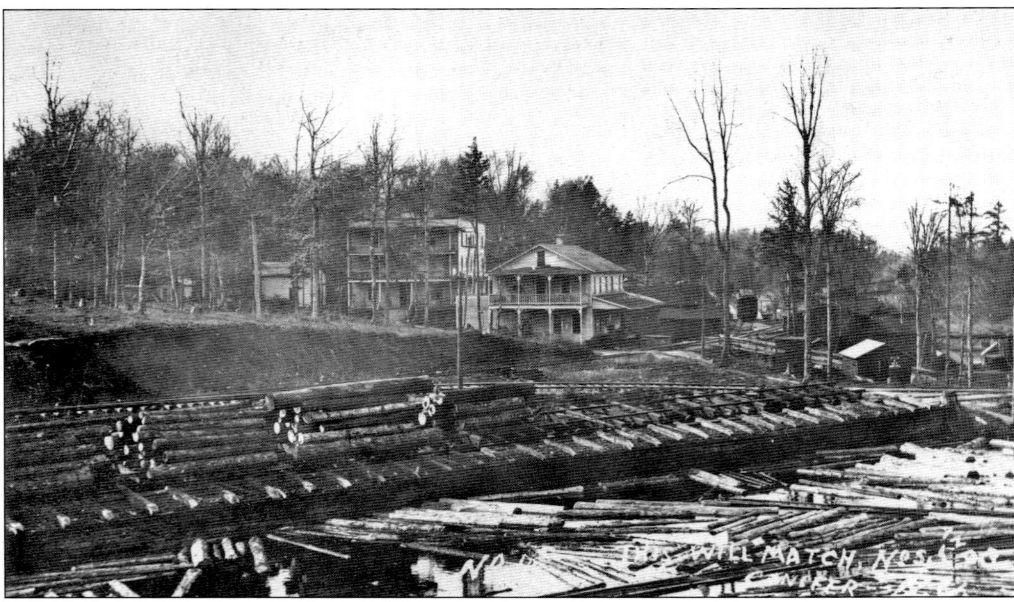

Emporium's store-depot and the Conifer Inn are at center in this card, along the main line of the Grasse River Railroad. The line ran in an east-west direction; the view is facing west, leading to Cranberry Lake 15 miles away. To the east, in a mile and a quarter was Childwold Station on the New York Central. The sawmill pond unloading ramp is in the foreground, with tilted track; several carloads of hardwood logs are ready to be rolled off. The adjacent track connects the main line with the sawmill complex.

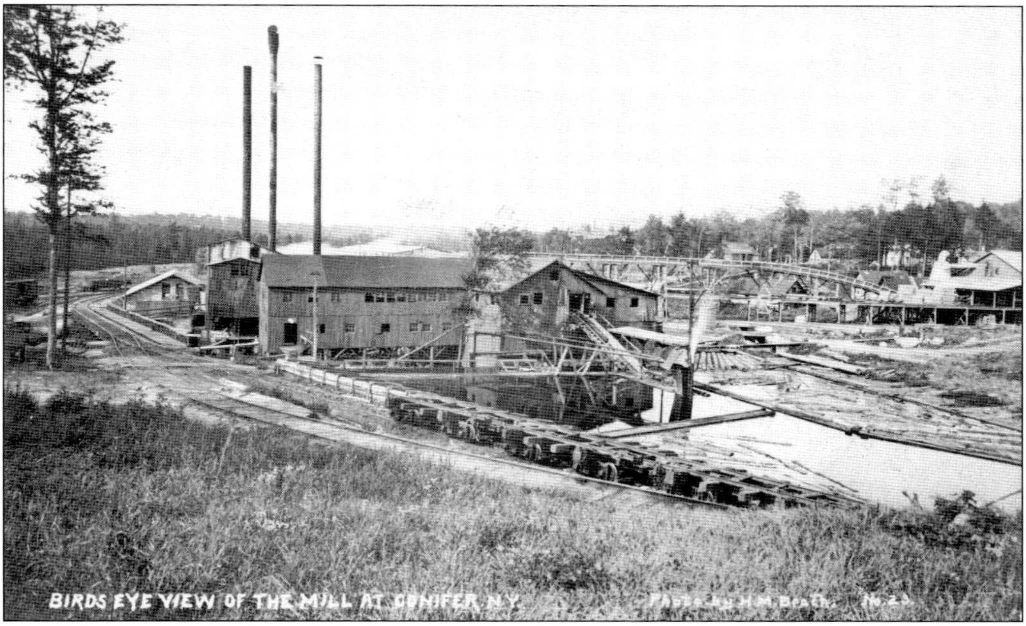

Emporium's large band sawmill began operation in October 1911, employing 100 workers and using machinery purchased from A.A. Low's sawmill at Horseshoe. A 1914 *Courier and Freeman* article described the early mill: "Logs are picked up from the mill pond by a chain conveyor and carried up to the saw room . . . band saws ten or twelve inches wide are used . . . the present output of the mill is 50,000 feet daily. Only rough-sawn lumber is produced, but a planing mill is under construction." The card above is a bird's-eye view of the sawmill by Henry Beach, postmarked at Conifer on April 21, 1916. The message notes, "The mill pond is kept warm all winter, by steam pipes." At far right is the planing mill, also pictured in the card below. The *Courier and Freeman* reported its burning on February 11, 1920: "The large planing mill owned by Emporium Forestry at Conifer was destroyed . . . the mill was operated by electric power and motors that may have started the fire . . . loss estimated at $25,000, fully covered by insurance . . . the planing mill will be rebuilt at once."

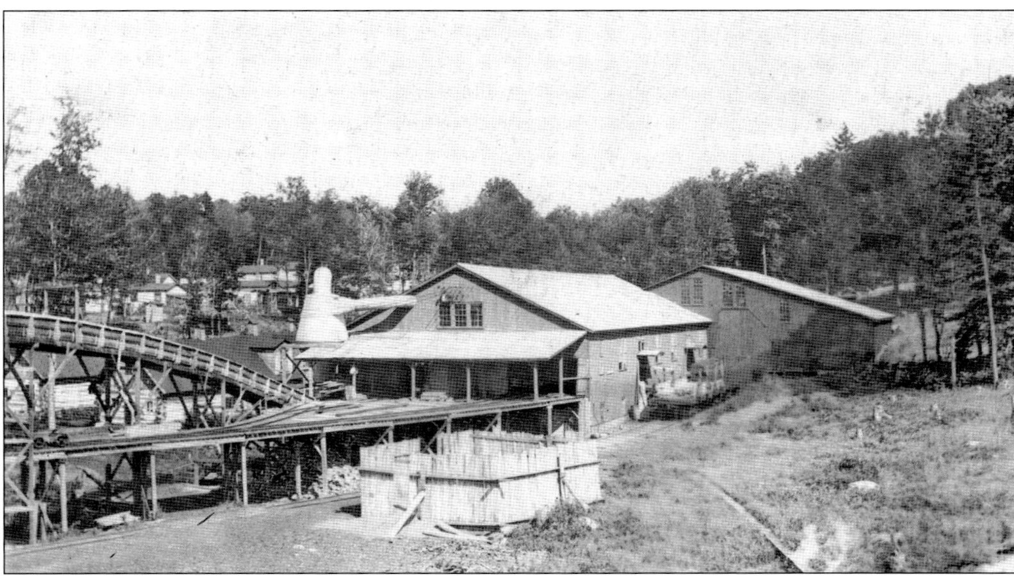

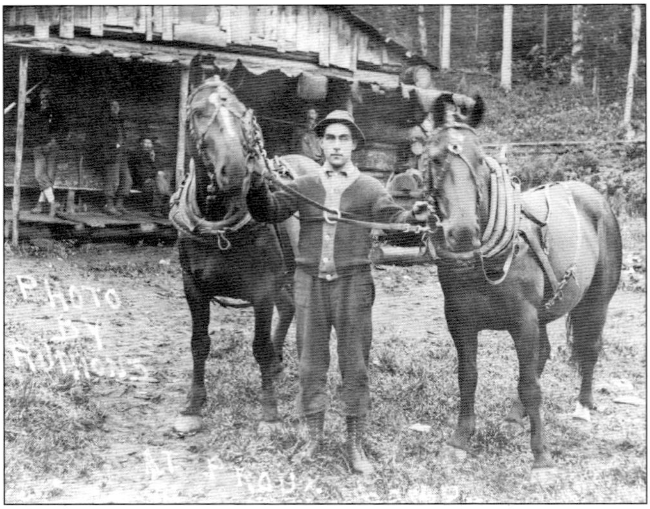

After 1920, Emporium's logging was done mainly by contractors. Jobbers agreed on price and then set up camps, built tote roads, and hired men and teams to cut and move logs to rail skidways. Emporium crews loaded the logs. This card pictures Oliva Proulx at one of his lumber camps. Proulx worked in the Tupper Lake area for Emporium, International Paper, and Oval Wood Dish. On one job, Proulx hired a team of men and 26 draft horses to haul 2,000 cords of pulpwood cut at Litchfield Park.

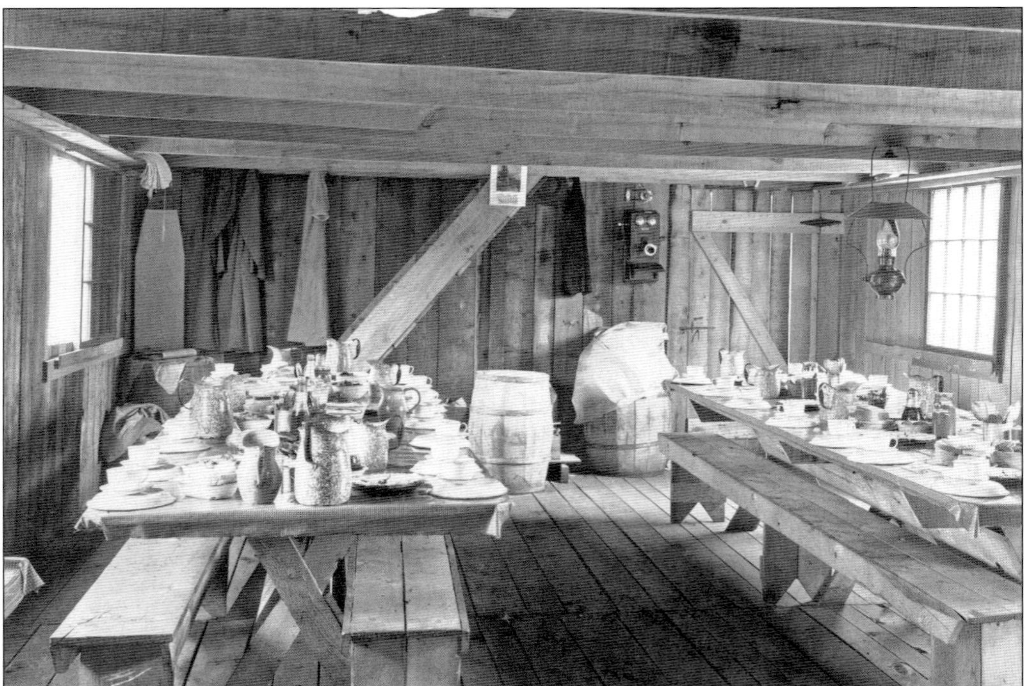

This photograph is labeled "Dining Room—Logging Camp near Cranberry Lake NY." Camp food was plain but abundant—loggers needed around 9,000 calories a day. No talking was allowed while eating. Cook stoves were used to prepare staples: bread, beans, and every variety of pork. The tables hold sturdy enamelware, with large tin spoons the only utensils. There are glass jars with pickles and condiments, bowls full of cookies, doughnuts, and bread, and several pies on each table. Either breakfast or dinner is about to be served to 28 hungry lumberjacks.

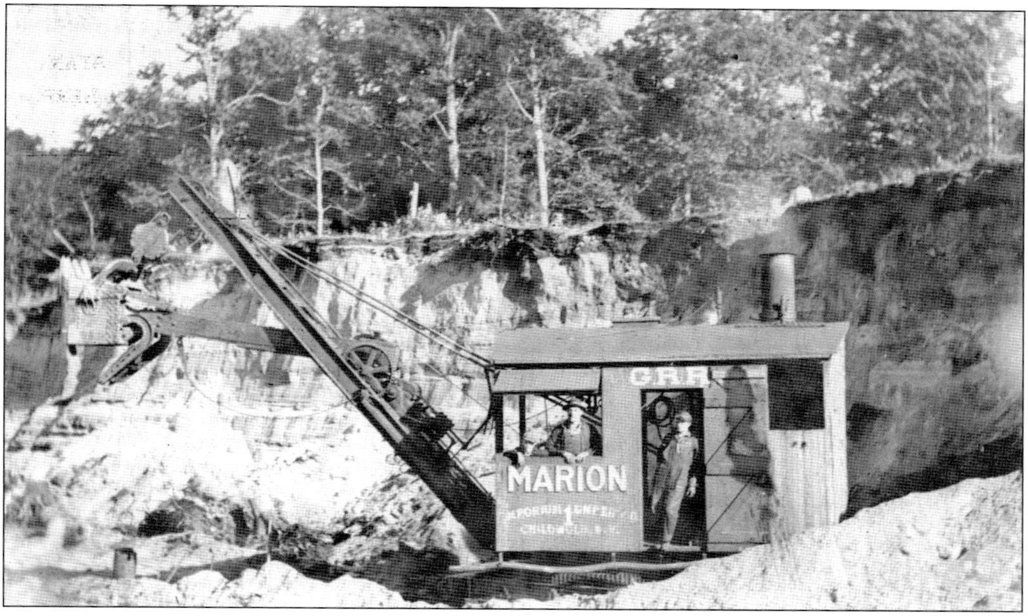

Emporium's construction of a railroad east from Conifer to Childwold Station was completed in June 1911. The extension west to Cranberry Lake was completed in 1913. The Grasse River Railroad was chartered in January 1915 as a common carrier, to haul logs and also carry passengers, freight, and mail. Some of Emporium's rolling stock—4 locomotives, 3 coaches, 10 box cars, 27 flatcars, 2 gas-powered cars, and a caboose—was transferred to the Grasse River Railroad along with a Marion steam shovel. The shovel would have been essential in building the railroad. In the card above, the shovel is digging fill from a pit. The card below was postmarked at Cranberry Lake on December 22, 1913, and shows the shovel widening banks along the right-of-way. According to the Gouverneur *Northern Tribune* of June 21, 1914, "the first trains were run over the completed Grasse River Railroad this spring. The road is of standard gauge with 75-pound steel rails. The roadbed has a good foundation and is well ballasted." Ballast refers to the gravel packed around railroad ties.

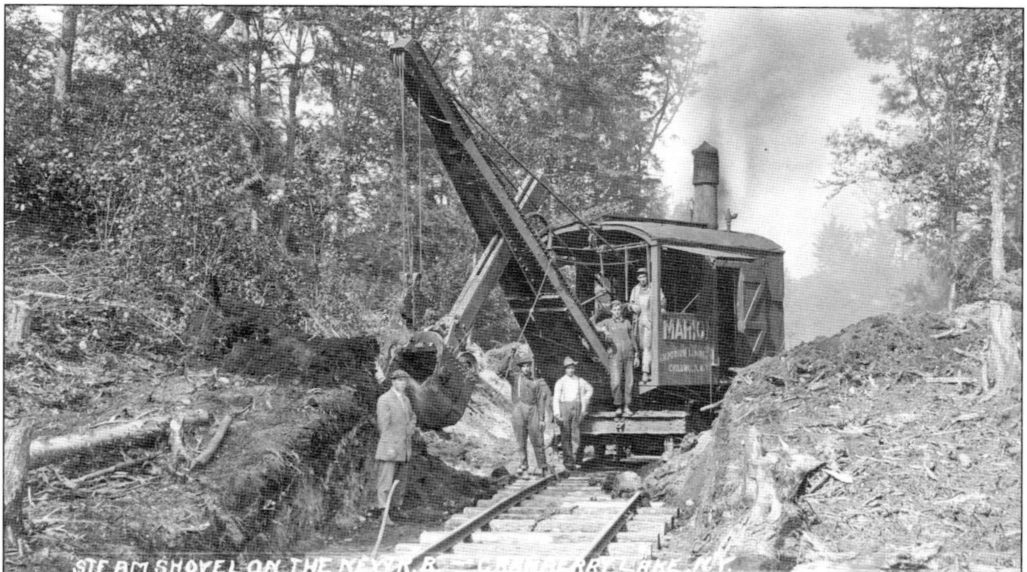

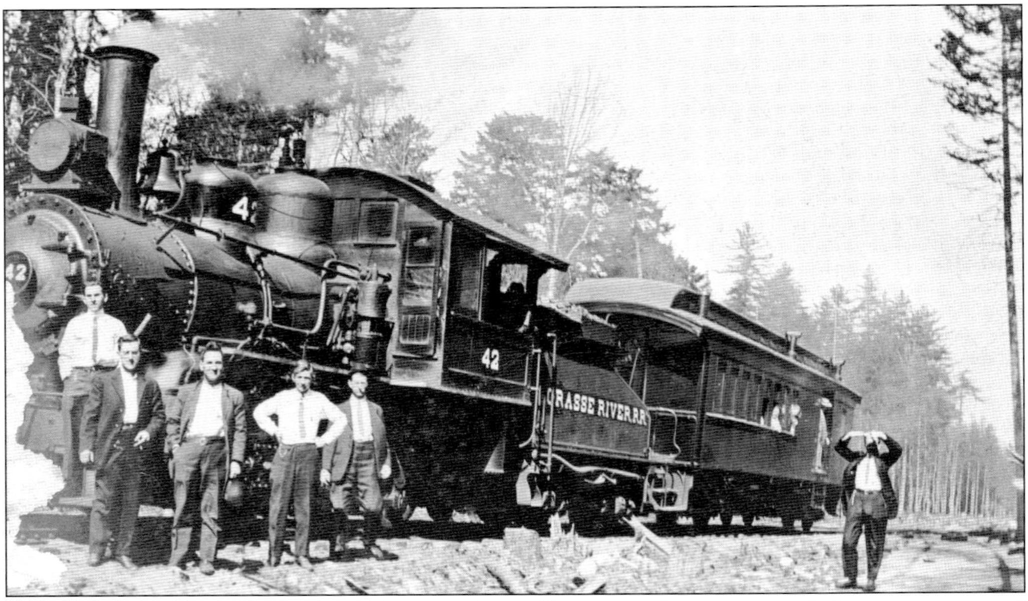

Grasse River Railroad engine Brooks No. 42 is pulling a combination coach for passengers and baggage in this card. In 1914, the *Northern Tribune* reported that "100 miles north of Utica by rail is Childwold Station. Connection is made here with the Grasse River Railroad. Two trains are run daily from Childwold Station to Cranberry Lake, leaving at 5:30 a.m. and 1:00 p.m., always awaiting arrival of the New York Central trains." The trip took about an hour. Passengers paid 5¢ per mile; baggage was a flat 50¢.

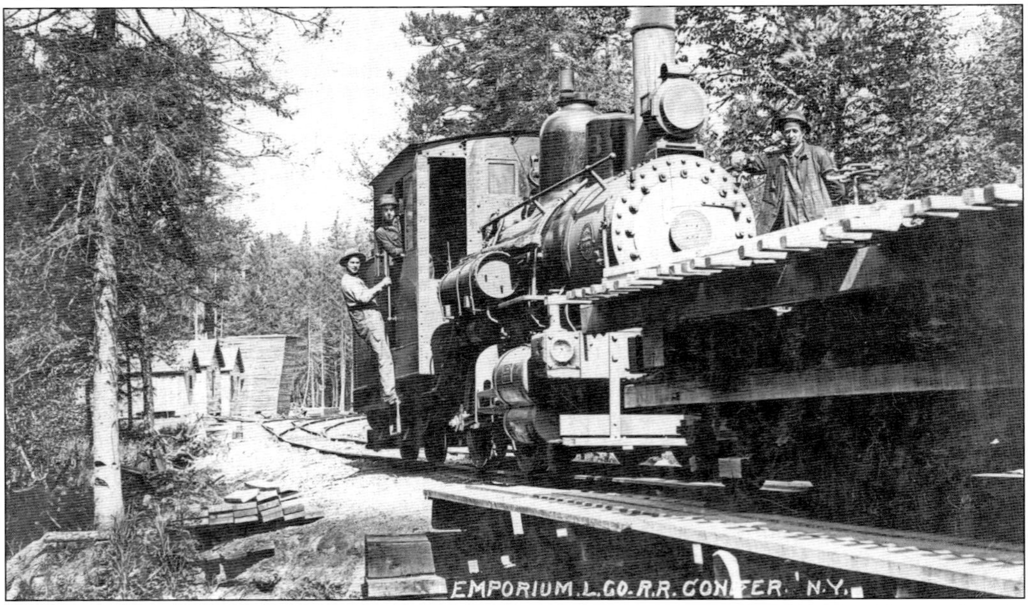

The Grasse River Railroad's Baldwin engine No. 38 is pictured in this card by Henry Beach, postmarked at Conifer on August 23, 1919. Built in 1892, the engine was used on the Chicago and South Side elevated railway, exhibited at the 1893 Chicago World's Fair, then purchased by Post & Henderson for use at Benson Mines. In 1909, it was sold to Emporium Lumber and used at the Galeton, Pennsylvania, sawmill. Emporium brought the 20-ton engine to Conifer in 1915. In 1923, it was sold to the Tupper Lake Chemical Company.

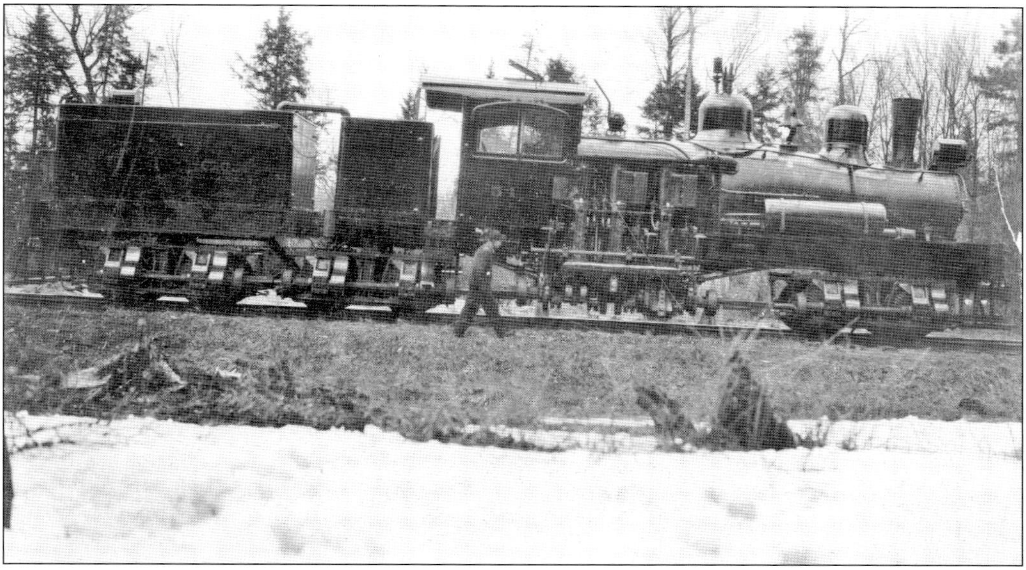

Emporium Forestry used geared engines—Shay and Climax—on its logging branches. Shay No. 51 is shown here; it was built in 1914 by Lima Locomotive Works. Emporium purchased it in 1930 from Jerseyfield Lumber Company. No. 51 was sold to Heywood-Wakefield in 1949 and scrapped in 1951. Emporium's crews preferred Shays; they could make 10 miles per hour sound like 100, but were smoother riding than the Climax. Old trainmen said that with geared engines, if all the parts stayed where they were supposed to, it was a good day.

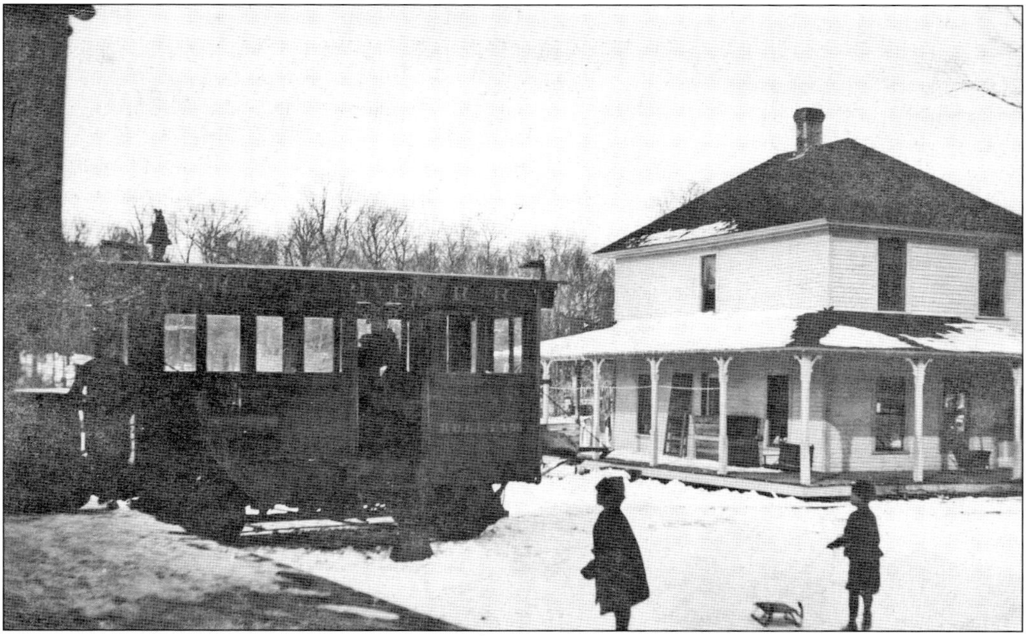

It was expensive to run steam engines on the Grasse River Railroad, so gas-powered speeder cars were often used. This card was postmarked at Conifer on July 11, 1918; the message reads, "This is a photo of our 'fliver' on our railroad here. I am leaving Conifer this AM for Cranberry Lake." Lettering on the side of the speeder reads, "Grasse River RR" and "Rolliam." The car was converted in 1916 by Roy Sykes from his 1905 Thomas Flyer automobile. Roy was the youngest son of Emporium's president William Sykes.

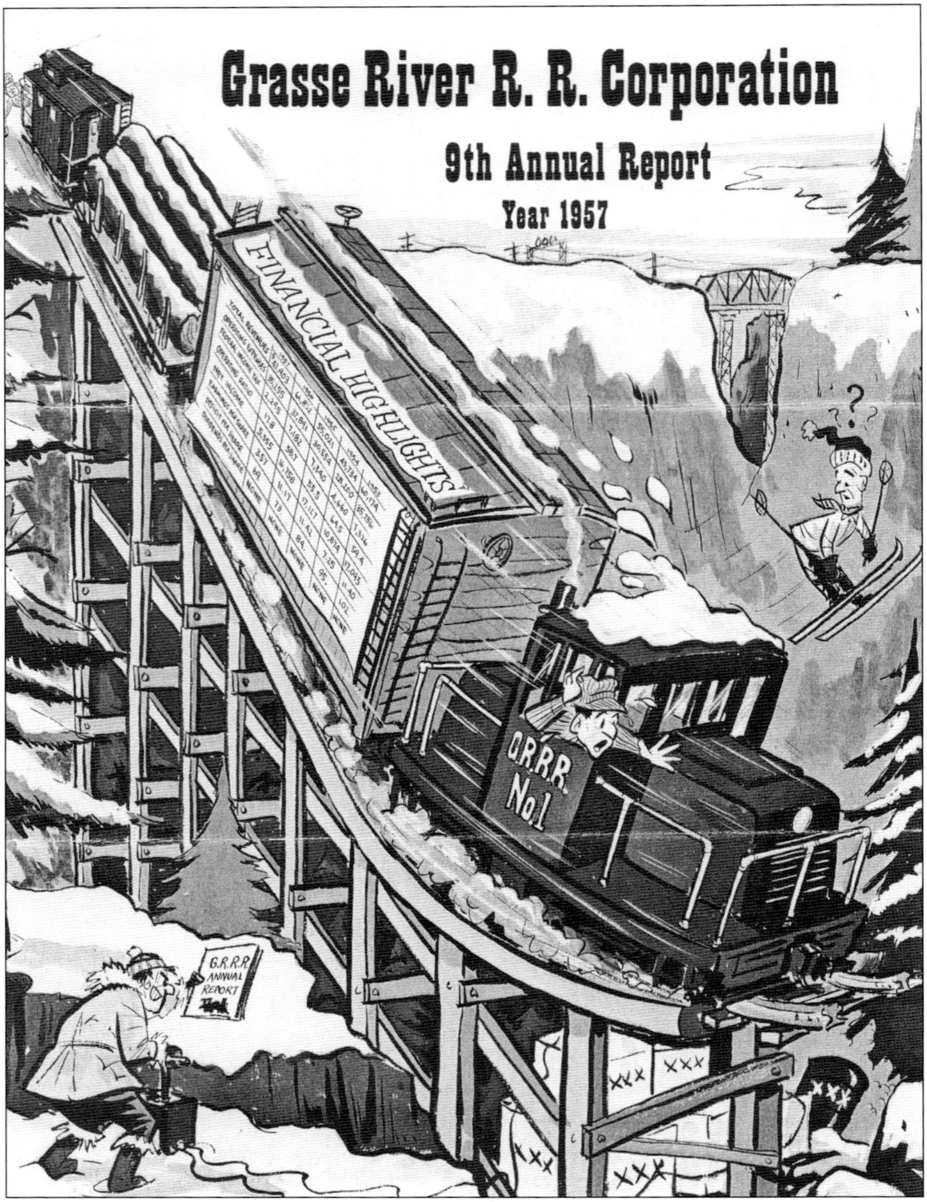

The Grasse River Railroad was generally profitable—until Route 3 was paved to Cranberry Lake in 1926. During the Depression, demand for lumber also dropped. By 1945, Emporium had sold nearly all of its timberlands and had to import logs. In 1948, the Grasse River Railroad was taken up from Cranberry Lake village to one mile west of Conifer, leaving it with about two miles of main track. From 1945 to 1949, Emporium's Conifer sawmill was leased to a furniture manufacturer, Heywood-Wakefield; in April 1949, the company bought the sawmill, railroad, and Conifer village. The Grasse River Railroad's president, Richard Greenwood, issued annual reports during Heywood-Wakefield's ownership; the cover of the ninth report, for 1957, is shown here. According to the president's tongue-in-cheek letter, "a few over-zealous stockholders stubbornly continue to associate railroading with profit. Our past experiences certainly should not have given them any such impression. . . . The downward "ski-jump" pattern of operations, illustrated on the front cover of this report, should be apparent at a glance."

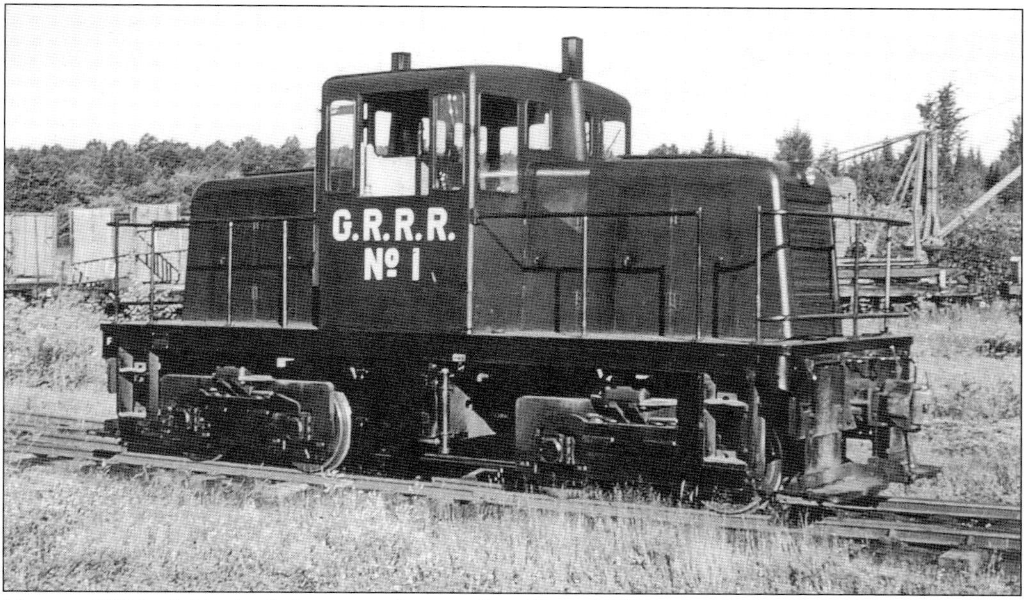

Heywood-Wakefield rebuilt Emporium's sawmill and installed new machinery. In 1950, a new 44 ton General Electric diesel locomotive was purchased, seen above. The line claimed to be the smallest 100 percent dieselized railroad in America. The engine took carloads of lumber from Conifer to Childwold Station and brought back flatcars loaded with logs left by the New York Central. When executives from Heywood-Wakefield visited, they were treated to rides in caboose No. 71, pictured below around 1954 with conductor William Tarbox. It was given a decorative makeover and lettered with "Perry's Pride" after company treasurer Henry Perry. Operations continued until a major fire, reported by the *Tribune-Press* on December 5, 1957: "The Star Lake Fire Department was summoned at 3:15 Friday morning to a fire which destroyed the sawmill at Conifer. Men remained until late in the forenoon assisting in saving other buildings including homes of mill workers." In April 1959, Heywood-Wakefield sold what was left at Conifer to a salvage company. Engine No. 1 was sold to the East Branch & Lincoln Railroad in New Hampshire.

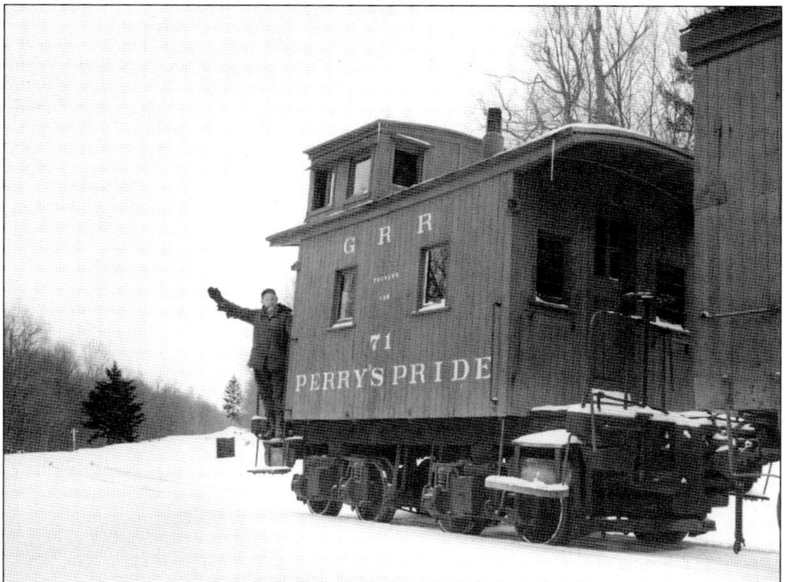

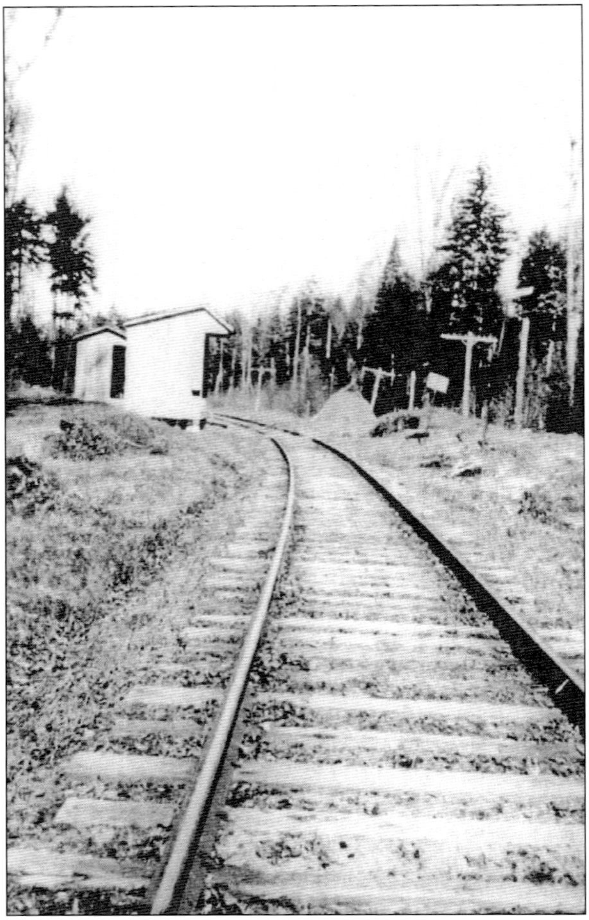

The Grasse River Railroad made several flag stops on its way to Cranberry Lake, from 1915 to the early 1940s. The first was at the Grasse River Club station, three miles west of Conifer, shown in this photograph. The railroad's local telephone system maintained call stations, including one at the club's guide house. Connections to the general stores in Conifer and Cranberry Lake allowed the club to order groceries and supplies, which would be delivered by train to the club station.

This 1896 photograph of the Grasse River Club shows the clubhouse at left along with three camps; access then was by wagon road from Childwold Station. In December 1911, the club sold its 10 square miles of property to Emporium Forestry, which allowed the club continued use of its camps; the Sykes family also became members. The land was sold in 1930 to Tri-River Power Company; in 1946, a total of 4,400 acres were sold back to the club. Emporium retained the 66-foot railroad right-of-way through the Grasse River Club property.

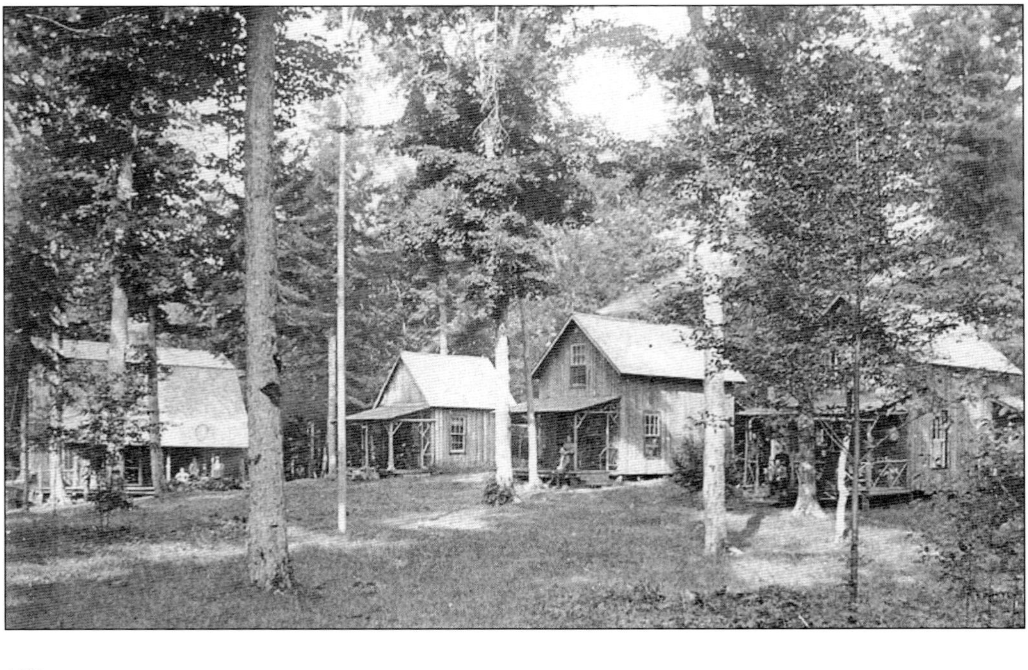

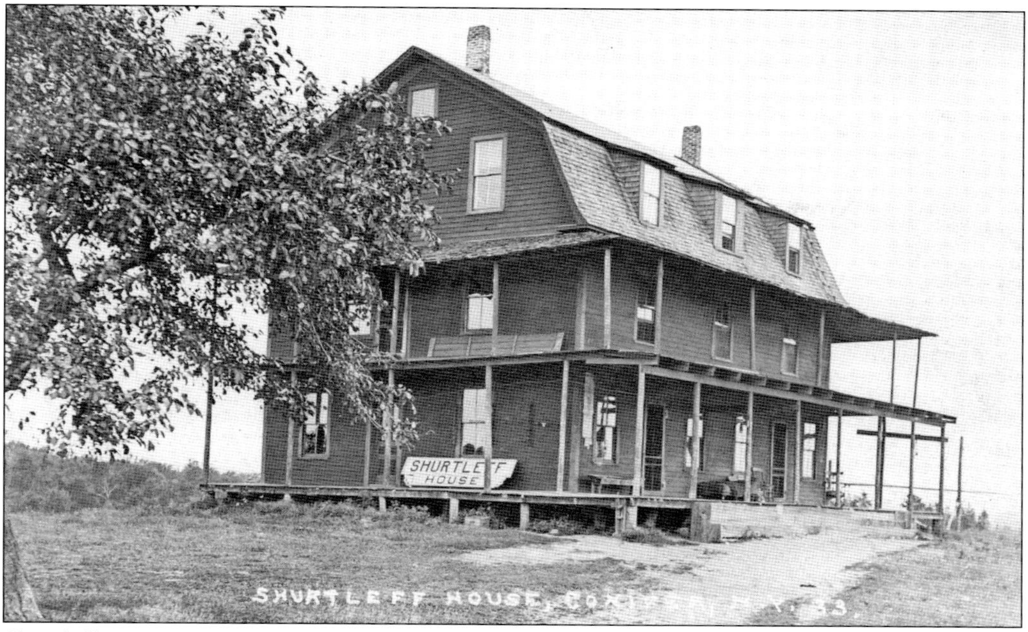

Shurtleff station was seven and a half miles west of Conifer; it served Shurtleff House, built in 1880 by Archie Shurtleff. The hotel catered to sportsmen willing to make a long trip on rutted, muddy roads to hunt and fish for trout. Easy access via the Grasse River Railroad expanded the hotel's appeal. This card, postmarked on October 31, 1927, shows Shurtleff House on a hill looking east over Grasse River Flow, dammed in 1872. The main hotel burned in 1935; outbuildings continued in use. The site is now a private club.

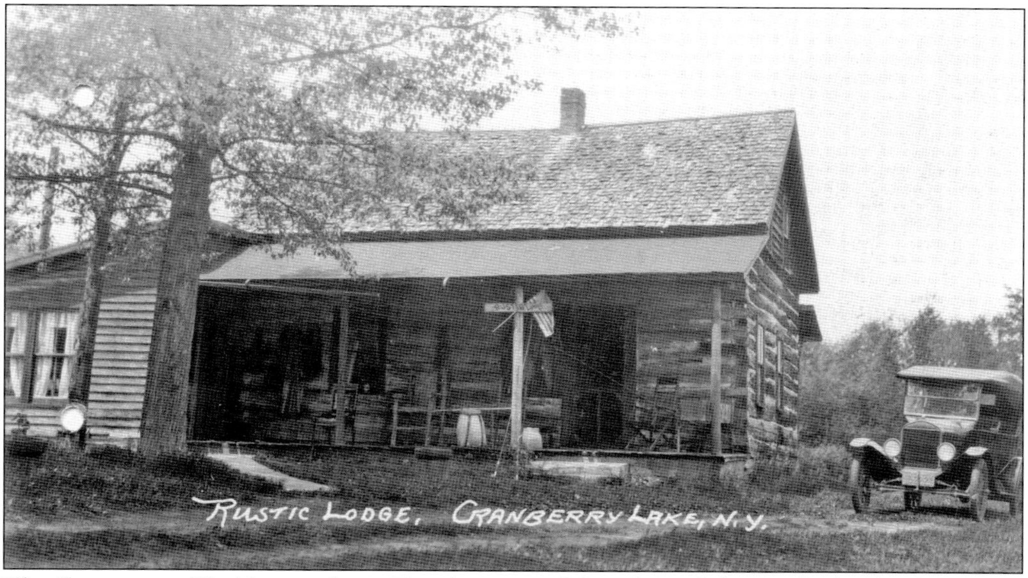

The flag stop at Clark's was about 10 miles west of Conifer and four and a half miles east of Cranberry Lake. The hewn-log cabin in this card dates to 1878; from 1884 until 1922, it was the home of Henry and Lucelia Clark. Lucelia kept a daily journal for almost 40 years, chronicling the family's life as pioneers of the Cranberry Lake region; it is preserved at the Adirondack Museum. An access road led from Clark's a half mile northeast to the railroad and station, via a bridge over the Grasse River.

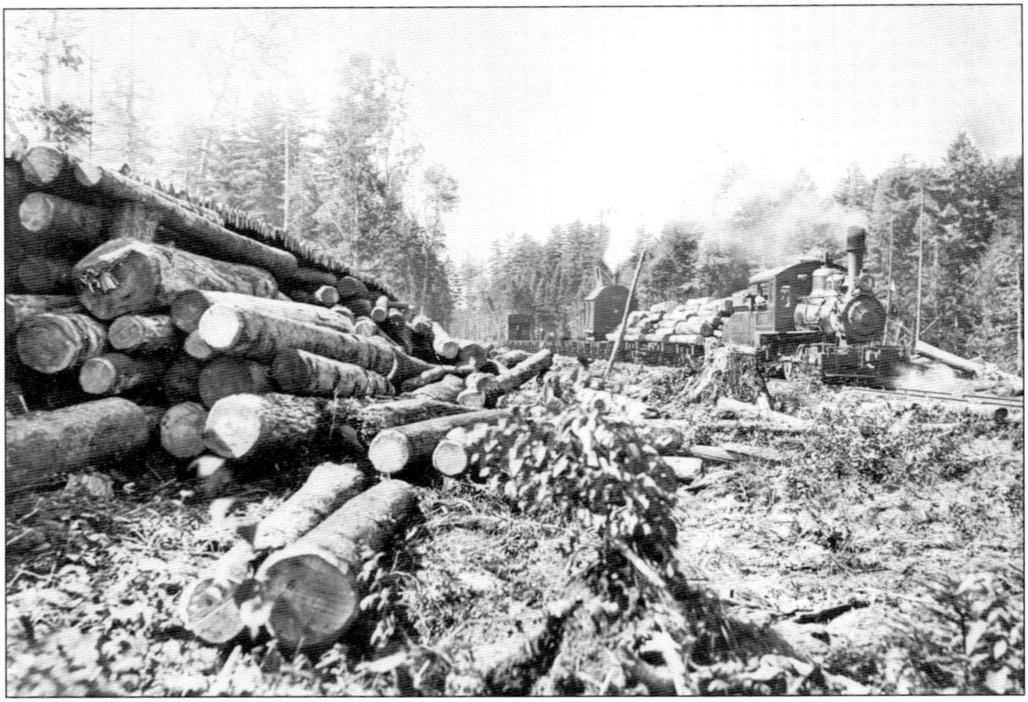

Emporium's North Tram was a network of logging lines extending 30 miles northwest of Cranberry Lake. It diverged from the main line a mile north of Cranberry Lake at the Dodge Brook Wye—where Grasse River Railroad passenger trains turned around and backed down to the Cranberry Lake depot. This photograph shows Brooks engine No. 43 and a Barnhart loader at work. The engine will pull the loaded log cars to either the Cranberry Lake or Conifer sawmill. The North Tram closed in 1941; the rails were taken up in 1945.

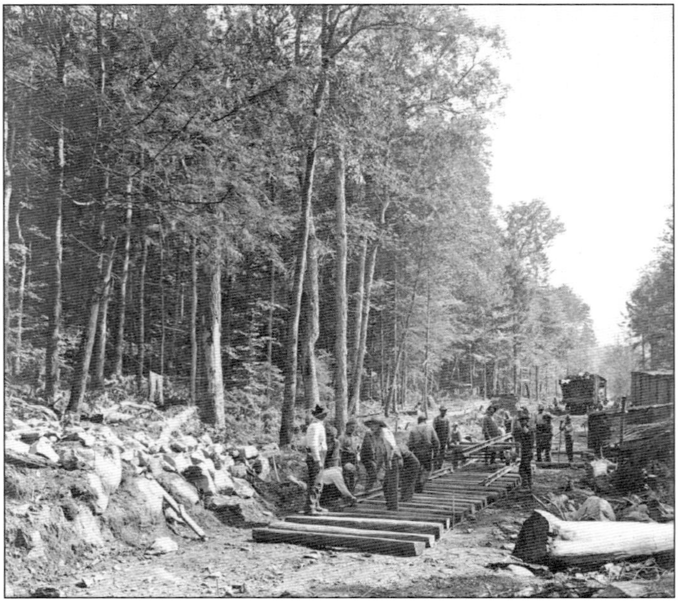

This magic lantern slide print is titled "Building a Wide Gauge Logging Railroad near Cranberry Lake 1913." The Grasse River Railroad's main line is under construction, as the bed has been well cleared and graded. Ropes guide placement of the ties, which are round with one side hewed flat where the rails will be spiked. Gravel fill will be dumped later over the ties and tamped. Behind the crew, an engine is pushing cars loaded with ties and rails. Most of Emporium's "gandy dancers," or railroad builders, were Italian immigrants.

Eight

Cranberry Lake

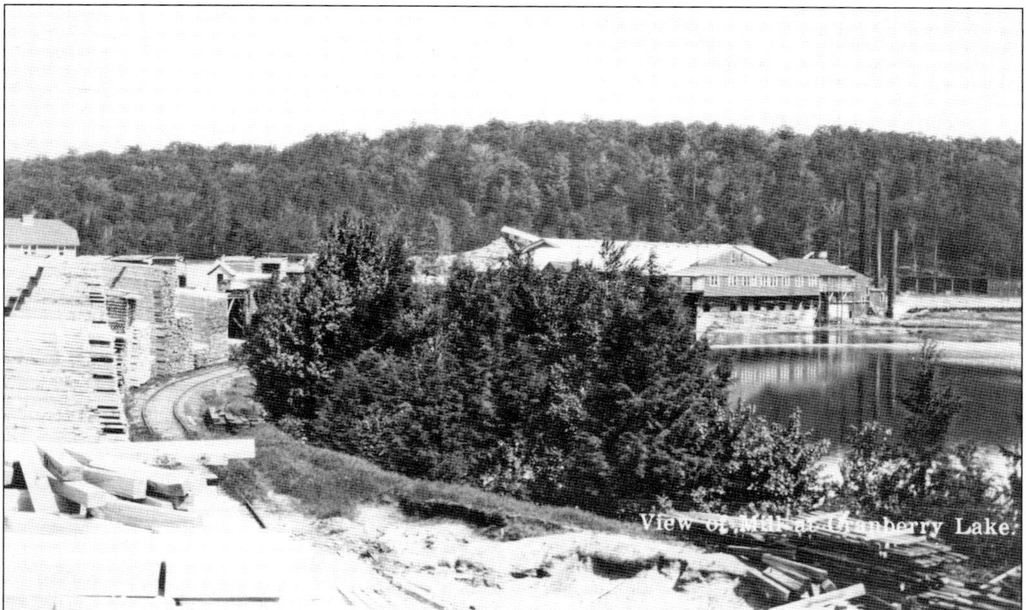

In early 1914, reports began on Emporium's plans to build a second sawmill at Cranberry Lake. A *Massena Observer* article stated that "The big lumber mill at Cranberry Lake starting construction this summer will employ at least 300 hands, and have double the capacity of the Conifer mill. The mill will be modern in every respect, and in addition to getting out hardwood lumber will manufacture wagon hubs. Estimated cost, completely equipped, is $500,000 . . . the railroad station at Cranberry Lake will be located near the present general store." On November 2, 1916, the *Republican-Journal* reported that "the new mill at Cranberry Lake has just been completed, and began operations this month . . . together the Conifer and Cranberry Lake mills have a combined capacity of from 35,000,000 to 40,000,000 board feet of lumber a year." This postcard shows the mill and some of its lumber docks; it operated for only 10 years, from 1917 to 1927. At upper left, Emporium's company office on Mill Street is visible.

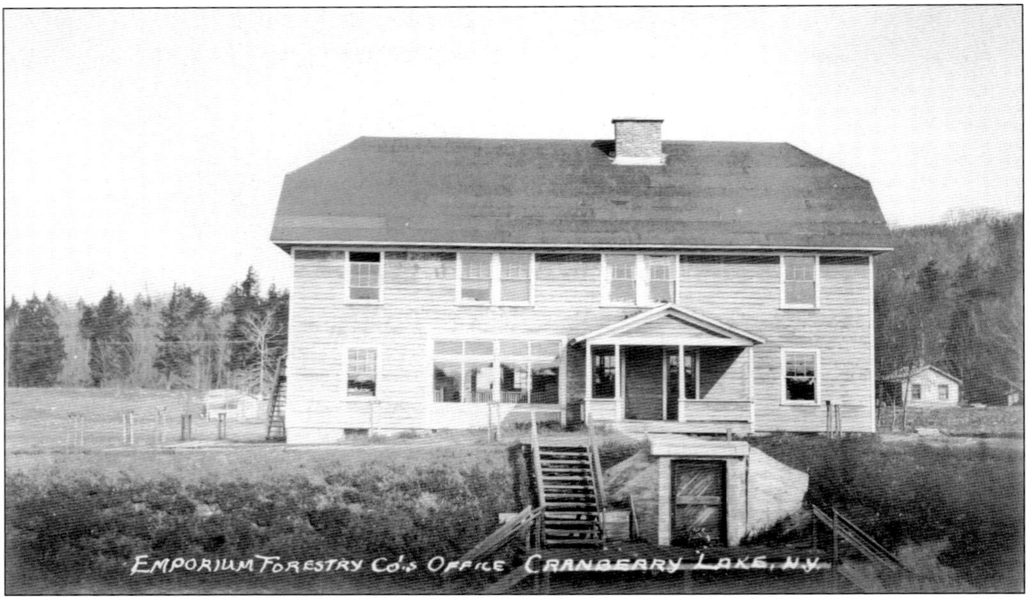

Emporium's office safe was robbed twice, in October 1920 and July 1930. The *Republican-Journal* headline on October 13, 1920, read, "Yeggmen get $3,000 in Cranberry Lake Robbery." "Yeggmen" was a term coined by the Pinkerton Detective Agency, after a nationwide pursuit of notorious safe-cracker John Yegg. Yegg returned the proceeds from his last job, hoping that agents would relent—they didn't. The 1920 robbery resulted in two men being jailed and some money recovered; the 1930 burglary of $1,000 went unsolved. Emporium's office is now a private home.

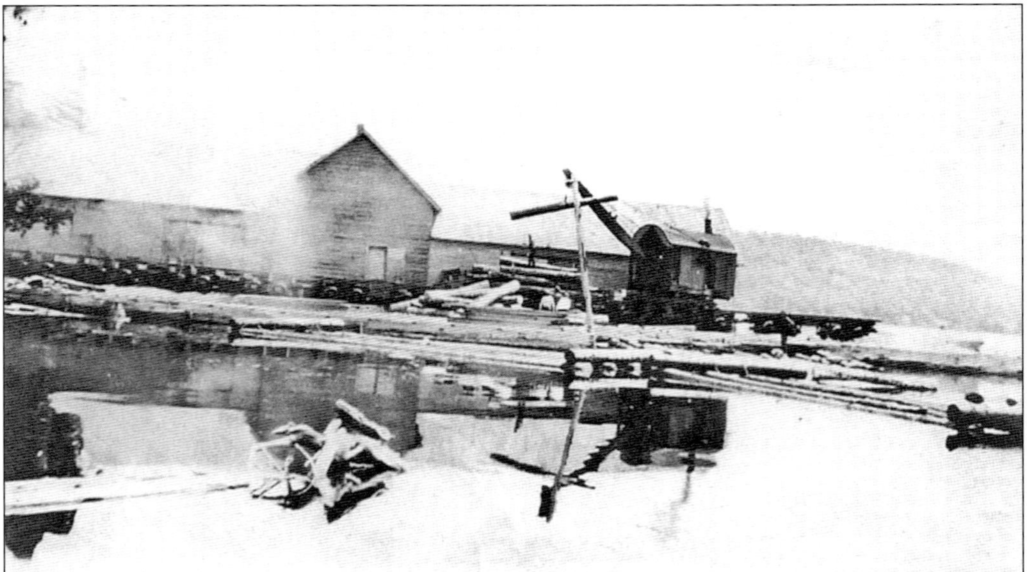

In the 1920s, Emporium purchased land on the south and east sides of Cranberry Lake from International Paper Company and logged it for hardwood. Tugboats towed the logs down the lake on spruce rafts, with the denser hardwood stacked on top. Emporium built a trestle next to the depot dock and warehouses in Cranberry Lake village, extending into the lake as shown in this photograph. A Barnhart loader lifted the logs from the rafts and placed them on railcars. The empty spruce rafts can be seen in the foreground.

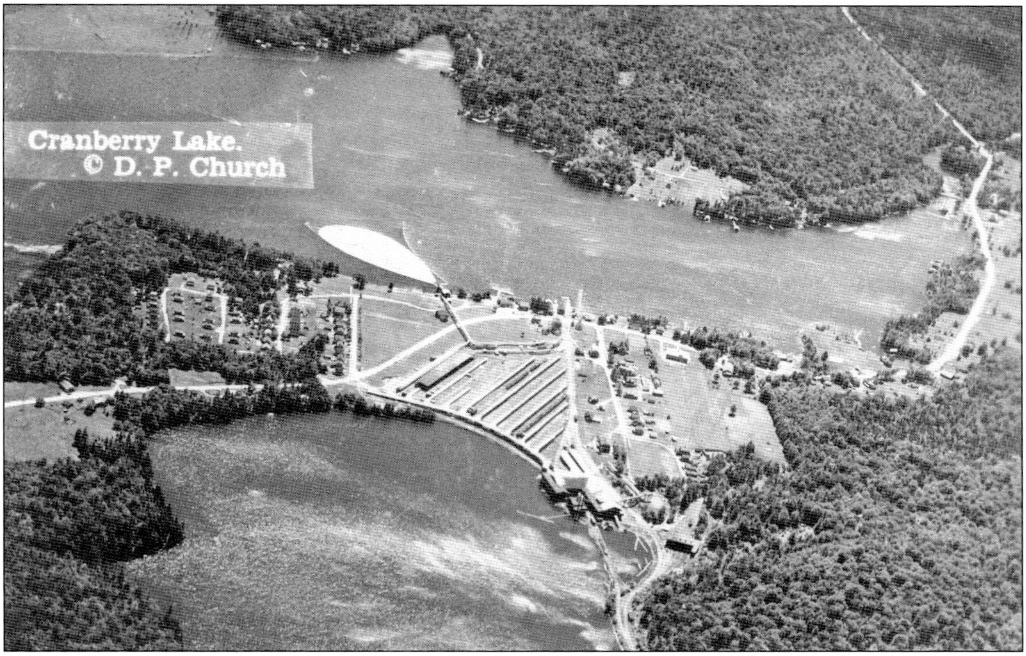

This aerial view of Cranberry Lake village by Dwight Church dates to the early 1920s. The mill is at lower right, with elevated lumber docks laid out along Silver Lake. The pulpwood boom on Cranberry Lake will be lifted by a jack mill onto an overhead conveyor and carried to railcars. Emporium logged pulpwood for other companies, sending some down the Oswegatchie River to Newton Falls. Much was hauled by the Grasse River Railroad to Childwold and then sent via the New York Central to International Paper Company's Piercefield mill.

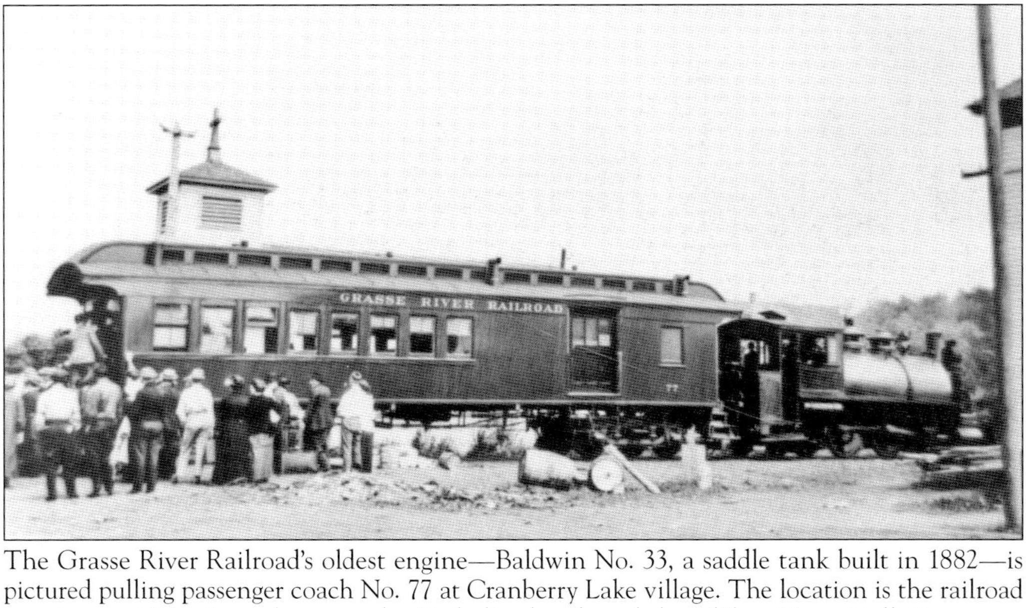

The Grasse River Railroad's oldest engine—Baldwin No. 33, a saddle tank built in 1882—is pictured pulling passenger coach No. 77 at Cranberry Lake village. The location is the railroad crossing on Main Street between the Catholic church and the Clifton Town Hall. Passengers with luggage are waiting to board at the rear of the coach. Trains headed into Cranberry Lake engine-first, but turned around a mile north at Dodge Brook Wye and backed into the village. A wye is a Y-shaped section of track used for turning locomotives or trains.

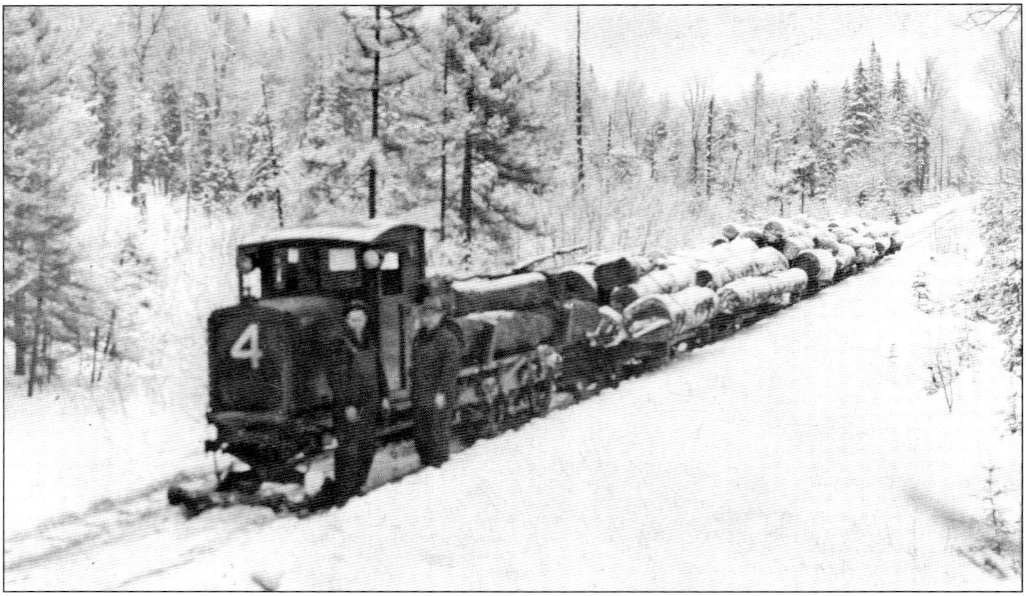

"Tractors Revolutionize Adirondack Lumbering . . . Long Hauls, Heavy Loads Mean Little These Days," read a headline in the February 1, 1934, Ogdensburg *Advance News*. An article described how gasoline-powered tractors—especially Linns—had transformed logging. Musician Holman H. Linn toured rural Maine with his large circus, featuring "wonderful educated dogs and monkeys," motion pictures, trapeze artists, singers, and comedians while working on a better way to transport his equipment. After moving to Morris, New York, he patented a design in 1918 that became a pioneer in Adirondack tractors. Dubbed the "torque monster from Morris," Linn's tractors were produced from 1917 to 1948. The initial cost was $6,000—equal to about $110,000 today, but Linn's showmanship served him well as he staged demonstrations for skeptical buyers. Emporium had four Linns; No. 4 is pictured in the card above, towing seven sleds of hardwood logs. The card below is dated 1931 and shows a Linn pulling sleds on Main Street in Cranberry Lake village. By then, the sawmill was no longer operating; the logs would have been loaded on railcars and sent to Conifer.

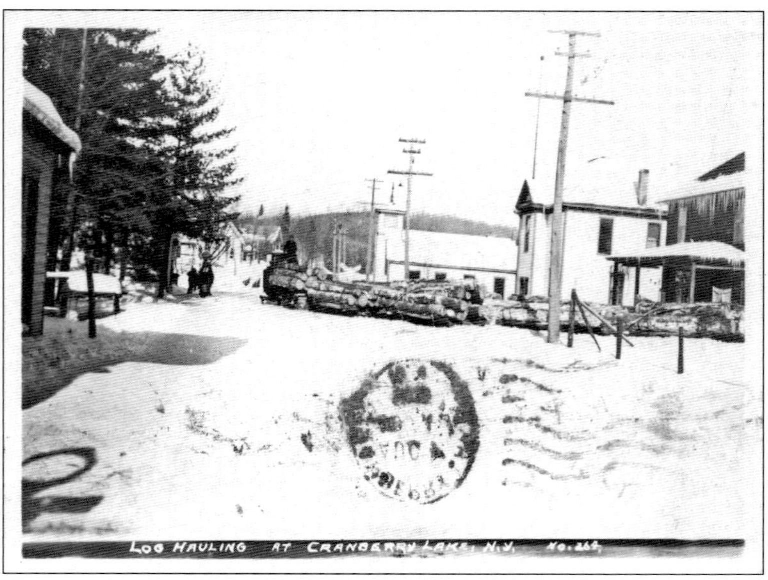

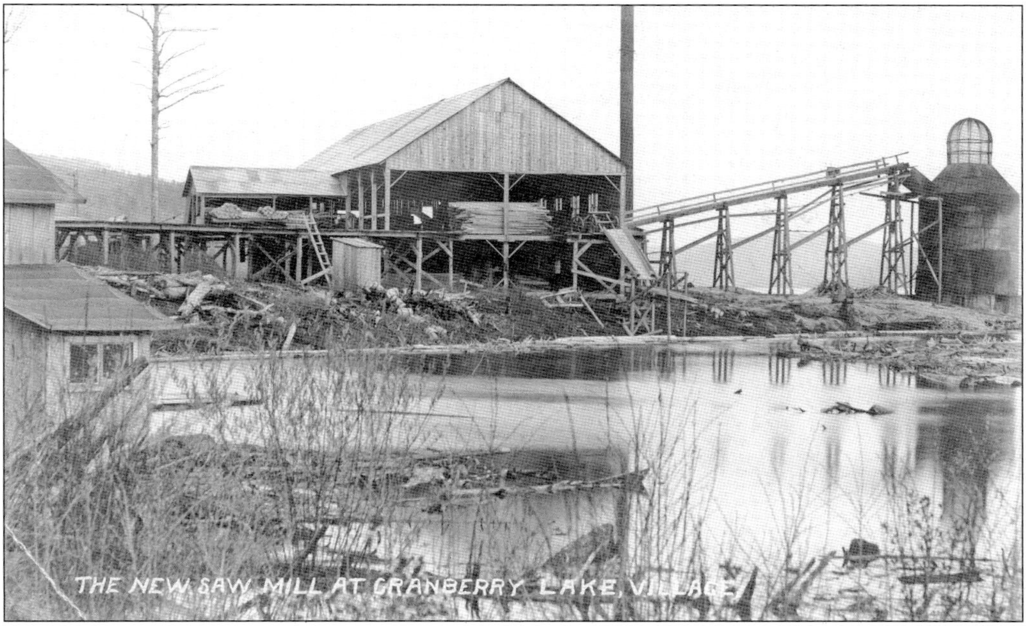

Emporium's was not the first sawmill at Cranberry Lake village; Abbott Lumber Company and the Bissell Brothers built earlier mills. The card above by Henry Beach shows Dana and Brahm Bissell's mill shortly after construction in 1908. An October 26, 1909, article in the *Ogdensburg Journal* reported that Emporium Lumber had secured an option to purchase the Bissell mill, which would serve as a central mill for its logging railroad system. Emporium's option was not exercised; the company decided to build its own larger and more modern mill. The Bissell mill continued to operate until November 4, 1912; according to the *Journal*, "Thursday evening the mill boys gave their farewell dance. The village regrets their departure. The firm will move to Big Moose." The photograph below shows the "Bissell Mill Boys" in 1911 or 1912. George Thompson, son of Cranberry Lake pioneer Albert Thompson, is marked with an arrow in the back row. Gaylord Westcott, son of Chauncey Westcott, another pioneer, is seated in the front row, also marked with an arrow. Mill foreman M. Bowen is standing at right.

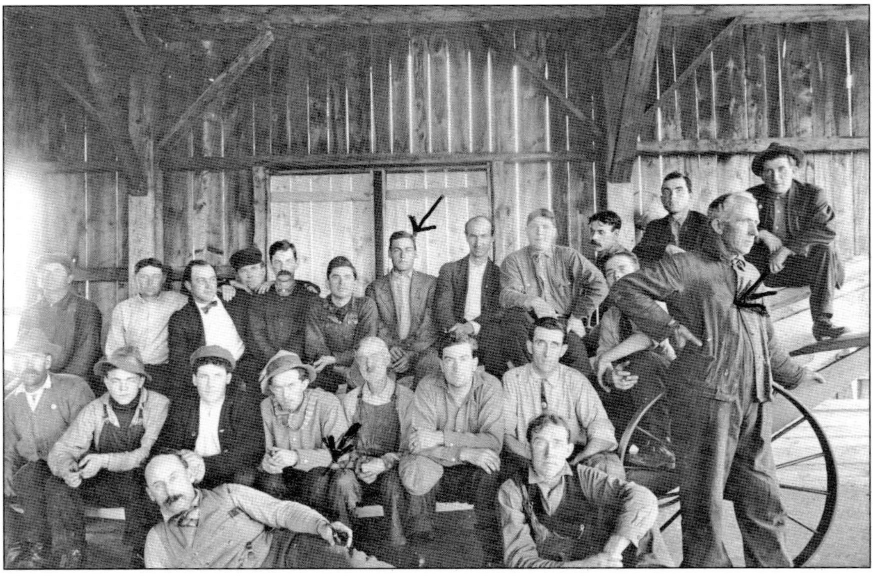

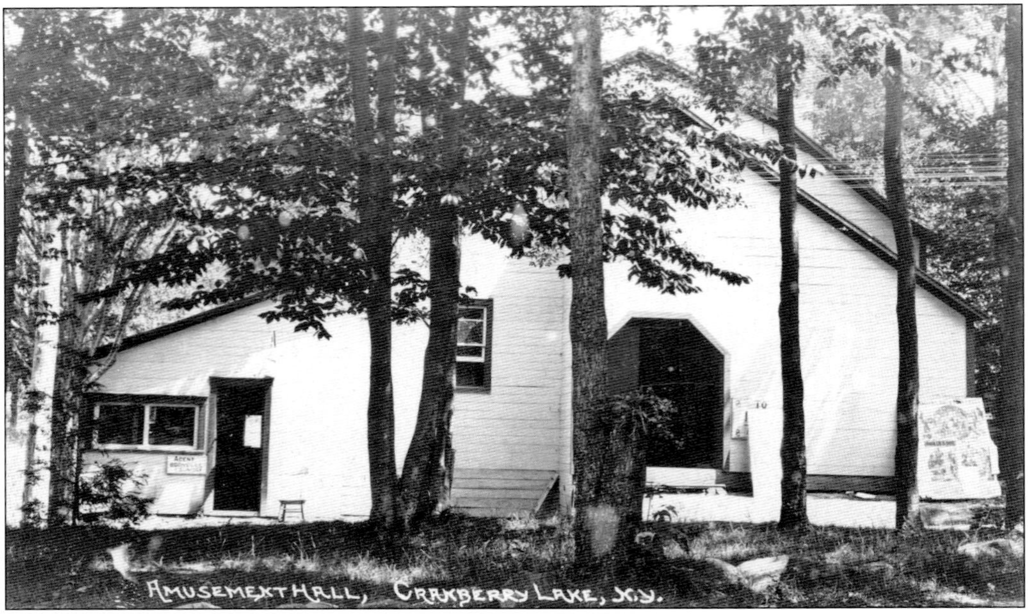

The amusement hall shown in this postcard was built in 1921 across the street from the Evergreen House. Owner E.F. Gaylord advertised it as "The Playhouse of Cranberry Lake," featuring movies, musicals, and a dance floor/basketball court. Its restaurant offered "lunches put up for picnic parties and motorists." Signs advertise "A Cent Laundry" and "Danglers's Dog & Pony Circus." On February 2, 1925, the *Republican-Journal* reported that the hall burned, with losses over $7,000. The fire began shortly after a party and dance held by the Married People's Club.

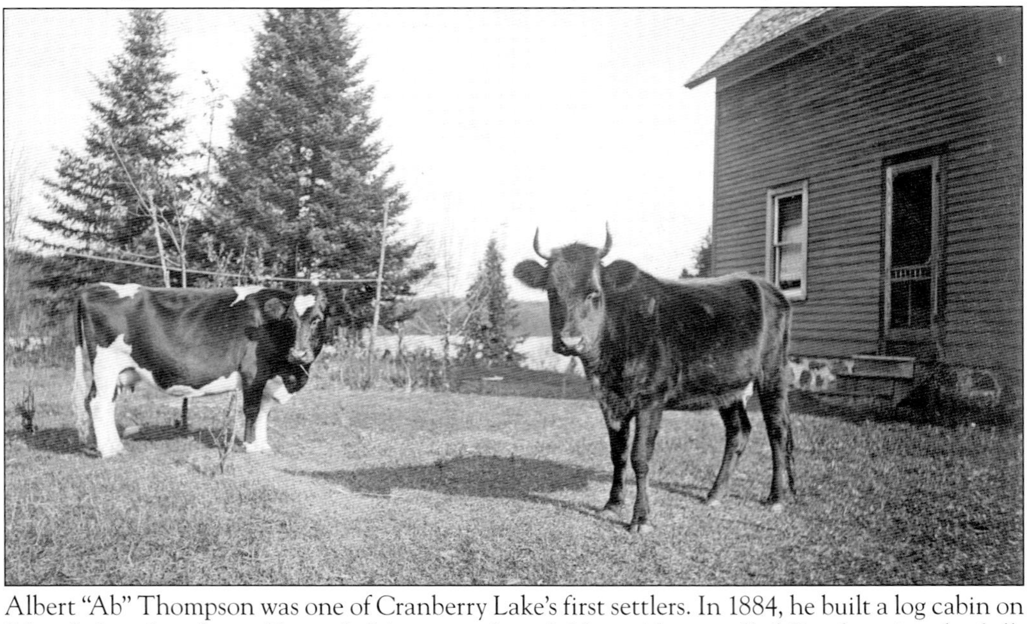

Albert "Ab" Thompson was one of Cranberry Lake's first settlers. In 1884, he built a log cabin on Silver Lake, where he and his wife, Mary, raised six children. Ab was called Cranberry's jack-of-all-trades: farming, carpentry, hunting, fishing, trapping, spruce gumming, and guiding. Around 1890, artist Frederic Remington painted his guide's log home; titled *Hunter's Cabin in the Adirondacks*, the painting is now at the Adirondack Museum. In 1898, the Thompson family moved into a new frame house on an adjacent lot, pictured in this postcard. Ab Thompson died in 1933.

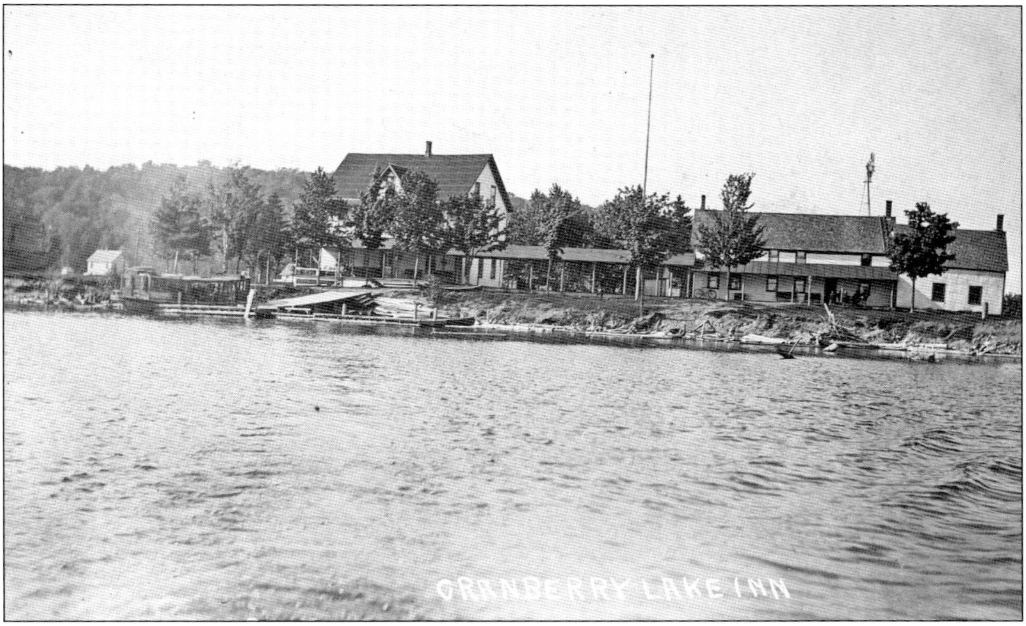

In 1910, Emporium purchased the Cranberry Lake Inn and advertised the lake's appeal to sportsmen and nature lovers. A motorboat, *Emporia*, was also available for charter. Tourists were needed to increase passenger revenues from the Grasse River Railroad. By June 1926, when the inn burned, Emporium was using it to board mill workers and loggers. Around 40 men were sleeping when the fire started; a barking "hero" dog and the night watchman's gunshots allowed all but one to escape. The *Wanakena* is at the dock in this c. 1910 card.

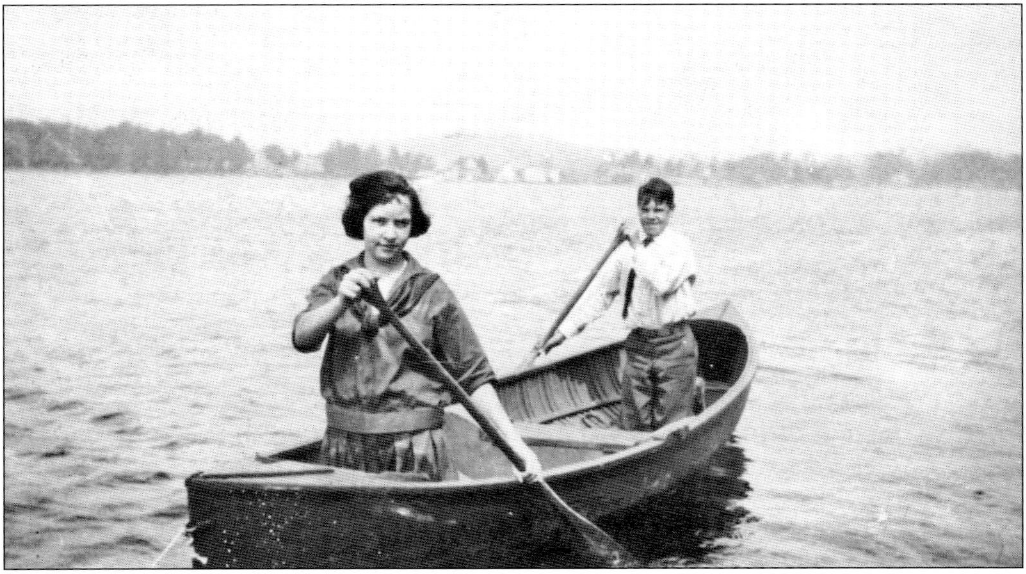

These two young people seem to be on their own in the middle of Cranberry Lake, with the village in the background, but on closer inspection, the canoe is safely tied to a dock or another boat. The posed photograph is dated 1923. Both look to be in Sunday best clothes, although public wear in the early 1920s was still formal, even for children. The girl's middy sailor blouse with a pleated skirt was a popular style. After 1925, the Roaring Twenties had more of an effect on fashion trends.

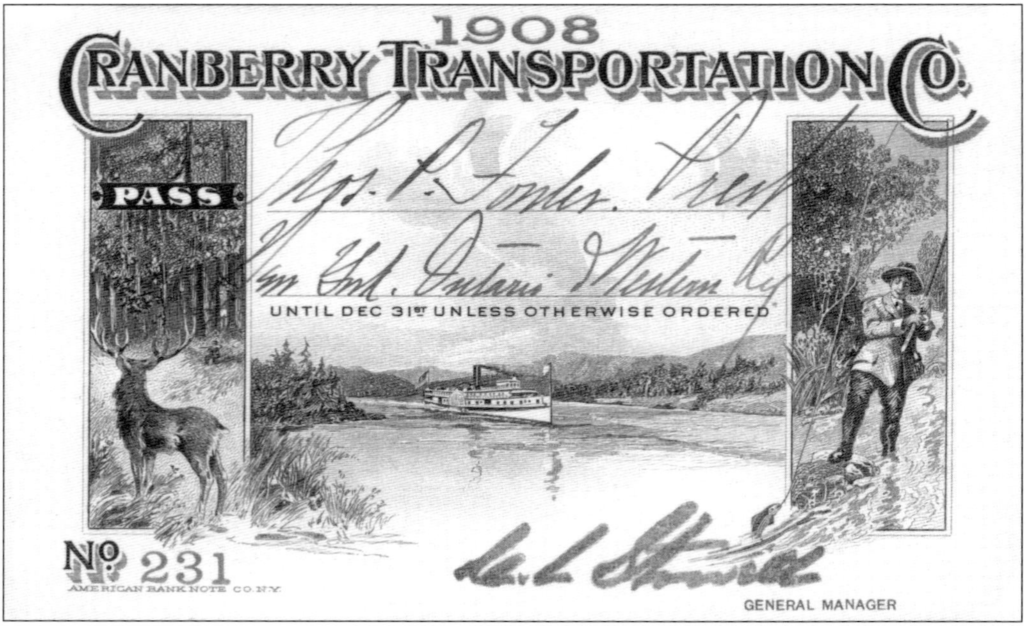

In 1915, the Cranberry Lake Boat Club distributed a 64-page booklet promoting the lake as a resort. It stated, "passenger service is well cared for by Howland Brothers, who operate a line of boats between Cranberry Lake village and Wanakena." This 1908 Cranberry Transportation Company pass was issued to Thomas P. Fowler, president of the New York, Ontario & Western Railway. The deer and fisherman engraved on the front are realistic, but the large paddlewheel steamboat never saw Cranberry Lake. The reverse states "The perfect Adirondack Lake, the Sportsmen's Paradise."

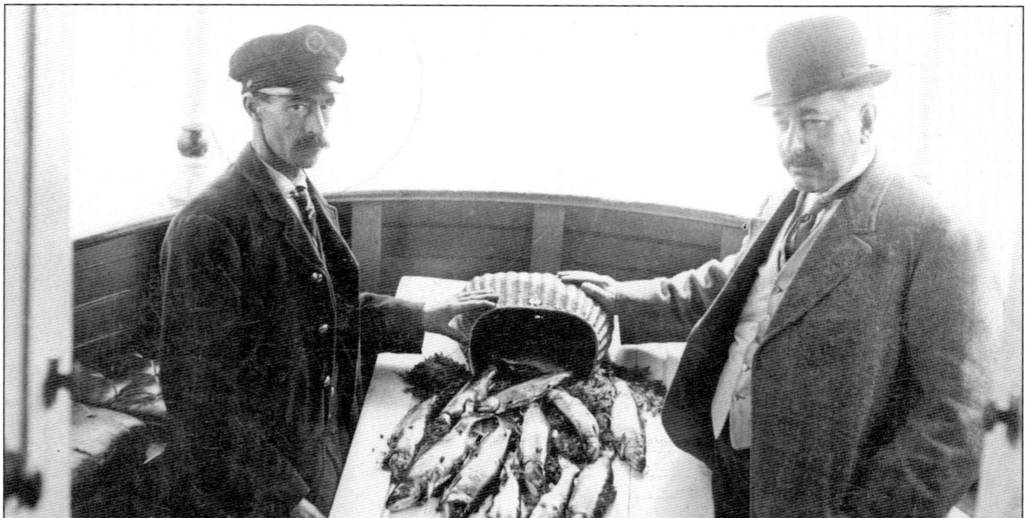

The Cranberry Transportation Company expanded its fleet by buying boats of competitors. The wood-burning steamer *Helen*, owned by Frank Wilder, was an early acquisition. Around 1910, the company bought *Zenda*, a small steamer brought to the lake by James Outterson. When Rich Lumber left Wanakena in 1912, its gasoline-powered launch *Wanakena* was purchased. This card is a view at the stern of the *Helen*; "A Nice Catch of Trout" is displayed, presumably taken by the "sport" in the bowler hat at right. The sender's message notes, "nice ones but small."

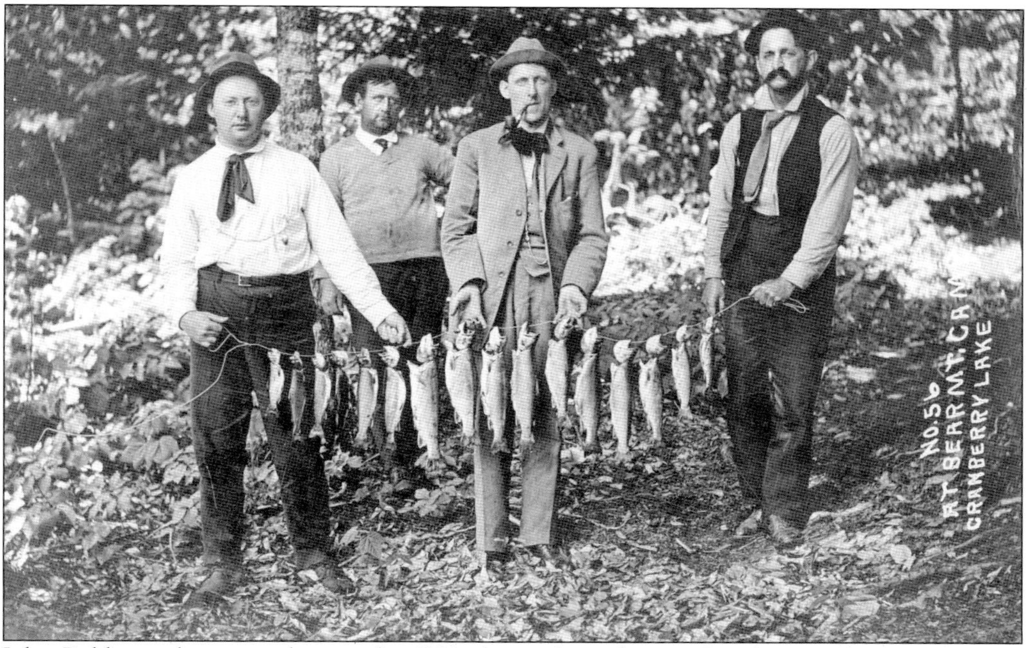

John Balderson began guiding in the 1890s from a log cabin on Cranberry Lake. His Big Deer Mountain Camp proved too small to house the hunters and fishermen drawn by Balderson's reputation as a guide and his wife, Anna's, skill at cooking game. In 1905, Balderson built Bear Mountain Camp, "a modern hotel, equipped with all the comforts of city life in the heart of the wilderness," and began touting the camp's appeal to "ladies, children and boaters." The card's message reads, "This is the kind of fish we catch here."

A group of hunters is pictured at Tramps Retreat in this 1907 card. The six men and women are armed with a variety of rifles and shotguns and accompanied by a hound dog and a large teddy bear. Theodore Roosevelt's refusal to shoot a helpless bear inspired the first "Teddy's Bear" in 1903, produced by Ideal Novelty and Toy Company. Steiff of Germany soon followed. By 1908, the bears had become so popular that ministers warned against replacing girl's dolls with toy bears, claiming it would destroy their maternal instincts.

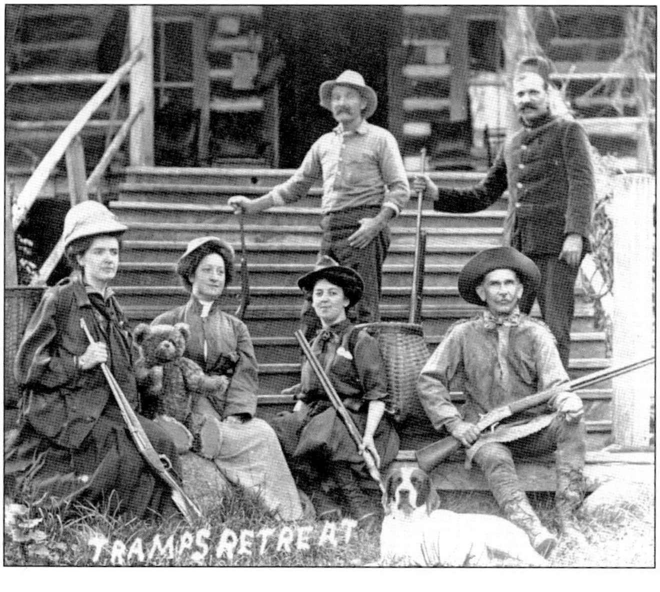

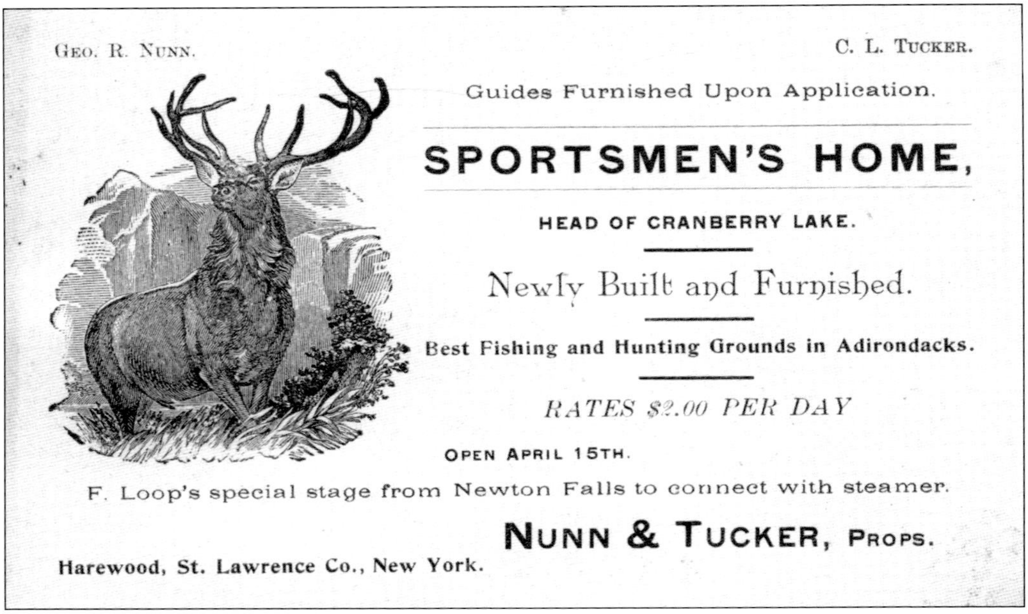

George Nunn began guiding at Sternberg's Hotel on the Inlet around 1890. Like other capable and popular guides, he was urged to build his own hotel. This he did, after securing land on Cranberry Lake at the foot of Indian mountain, with a small existing camp. After acquiring C.L. Tucker as a financial partner, a new large hotel was built that would become part of an expanding complex. It was initially called Sportsmen's Home, as seen in the upper advertising card from 1898, the first year of the hotel's operation. Early brochures claimed, "First Class Fishing and Hunting . . . Speckled and German Trout, Deer, Bear, Ducks, Partridges and Rabbits . . . Choice Wines, Liquors and Cigars." By the time of the 1905 brochure pictured below, Nunn was advertising to a wider clientele and had renamed his hotel Nunn's Inn. While still attracting hunters and fishermen, the inn was now "Strictly First Class," with amenities like "Spacious Verandas, Airy Rooms, Home Comforts and Modern Sanitary Arrangements." Vacationers, nature lovers, hikers, and campers soon made up the largest share of the inn's guests.

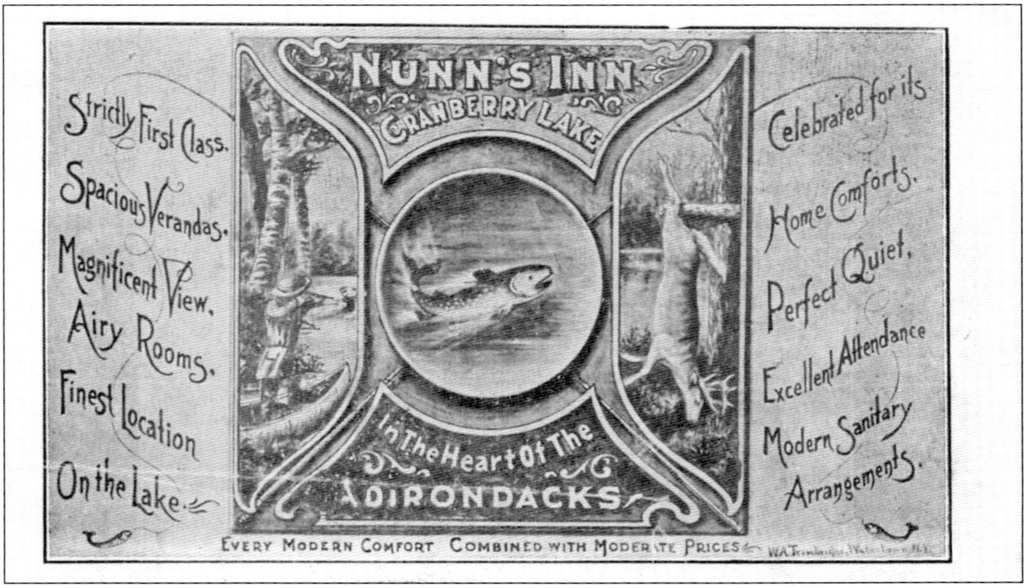

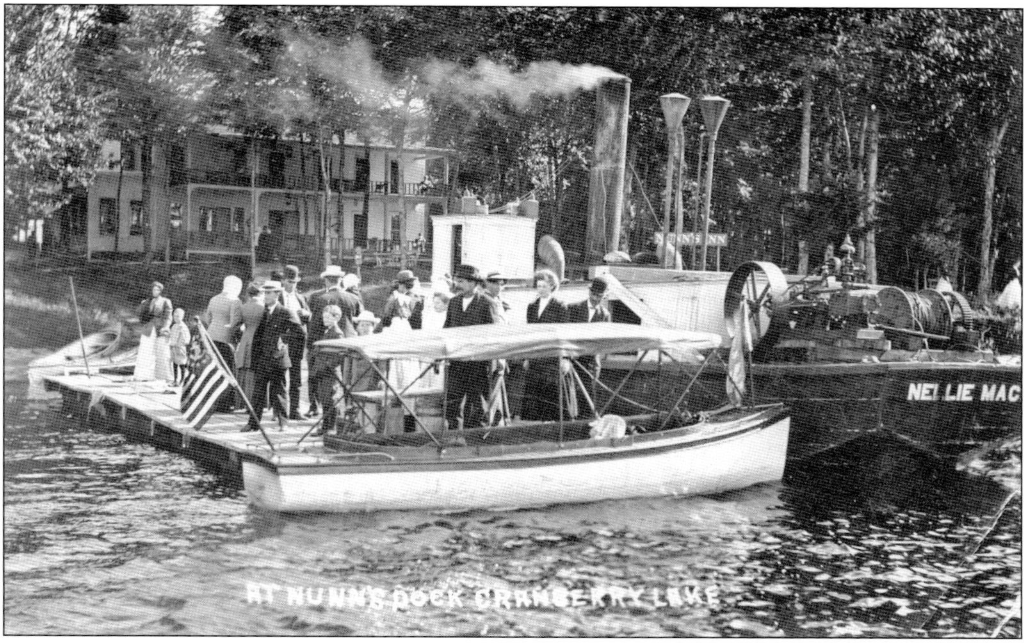

After George Nunn died in June 1910, the *Ogdensburg Journal* eulogized him in an article dated October 20, 1910: "George Nunn was a real woodsman. He was born and brought up in the big woods and knew every trail and stream. He was a guide by instinct and by training, and he was a good fellow as well. The guides that he had for the benefit of his patrons were qualified, and hunters who went into the woods for real sport found what they wanted at Nunn's." By the time of Nunn's death, his hotel was more than a sportsman's rendezvous. These two cards by Harris Locke are postmarked 1909 and illustrate how the inn was a focus of social activity at the head of the lake. Families crowd the dock and grounds in both images, with the main boardinghouse in the background. The steam tugboat *Nellie Mack* and a small gasoline launch are at the dock above, while the *Helen*, heavily loaded with passengers, is docked below.

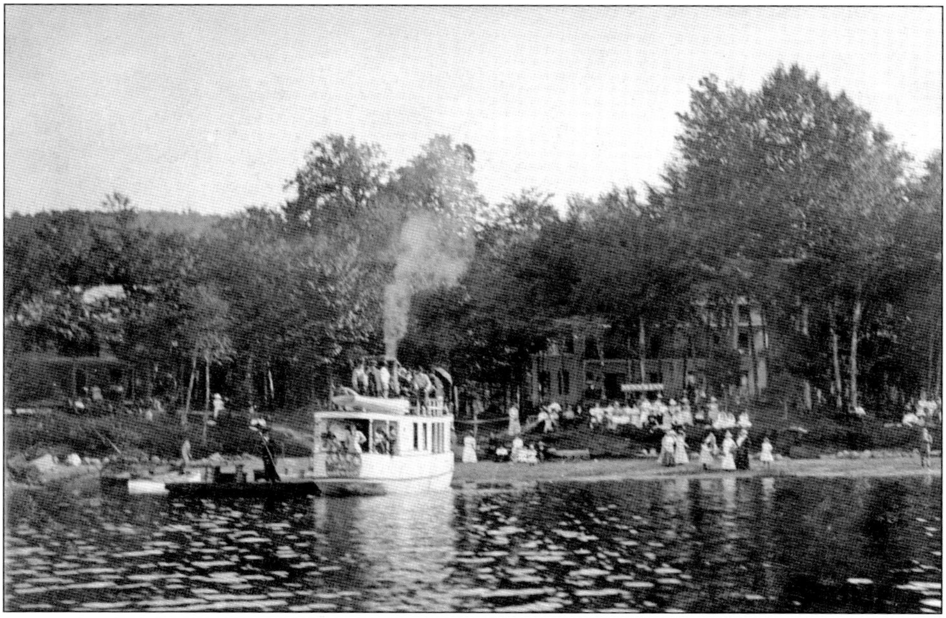

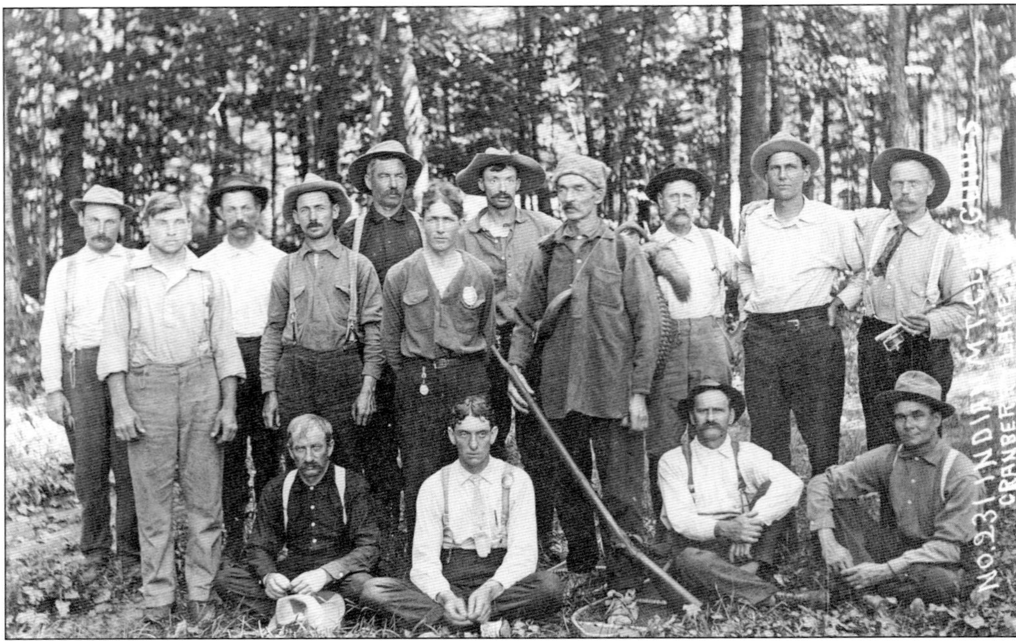

Nunn's Inn was purchased by Richard Jesup, who organized the Indian Mountain Club. The *Ogdensburg Journal* reported on March 10, 1911, that the club would make extensive improvements. Camps would be built on leased land, and "a guide will be provided for each to cook and care for members there. Most of the old guides, under George Preston, have been employed on a yearly salary." Experienced guides were essential, and were more important than the guests. They led sportsmen to fishing and hunting grounds and escorted families on hikes and camping trips. The card above is labeled "Club Patrol Force, Camp Keepers and Guides." Head guide George Preston is seated second from left; Wilfred Morrison stands to Preston's left. Art, John, Willard, and Nelt Howland are part of the group, as are Chan Westcott and Sherm Hazelton. Guides competed in rowing, water-boiling, and wood chopping contests. A boat race is shown below; the message reads, "This is the start of the guide race. George is the lead man. This all took place on the 4th of July."

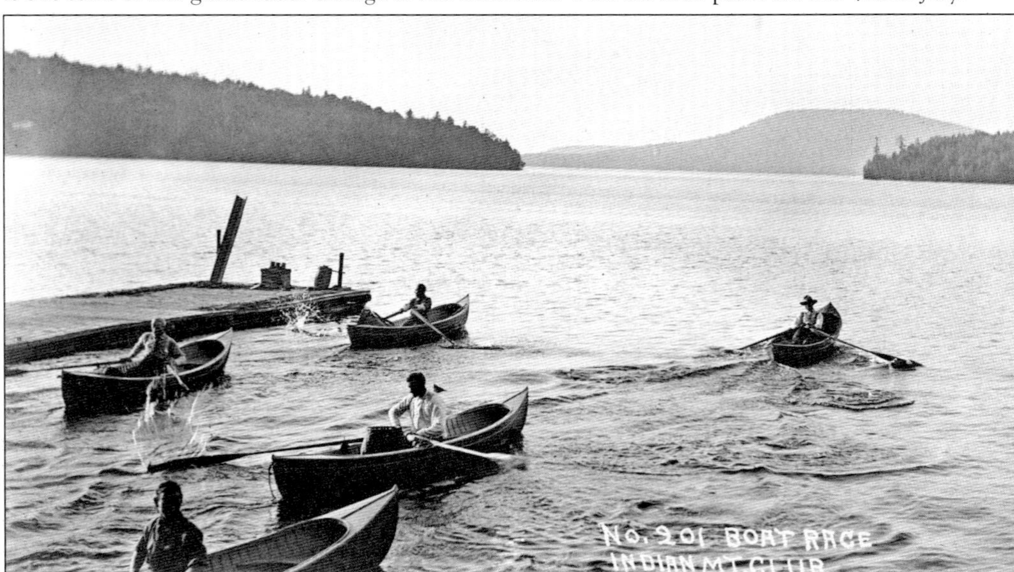

Meno or Manee

(American French as She Spoke)

WHOO AH--- COCKTAIL

Yellow Mill Pond Trunk Sewer Oyster on 3/4 Shell
Clams (Rubber or Low Neck) Patty du Clams

Potage

Lincrusts Walton Celluloid Bog Boiled Oyster Stew
Milk Weed Oleomargarine Bill Board Paste Guano

INDIAN MOUNTAIN CLUB COCKTAIL

Poisson

Trout (Brook, Speckled, Brown, Rainbow and Red Throat)
Pin Fish Baked Whale Codfish
Skates Suckers Shiners
Swimmers, on Toast, i. e. Picked up Fish
Sea Spiders with Mayonnaise Perwinkles, Dandruff Sauce
Sardines (from Mohawk) in good Cottonseed Oil
Fiddlers in Jelly

DOG POND PUNCH

Oufs

Tired Eggs Antique Eggs Eggs Just Snared Eggactly Other Eggs

HOLLOW HORN BEARS—COW HORN RICKEY

Gibier

Fire Sniff Birds Politician Crow Iguano Suffle
Wharf Rats—Kalsomined Pensioners Soaked in Tobasco Sauce
Mud Hens Stuffed with Blasting Powder and Roasted in Hades
Snipe with Asbestos Dressing Sea Gulls Pigeon (Clay or Stool)
Blue(and other) Jays Shitepokes Hell Divers Razzooed
Ostrich Lungs Fricasseed Gutter Snipes Skunk Stuffed with Poultice

THE MOHAWKS' HIGH BALL

On the Side

Flamingoe's Eyebrows Stewed in Tar Grilled Rhinoceros
Kosherwurts with Catch--Booze Balls Steak from Mantanzas Mule
Bubble and Squeak from Hold Holland
Bug Hash a la Delmonico Canada Thistle Salad
Yucatan Toad Cutlets with Saurekraut

UTICA'S SPECIAL DRINK (EVERYTHING)

Chaud

Sugared Icicles Gedampfier Snow Balls Pitasche

DESSERT

Pipe of Peace Holstein Milk—Barnyard Flavor

On August 6, 1912, the Potsdam *Commercial Advertiser* asserted that "the Indian Mountain Club is now the aristocratic place on the lake." Elaborate events were presented, such as the banquet held on May 9, 1914: "Planting Time of the Green Corn Indians." Officers assumed Indian names—Jesup was Tecumseh—and a souvenir booklet included the fanciful menu seen here. The exclusive club never attracted enough members to support it. In April 1916, Jesup sold the club to John Howland, who opened it to the public as the Indian Mountain House.

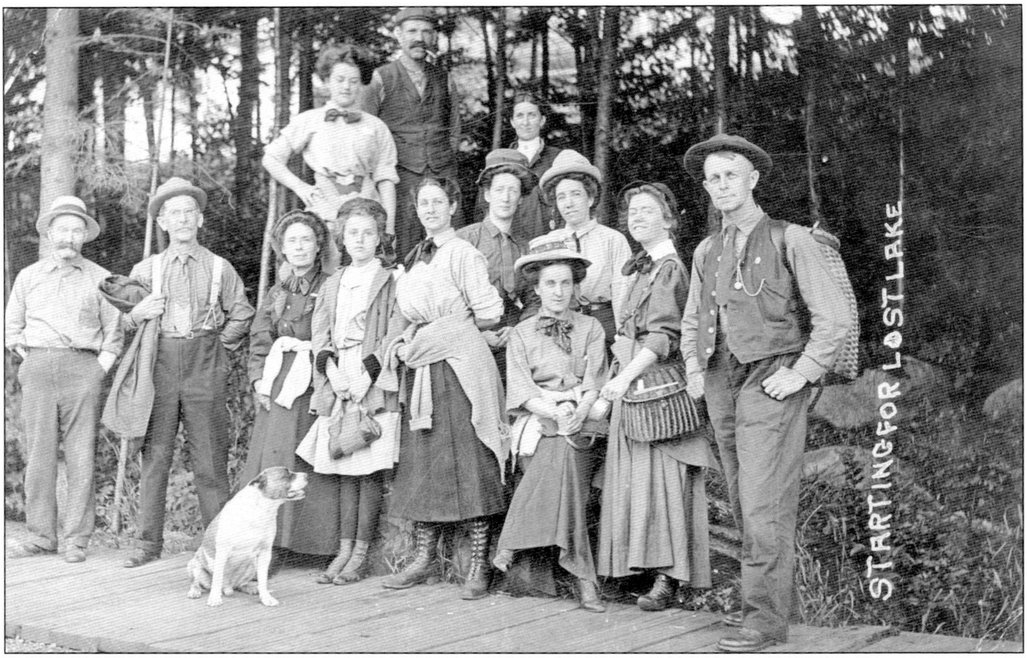

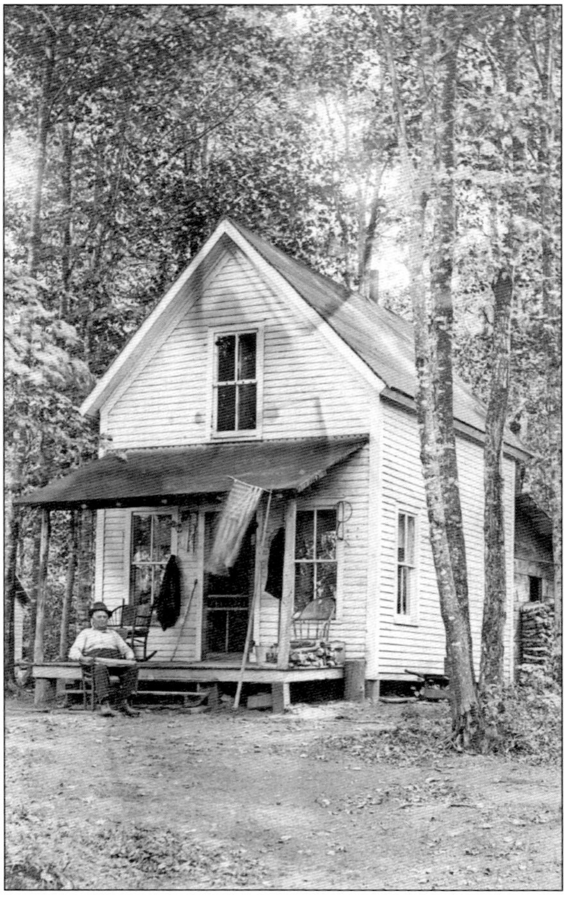

A mixed group of hikers from the Indian Mountain Club is "Starting for Lost Lake." Also called Big Deer Pond, the lake was home to famous hermit Philo Scott. After Scott's death in 1911, the club maintained his camps for use by members. Big Deer was a six-mile hike south from the club, but the group seems equipped with little more than water cups, and only one carries a pack basket. An overnight stay was probably planned. All of the club's camps were well stocked with bedding and staple foods.

This card is labeled, "S. Ward's Camp, 3-8-24." Steven Ward, pioneer hunter and trapper, was born at Lake Bonaparte in 1837. In 1863, he enlisted in the Union Army, joining Company A of the 95th New York Regiment. After recovering from a leg wound in 1864 during the Battle of Weldon Railroad in Virginia, he returned to Cranberry Lake. He built this cottage in 1905 near Nunn's Inn; his winter home was in the village of Oswegatchie. "Uncle Steve," the "guide's guide," died on August 13, 1928, at his cottage.

Steve Ward guided from Camp Uncle Sam on the Oswegatchie River above Inlet, near Griffin Rapids. He is standing at center in this 1890s cabinet card. On November 24, 1926, the *Northern Tribune* published a tribute to Ward, declaring that "to become a good guide a man must have something on top of his shoulders, also years of experience. Mr. Ward had both. A fine cook, the best man with a paddle we ever saw, optimistic, witty, Steve Ward had all the good points that make a first class guide."

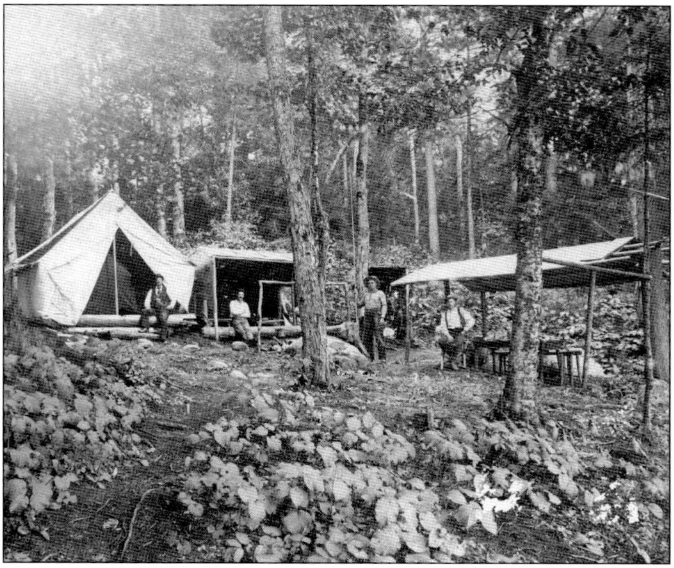

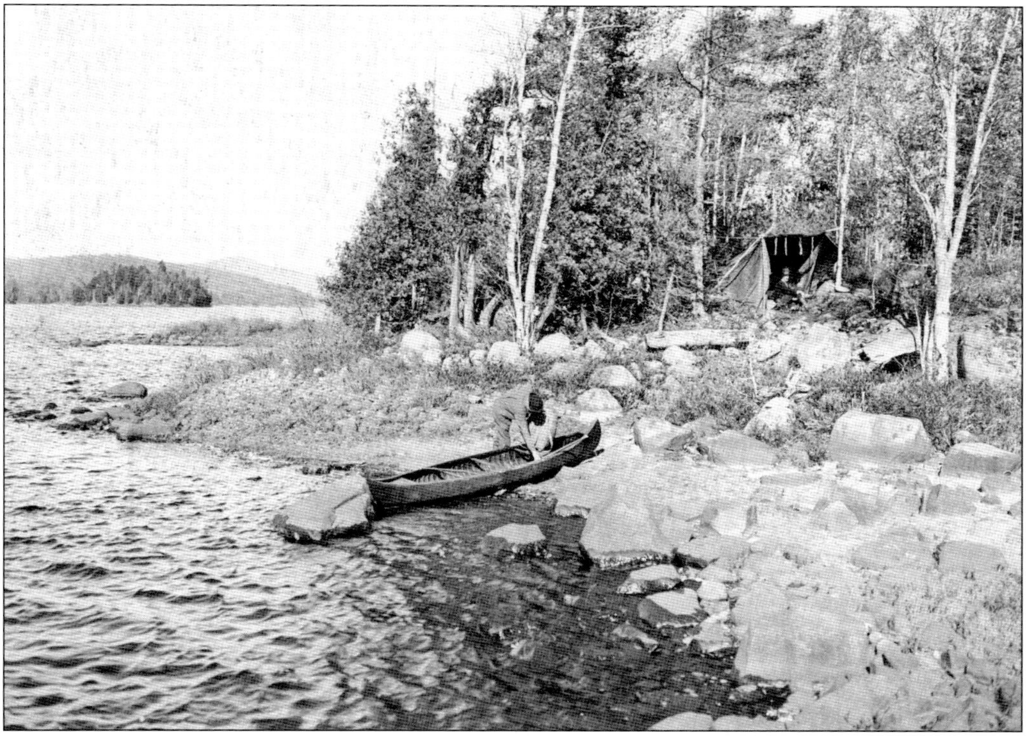

This early photograph of canoe campers on Cranberry Lake—with Buck Island in the distance—is timeless. The two men might have recognized this verse by American poet Richard Hovey, from "Along the Trail," 1898: "I have need of the sky, I have business with the grass; I will up and get me away where the hawk is wheeling lone and high, and the slow clouds go by. I will get me away to the waters that glass the clouds as they pass. I will get me away to the woods."

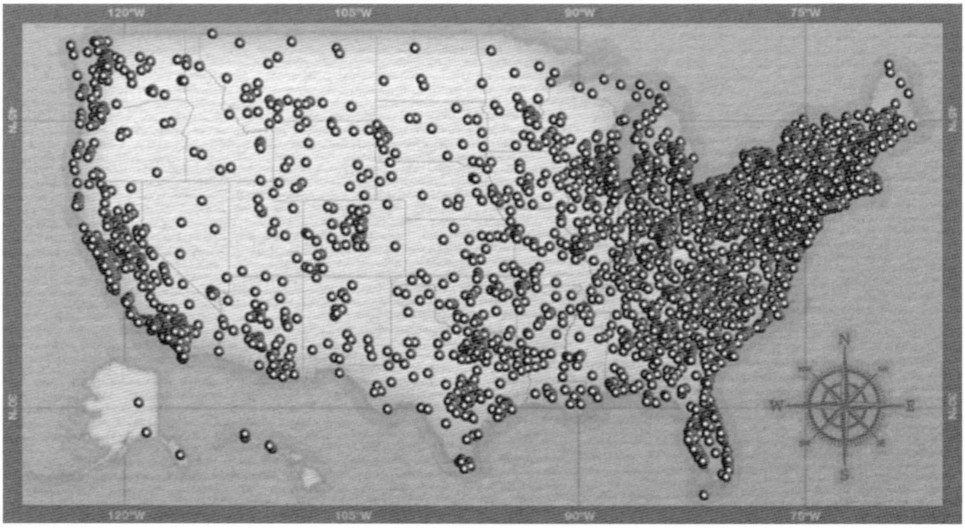